Waterton and Glacier in a Snap!

Fast Facts and Titillating Trivia

by

Ray Djuff and Chris Morrison

Rocky
Mountain Books
Calgary—Victoria—Vancouver

ROCKY MOUNTAIN BOOKS
#108 – 17665 66A Avenue
Surrey, BC V3S 2A7
www.rmbooks.com

Distributed by
HERITAGE HOUSE PUBLISHING CO. LTD.
#108 – 17665 66A Avenue Surrey, BC V3S 2A7
greatbooks@heritagehouse.ca

Library and Archives Canada Cataloguing in Publication

Djuff, Ray
        Waterton and Glacier in a snap! : fast facts and titillating trivia / Ray Djuff and Chris Morrison.

Includes index.
ISBN 1-894765-56-7

        1. Glacier National Park (B.C.) 2. Waterton Lakes National Park (Alta.)
I. Morrison, Chris, 1946- II. Title.

FC215.D59 2005   971.1'68   C2005-901216-1

First edition 2005

Book design by Ray Djuff
Cover design by Erin Woodward
Back cover photo courtesyTravel Alberta
Printed in Canada

Rocky Mountain Books acknowledges the financial support for its publishing program from the Government of Canada through the Book Publishing Industry Development Program (BPIDP).

Acknowledgements

Heartfelt thanks to: Thomas White, curator, and Eileen McCormack, associate curator, James Jerome Hill Reference Library, St. Paul, Minnesota; Greg Ellis, archivist, and Trish Purkis, archives assistant, Sir Alexander Galt Museum and Archives, Lethbridge, Alberta; Rob Watt, senior park warden, wildlife, aquatics and cultural resources, Waterton Lakes National Park; the reference librarians of the Lethbridge Public Library and the University of Lethbridge library; Rebecca Hill, computer guru, Lethbridge, Alberta; Acea Hill, sanity specialist, Lethbridge, Alberta.

Also: Deirdre Shaw, curator, and Ann Fagre, museum technician, Glacier National Park archives, West Glacier, Montana; Scott Tanner, Bill Lundgren and Bob Jacobs of the Great Northern Railway Historical Society; John Mauff of Chicago, Illinois; Millie Jean Perkins of St. Paul, Minnesota; Doug Follett, seasonal ranger, Glacier National Park; John Hagen, Rolf Larson and Tessie Bundick, Glacier Park Foundation, St. Paul, Minnesota; Burlington Northern Santa Fe; and the Minnesota Historical Society, St. Paul, Minnesota.

And to the many others unnamed, who were helpful in countless ways: you are by no means forgotten.

Chris Morrison and Ray Djuff

Dedications

To Jim
For his support, interest and encouragement
C.M.

To Monika and Michael
My interested companions on many travels to the parks
And Gina
For her love
R.J.D.

About the cover

Great Northern Railway fans will recognize the image used for the cover as coming from a 1929 brochure promoting Waterton and Glacier. For design purposes, the illustration was flopped. While purists may cringe, the practice of tinkering with images was more common in the railway's public relations department than might be imagined. See Chapter 8, What Were They Thinking, for examples of the truth being manipulated.

Table of Contents

Introduction

How much do you know about Waterton and Glacier National Parks? Let's see. They straddle the Canada–U.S. border. Glacier is in Montana, Waterton is in Alberta. Combined, they became the world's first international peace park in 1932. There are some big, lovely old railroad hotels. There's that Going–to–the–Sun Road. Roosevelt was in Glacier, wasn't he?

Obviously, you know something. And you picked up this book. Try these tidbits:

- Before George Bird Grinnell lobbied to preserve Glacier as a national park, he was drawn to the region for its excellent big game hunting, an activity today that would land the participant in court faster than you can say Jack Robinson.
- At 500 feet (150 m), Upper Waterton is the deepest lake in the Canadian Rockies.
- Sixty percent of the Going–to–the–Sun Road required excavation through solid rock.
- John Diefenbaker is the only Canadian prime minister to have visited Glacier National Park, arriving in June 1960 to address the 52nd annual Governors' Conference held at Many Glacier Hotel.
- The worst forest fire year ever recorded in the U.S. Northwest was in 1910, when some 100,000 acres (40,000 hectares) of forest, including 10,000 (4,000 hectares) in Glacier National Park, were destroyed. Edward Pulaski, as a result of his efforts to fight the fires, later invented what would become the most essential tool used by future fire fighters: the Pulaski, a combination hoe and axe.
- The bottom of the *Motor Vessel International*, Waterton's largest excursion boat, was once filled with rocks, ballast, in the age-old tradition of mariners to keep the boat on an even keel.
- Drifts on the famous Highline Trail between Logan Pass and Granite Park Chalet sometimes have to be blasted clear of snow and downfall to accommodate the demand from tourists for access to the area.
- Chief Mountain border crossing is the highest in Canada.

- Between 1912 and 1928, 18 million fry were released into 500 lakes and streams in Glacier. Prior to 1928, when Waterton's fish hatchery was opened, Glacier provided this Canadian park with a limited quantity of fry as well—a major transportation undertaking in its time.
- While the U.S. federal government awarded a construction contract for nearly $90,000 to build the Montana side of the Chief Mountain International Highway, the Canadian government built the Alberta portion of the road using relief camp workers who were paid less than 50 cents an hour. The road was opened in 1936.

Did you know any of those facts? Maybe a few. Possibly none. Don't worry, there's no test. The point is you're not alone. And you are curious, otherwise you wouldn't have read this far.

Welcome to *Waterton and Glacier in a Snap!*, an all-purpose primer to two of the most popular and scenic national parks in North America.

As you've already figured out, this is not your typical tourist guide to Waterton and Glacier. Nor is it meant to be.

Waterton and Glacier in a Snap! completes the parks picture, providing you with details, trivia and information you'll find difficult to get any other way. It's the ironic and humorous stuff the rangers and wardens tell each other. The stories locals might know, but only tell their family and friends. The facts tour guides should know, but probably don't. It's also information long forgotten and now dusted off for another go-round.

We had a lot of fun finding this information. We hope you get as much pleasure reading it and sharing it.

Ray Djuff and Chris Morrison
2005

A bear near a park road can stop traffic faster than any red light. In bygone days, everyone tried to get a close-up view by feeding bears. Today, two safety rules dominate: drive to the road's edge and stay in your car.

1

Gertie and Other Animals

They are Number One

Over the years, Waterton and Glacier visitors who return home without a least one personal story of a bear are seen as something of a failure. Among park employees, collecting bear stories is nearly a rite of passage. While entire volumes have been written on the deadly side of bear encounters, thousands of people each year are thrilled at the sight of a bear, the number one animal on the must-see list of park visitors.

Gertie the Grizzly

One of the best-remembered and most photographed bears in Glacier history was Gertie, a honey-colored grizzly that used to beg morsels from tourists below the Garden Wall on Going-to-the-Sun Road during the 1940s. She learned to sit on her haunches and beg, with front paws outstretched, sometimes in the middle of the road as traffic passed on either side. Gertie was the epitome of the cute bum bear, a Yogi prototype, and her photo appeared in many publications, including *National Geographic*. When Gertie had cubs, she would bring them along and they quickly learned the benefits of the mooching routine. Gertie's begging days came to an end in 1949 after several minor biting and scratching incidents. Despite being a photogenic host for the park, she was trapped and moved, returning once before being trapped and moved again—never to return.

Treat or trick

When Mr. and Mrs. Fred Burns and their daughter, of Coutts, Alberta, got caught up in a "bear jam" while driving through Glacier in 1937, they discovered not having food for the bear could be as dangerous as feeding one. When a begging bear walked over to their car to see what morsels were available and found none, it reached through the open window with its front paw and struck Mr. Burns a husky wallop on the back of his neck causing him considerable pain for a few days.

Mr. Burns said later that if the bear could have spoken, it would have said something like, "You tightwad, I'll fix you."

A swim always makes them hungry

It's a real treat to see a bear swimming across a lake. Bears take to the water because they can or because they are motivated to do so—and nothing motivates a bear like an empty stomach.

That was the case in mid-summer 1927, when a small encampment of Blood (Kainai) Indians set up their teepees on the far shore of Waterton's Emerald Bay. They had brought with them some 20 pounds (9 kg) of raw beef, which they kept in a wagon beside their teepees.

A bear, which was known to frequent the other side of the lake, got scent of the beef and one evening was seen swimming across the Narrows toward the camp. He landed and then disappeared. A few moments later, an Indian youngster popped his head out of the teepee's canvas slit when he heard a noise. Sure enough, there was something in the wagon. One big black bear—but no meat. The bear had gorged itself on the raw beef in a few gulps!

Alerted by the lad, the whole encampment clamored out of their teepees and the frightened bear took to a tree.

Then the Indians got scared. That tree was right beside their teepees and it was pitch dark now. Perhaps their forefathers relished sleeping with bears as neighbors, but most assuredly these tribe members didn't. So they did what any sensible camper would do: they called park warden Bert Barnes.

The seasoned Barnes rushed down with a good load of buck shot to pepper the bear and scare him away. The bear must have sensed danger, for he clambered down from the tree and went elsewhere to digest his dinner.

Where there's bacon, there's a way

Big Lena, a female black bear, made a monkey out of the cook at Granite Park Chalets, where she used to hang out with her cubs in the mid-1920s. Fed up with the bear raiding his larder, the cook stripped a thin lodge pole pine of branches and hoisted his meat supplies to the top. The cook and his attendant had a good laugh for a few days as the chubby Lena tried but failed to climb the slender tree to reach the goods. On the third day, however, the cook came out to discover the sow and two cubs munching on some bacon and slabs of ham. A third cub was at the top of the tree trying to dislodge another ham.

"Uncatching" a bear

Four southern Alberta men returned home from Waterton in August 1922 with a whopper of a "fish" story that, had it not been for their standing as well-respected citizens, might have provoked snickers.

The four were: Archie McLean, retired provincial politician, George Skelding, a Fort Macleod old-timer and former politician; Jimmie Acheson, superintendent of the Canadian Pacific Railway's agricultural branch; and A.L. Wood, a Taber citizen of prominence and fisherman of note.

While fishing in a motor boat at the Goat Haunt end of Upper Waterton Lake, they saw what appeared to be a log rolling about in the water and steered closer for a better look. The log turned out to be a bear, swimming across the lake. Both curious and interested, they circled round and round the swimming bear, which was beginning to tire.

Taking pity on the bear, they decided to try to fish him out and Skelding, as the cowboy of the outfit, was put on the prow of the boat, handed a rope and given the assignment of lassoing the animal. He made a number of casts and nearly succeeded in getting the bear around the neck, but the rope was just too short.

At that point, the men began to think a little further ahead: What if they were successful in catching the bear? What was the possibility of "uncatching" it once ashore? Not wishing to tempt fate, the party left the biggest animal they had ever seen in the waters of the park and went home, leaving the bear to make its own way to land.

All four resolutely stood by their tale.

It seemed like a good idea at the time

English sculptor and writer Clare Sheridan (1885–1970) spent much of the summer of 1937 at the St. Mary art school, operated by Winold Reiss (1886–1953), where she became enchanted by the bears. After her sojourn in Glacier, Sheridan decided she had to have a black bear cub of her own.

Courtesy, Karola Miener

Clare Sheridan was so fascinated by bears during her 1937 visit to the parks that she bought a cub and planned to take it home to England, until reason prevailed.

She was able to purchase one in Babb, Montana, and had a box specially made and mounted on the back of her Ford V-8 in which it could ride.

With the bear aboard, Sheridan headed to Alberta to spend some time on the Blood Indian Reserve, north of Cardston, visiting new friends. As the days lengthened to weeks, the cub grew rapidly and his impending need for hibernation became as problematic as his sometimes cross temper. Sheridan had also completely underestimated the problems of returning to England with a live bear.

Finally in late fall, with the encouragement of her Blood friends, she drove to Banff and released the young bear into the wild and whatever fate awaited him.

A modified idea whose time finally came

Don Hummel (1907–1989), president of hotel concessioner Glacier Park Inc. from 1960 to 1981, hit the nail on the head when he said Glacier's bear management policy was really a people management problem. Separating bears from people has long been seen as a solution to a potentially deadly problem.

Courtesy, Jack Sheaffer

Don Hummel

Hummel's suggested solution was bear-aversion, using a firearm to scare bears away so they'd come to associate people with the potentially deadly noise. His advice was in part fostered by the fact that in his 21 years in the park, four of his employees had been killed by bears while in the previous 40 years there'd never been a human fatality.

Ironically, bear aversion tactics are now used around Glacier, using Karelian bear dogs, and in Waterton, where "rubber bullets" and high-power noise-makers are used.

Death and destruction are sad postscripts

A children's book about a Glacier grizzly and its cubs that was supposed to be a happy story had a sad postscript. *Chocolate Legs, A Glacier Grizzly* by Peggy Christian and illustrated by Carol Cottone-Kolthoff, was the idea of the humane society, which wanted to publish an uplifting bear story.

Glacier bear researcher Kate Kendall suggested the story of Chocolate Legs, a grizzly sow that had been successfully relocated from the Many Glacier valley in 1983 and went from being a nuisance bear to model citizen of the animal kingdom.

Just months after the book's debut in 1997, Chocolate Legs mauled and killed hiker Craig Dahl near Appistoki Falls. The sow and her pair of two-year-old cubs were destroyed.

In May 2001, naturalist Roland Cheek wrote another version of the story for adults, *Chocolate Legs, Sweet Mother Savage Killer*. This thought-provoking account of the life cycle of bears mixes fact and speculation to stimulate readers into considering a bear's place in the environment.

Adding a little spice to their life

Cooks and kitchen staff at hotels and chalets have tried a variety of methods to keep bears out of their larders. During the Depression, a particularly headstrong bear kept raiding the shed where kitchen waste was kept at the Prince of Wales Hotel.

No matter what the staff did, the bear would return, break into the shed and knock over the garbage cans to paw through their contents, making a mess the staff was getting tired of cleaning up.

After one such raid, the chef had an idea. That evening, he and the staff took a bunch of bread, buttered it and then topped it with cayenne pepper. Then they retreated to their cars and waited for the bear to arrive. It did, entering the garbage shed and disappearing for a while. Within minutes, there was a roar of pain and the bear fled as fast as it could, never to be seen again that summer.

A never-ending hunger and acute sense of smell traditionally led bears to garbage cans left outside. It was an invitation that led to trouble.

Getting the point

Fed up with bears repeatedly raiding the larder at Granite Park Chalets, someone in the 1930s came up with the idea of driving long nails through the heavy wooden door with the points sticking out. The door looked like some sort of medieval torture device or a bed of nails a swami might lie on. The idea worked, and visiting bears could no longer help themselves.

Not to everyone's taste

Butcher Alvin Caldwell found an unusual marketing niche for his Waterton store in July 1924. When a large bear was shot outside the park, he butchered the animal and sold cuts to tourists so they could taste bear meat. The meat was not to everyone's liking. Not wishing to waste her purchase, one woman used some of the bear meat as fish bait and succeeded in catching a 19-pound (8.7 kg) lake trout. Sales of bear meat reportedly increased after word of the incident spread.

Twice in one night

Some bear encounters over the years have lead people to temporarily replace fear with anger. Three Lethbridge boys, Bonar Peat, Stafford Peat and Bob Bletcher, who were camping in the Waterton townsite in 1931, were visited twice during the night by a bear that entered their tent, broke all their eggs, and carried away their bacon, meat and butter. The bear apparently didn't care for the butter as it was found about 100 feet (30 m) away in the morning, ruined. The boys said the scare the bear gave them was not nearly as bad as the experience of going without breakfast.

Ted Marble postcard, Ray Djuff collection

In the early years, feeding bears was not strictly forbidden as it is today. A 1939 warning in a Glacier brochure noted that, "if you feed or photograph them you do so at your OWN RISK AND PERIL."

Do not feed the bears

A number of incidents between bears and tourists, likely some involving Gertie, prompted this 1949 warning to Glacier tourists: "For your protection and safety while visiting Glacier National Park, you are warned that b e a r s are wild animals and cannot be fed, teased, or molested with impunity." The warning went on to note that feeding animals was prohibited, and campers were urged to keep their sites clean and not leave food unattended in tents or automobiles.

Despite a desire to make that point clear in Waterton, wardens were able to only make suggestions to the public: "Visitors to the National Parks of Canada are warned against teasing or otherwise molesting wild animals. Any animal is dangerous at close range and should not be fed or encouraged to be friendly."

Some tourists continued to disregard the notices and each summer the local newspaper reported close calls. One article noted the real tragedy was the required destruction of bears who caused injuries. "Perhaps," one park official said, "someday people will become educated enough that they will be able to read and understand that signs mean what they say."

It was not until 1959 that a Canadian regulation was enacted making it a punishable offense to feed bears.

Out popped the bear

In 1927, when Waterton's Prince of Wales Hotel was being built, contractor Douglas Oland (1884–1964) and his family lived in a cottage beside Linnet Lake, not far from the construction crew's quarters. The camp had a cesspool with a plank lid, which covered an opening about two feet square.

Courtesy, Oland Family

Douglas Oland

For reasons known only to the animals, bears would remove the lid and get in.

One night, Oland and the construction laborers heard a noise coming from the direction of the cesspool. With Oland in the lead, a group of five or six men snuck along the narrow path to within about two feet of the opening. Out popped the bear.

Oland, 42, was the first one back to the house, easily beating some of the younger men. He said afterwards that he didn't know until then that he had such sprinting ability.

Guess who's coming to dinner?

One of the big perks of visiting Glacier in the winter was the fact that there was no need to watch out for bears, which usually hibernate from late November to April.

Since the early 1990s, however, rangers have reported seeing bears year-round in a few locales. This change in habit has been linked to the arrival of wolves and an increase in the number of cougars. The bears have been raiding the wolf and cougar's deer and elk kills, which provide the bruins with a good food supply throughout the winter.

Biologists say the uninvited dinner guests have caused the mountain lions to change their eating habits. Rather than feeding off a carcass for a few days, cougars immediately chow down on their kills to take as much food as possible.

They just loved that soap

It's not always just the smell of food that attracts black bears, as a trail crew cook in Waterton found out the summer of 1928. At first, the bears stole meat and supplies from the crew's camp near Bertha Lake.

When they were foiled at those efforts, the bruins turned to pure mischief: they began to steal washing off the line. The cook had put some heavily soaped towels on the line to dry and two bruin brothers made off with them, perhaps delighted with the smell.

Naturalist Karen Chin often helped lead Saturday peace park hikes, regularly stopping to point out this sign damaged by gnawing bears that frequently left tell-tale tufts of hair behind as well.

Educated bears

It could be coincidence or it could be something else, but in several instances in Glacier bears have been known to destroy signs warning against their species. In 1932, a newspaper reported the destruction of a sign that read: "It is dangerous and it is prohibited to feed the bears." Close by was another sign describing a trail—that sign was untouched.

In the 1980s, a sign warning about bears located on the Glacier side of the international border on Upper Waterton Lake showed signs of claw and teeth marks and even had bear hair clinging to it. It became a frequent stopping place on the weekly international peace park hike so park interpreters could point out that Glacier's bears had learned to read.

Good manners

A wrangler and a group of nuns stopped for a rest and a drink along the trail when a grizzly approached. The wrangler told the nuns to follow his lead and take one step backwards.

They all did and the bear took a step forward. Then the wrangler told the nuns to all take two steps backwards. They did, and the bear took two steps forward.

Fearing for their lives, the nuns decided to kneel and pray. The bear appeared to mimic them, kneeling and folding its paws as if in prayer. The nuns told the wrangler that it was a sign God had intervened and the bear wouldn't bother them.

The wrangler replied: "Can't agree with you there, sister. He's just saying grace."

Grasp and groaning

The change in public perception of bears, from roadside novelties to potential killers, has prompted all sorts of bear humor, ranging from cute to faintly morbid:

Wrangler: Do you know how to stop a charging bear?
Tourist: No
Wrangler: Take away his credit card.
Tourist: Groan

For whom the bell tolls

A story often told for the benefit of newcomers to bear country is one about bear bells. Grizzled park and trail veterans, and hotel employees with a wicked sense of humor, like to advise the use of bear bells that warn away black bears but can't be relied on to scare grizzlies.

Tourists are cautioned to watch the ground, paying particular attention to bear droppings to be alert for the presence of grizzlies.

One can easily spot a grizzly bear's droppings: they're the ones that contain those shiny bells.

And all those other animals

Other animals, especially when observed close at hand and without fear of danger, have provided park visitors with lots of amusement and wonder over the years. They may not be as dramatic as bears, but they are entertaining in their own ways.

Flying laundry

A.H. "Pop" Harwood (1876–1971), a longtime Waterton postmaster, was admiring the rack of antlers carried by a mule deer in October 1933 as the animal foraged in his yard.

Nearby, a clothesline hung full with the weekly wash. The breeze fluttered and in a matter of seconds the deer, line and laundry were a jumble of confusion, with the buck on the move over the fence to find open spaces and, presumably, freedom. The jolt of landing on the other side of the fence separated the buck from the clothes.

When Harwood got the tucks out of his sides, he found he had rents in the shirts and unmentionables. His humor quickly turned to consternation when he discovered several articles torn beyond all hope of repair.

White, bright and gone

In the days before clothes dryers, everyone hung washing on the line outdoors. A popular radio program offering household advice suggested adding salt to the starch for better laundering results. Waterton folk who followed this advice found out the deer and the bears liked it, too, and ate the clothes and expensive linens right off the line.

Hold that horse

Laundry lines have, from time to time, caused a variety of human-animal interactions, such as happened to one of the musicians at the Palace Dance Hall in Waterton one afternoon in 1923.

He was in a shed at the back of the dance hall when the horn of a saddle on a horse grazing close by got caught on a low-hanging clothes line attached to the shed and pulled the building over with the door to the ground, imprisoning the musician.

The horse became excited and started to drag the shed along, with the man vociferously yelling for help. Hearing his cries, Ernie Haug (1892–1952) and two others quickly rushed out and caught the horse, removing the line from the saddle.

The building was righted and the thoroughly scared occupant fell out through the doorway, suffering nothing other than a few bruises and shock.

When they get tired of climbing, they swim

Mention mountain goats in Glacier and most people's first impression is of animals skittering among the rocks on steep slopes at incredible elevations. But that's not always so. Montana senators Thomas Walsh (1859–1933) and Burton K. Wheeler (1882–1975) were on a fishing jaunt in the northeast portion of Glacier when they spotted a mountain goat swimming across Lake Elizabeth. It was a never-to-be-forgotten sight.

What the heck was that?

Chris Morrison

Mountain goats often take to park trails and, when they do, they expect the human traffic to yield the right of way.

Occasionally, an animal will be found in the parks that baffles even those with wildlife expertise. In 1924, Ancey Bainer of the Belly River district of Waterton, who had been hired to trap predatory animals to ensure the protection of game, caught what he described as a freak animal one February day.

The animal, although not quite as large as a lynx, had the tufted ears and head of the lynx, but was a different color, with the much longer and ring-marked tail of the bobcat.

Rangers were baffled by two reports in August 1951 of a strange creature near the south shore of Lake McDonald. The beast was described as being about three feet long (90 cm) and two feet high (60 cm), with longer back legs than front and a poodle-type face. Park officials guessed that it was a wolverine, rare in Glacier.

Small but ugly

Tales of strange creatures in the park lakes abound. In the summer of 1936, a strange reptile was discovered at Waterton. According to reports of the day, the three-inch long (7.8 cm) creature was an "Oxtolata." It had three sets of short, feathery gills, a fish-like tail, short feet and a large, animal-shaped head.

Unidentified swimming object

Large bodies of water, such as the three main lakes in Waterton, tend to conjure up stories of big things that swim. The first report of a large, unidentified lake dweller was made sometime in the early years of Waterton's existence by Isabella, second wife of John George "Kootenai" Brown (1839–1916), forest ranger in charge of the park. While fishing alone, she hooked something so terrifyingly large that she dropped her line over the side of her boat and rowed quickly to shore.

There have been many stories told since about a large, gray apparition in the lakes, inevitably dubbed Ogopogo.

* * *

In 1909, a party driving to the park in a carriage noticed something in a pool in the bend of the river near the present day Waterton bridge. The creature was reported to be about six feet long (1.8 m) and estimated at 300 pounds (136 kg). It left the pool with the speed of greased lightening and disappeared into the river, reportedly creating a wake like that of a boat.

* * *

Enormous size and speed became the two common denominators of all of the sightings that followed.

A widely circulated sighting was reported in July 1938 when three Prince of Wales Hotel employees watched as a serpent or fish gamboled in the water for more than an hour, diving and swimming back and forth across Upper Waterton Lake near Cameron Bay. Local skeptics were quick to speculate about what the threesome "actually" saw, offering explanations that ranged from beavers to logs to sturgeon or ling.

The discovery of eels in the lake the year before provided grounds for speculation, as well.

* * *

Six years later, in 1944, another mysterious creature was sighted. Passengers aboard the private boat *Donna Kay* briefly spotted something within 15 feet (4.5 m) of them.

* * *

In 1945, two prominent Lethbridge citizens, who were not named, glided up to the Ogopogo while fishing on the lake. The men were convinced the creature had reptilian characteristics and became believers.

* * *

In 1946, there was another sighting, this time in Cameron Bay. Ten years went by before the Ogopogo made another showing. This time, Ron Boyce, skipper of the *Miss Waterton*, spotted the creature near the head of Upper Waterton Lake.

What was this thing? Those who saw it weren't sure, but they would not be dissuaded—they had seen something. Then the reports stopped.

* * *

Finally, in 1977, the Chamber of Commerce decided that since the Ogopogo had not been reported since 1956, it was time to take matters into its own hands and import a replacement.

The Chamber sent a letter to British Prime Minister James Callaghan offering to pay $10,000 for the Loch Ness monster and proposed to approach marine scientist Jacques Cousteau (1910–1977) to supervise the transfer of the beast.

No reply was received.

Breakfast for everyone

Glacier officials couldn't figure out for the longest time why ranger Lewis Hanson was forever reporting a shortage in his flour ration.

The explanation was that the isolated ranger, who was staked out over the winter in the Two Medicine Valley, was feeding a host of critters flapjacks every morning. The breakfast guests included a mink, a weasel, two gray squirrels and a skunk. Many of the creatures became downright friendly, Hanson reported, and would eat out of his hand, although he did have some doubts about getting friendly with the skunk.

"I just couldn't bring myself to fondle him, although the poor devil almost wagged his tail as friendly as a dog when he approached me begging for the flapjacks which he had seen me feed to the other animals. I had to laugh at myself at times, when I was almost convinced that he was sincerely friendly in the wagging of that tail."

Two parks, two Fannys

The longevity of some wildlife, despite the harsh winters and potential predation, is surprising to many visitors, and the return of individual animals year after year to the same area is a delight.

At the Lake McDonald Lodge in the 1920s and 1930s, a white-tailed deer named Fanny became a regular, scrounging for tidbits with her twin fawns every summer. Tourists would delight in feeding and petting her, and—despite this uncharacteristic lack of fear—she lived to be some 15 years old.

In Waterton, a mule deer, also named Fanny, showed up like clockwork at the first sign of activity around the Prince of Wales Hotel each spring, beginning in the late 1920s. Easily identified by a nicked ear, Fanny paid daily visits to the hotel's power house, walking into the noisy steam engine room to receive snacks from the engineers.

When the hotel closed for three years in the 1930s, Fanny frequented the townsite and became a regular at a lake shore cottage, where she received a dish of salt or sugar each morning. When the hotel reopened in 1936, Fanny again took up that territory and was seen there for many years.

Those cheeky deer

Glacier has had its share of unusual deer, which the weekly *Hungry Horse News* has documented in words and photos to the delight of its readers.

Deer of the year in 1963 was Suzie, who was often seen lying under Trick Falls near Two Medicine Lake. She chose the location to keep the flies away. Rangers received so many reports of a dead or wounded mule deer, a trail man finally put a red ribbon around her neck with a sign that read: "I'm not wounded."

In 1950 a mule deer doe named Toni followed John Blankenship of the

Waterton old-timer Billy McEwen never failed to marvel at how easy it was to convince the deer they had nothing to fear from him, often getting them to mooch bread crusts.

Glacier area River Cabins home one spring and stayed. If doors on the family's residence were left ajar, Toni took full advantage of the opportunity to go in and raid any food in easy reach.

Not content with board, Toni insisted on a room, as well, and took over a less-frequently used tent, where she was photographed laying on a bed.

According to the *Hungry Horse News*, during the Fourth of July holiday, the cabins were full and the tent was turned over to the mayor of an eastern Montana city. Toni was not pleased about losing her quarters, and at sunrise she walked into the tent and tugged off his honor's blankets. The bossy doe was finally taken way by a ranger.

A matter of taste

While tourists are taken with the sight of deer close at hand, residents of Waterton who want to beautify their property with flowers in the summer have a different opinion of deer. The voracious deer have been winning the "battle of the blooms" for decades and their feasts have been slowed only where protection, such as chicken wire, has been carefully installed over bedding plants.

The gardening staff at the Prince of Wales in 1928, intent on laying out decorative flower beds amid grass plots along the sides of the hotel, did not realize their mistake in mixing red geraniums, showy pink phlox and the ever-hardy pansy in their display. The deer, ignoring the geraniums and phlox, devastated the pansies, even going so far as to find where the hotel's garden supplies were stored, gorging on baskets of pansies set aside for future plantings.

Eventually, the hotel gardening staff resorted to hanging flower baskets well out of the reach of the deer, and planting a perennial called monkshood, all parts of which are inedible.

Park people to the rescue

Deer don't always have as much good sense as people give them credit for, and can get into serious trouble. Such was the case in the spring of 1924, when Ernie Haug and Scotty Morris of Waterton spotted a large male mule deer struggling well out in the lake, where it had fallen through the thin and badly honey-combed ice. The pair arrived in a boat and towed the buck to shore by the ears.

They're "bison" not buffalo

There is one major animal found in Waterton but not Glacier: bison. A park paddock contains an exhibition herd of less than two dozen of the animals. While once native to the area, these animals are the descendants of six bison transferred in 1952 from Elk Island National Park, just east of Edmonton, Alberta.

Nearly eighty years before, a man named Samuel Walking Coyote captured four bison in southern Alberta by the banks of the Milk River, bred a small herd and sold 10 animals to Charles Allard (1852–1896) and Michel Pablo (ca.1845–1914), ranchers from Ronan in Montana's Flathead Valley. Allard and Pablo had realized that bison had just about disappeared from the plains and were gathering as many animals as they could. In 1907, the Canadian federal government purchased 716 bison from Allard and Pablo's growing herd. The Waterton animals came from descendants of that group.

In 1959, a loop road, defended by a Texas gate, or cattle guard, was built in the bison paddock so visitors could get a better look at these sometimes elusive beasts as they grazed in the hilly terrain. There's a strict rule that visitors must remain in their vehicles while driving through the paddock.

Ray Djuff collection

This photograph shows everything tourists shouldn't do when visiting the bison paddock in Waterton. While the animals are large and appear docile, they are extremely powerful and quick. These bison are descendents of the Pablo-Allard herd.

Objects closer than they appear

Like bears, bison can appear docile and, due to their large size (they can weigh as much as a ton), sluggish.

Karl Jentzsch of Springfield, Oregon, learned otherwise during a July 1984 trip to the bison paddock in Waterton. Ignoring signs to stay inside his vehicle, Jentzsch got out of his car and started taking photos of a bull bison some 40 feet (12 m) away.

"I was looking through the viewfinder and whammo! He charged me.... I tried to outrun him but I didn't make it."

The animal butted him in the rear and sent Jentzsch flying. "I felt like I was clubbed by a baseball bat," he told the *Calgary Sun*. "He charged again and drove his horns into my side."

While recovering in Cardston hospital with 30 stitches in his stomach, Jentzsch ironically noted: "I realized later I had no film in my camera."

Buffaloed by the bison

During the 1920s, there was discussion of reintroducing bison to Glacier. The plan was scrubbed for lack of money to build an enclosure to contain the bison to a single area/valley of the park.

23

In 1992, Waterton's management plan called for an assessment of reintroducing bison during the fall and winter into the Blakiston and Waterton Valleys. By 2004, two feasibility studies were completed and park managers felt it was a workable idea that would also conserve the plains bison as a species. However, a number of outstanding problems have yet to be solved and public consultation will be necessary before any plan can be implemented.

Thinning the herd

The Waterton bison herd must be culled periodically to prevent over grazing, and new animals must be introduced to keep a good genetic mix. In the first few years, Waterton's bison herd was reduced by slaughter, with the meat going to local Indian reserves and to the park's cookhouse to feed park laborers. Sometimes, animals are moved to Elk Island National Park.

In 1982, the surplus animals were shipped to a Metis community near Lac la Biche, in north-central Alberta, as part of an experiment to raise meat-producing animals on marginal land. Today, the excess bison are taken to auction, where they may be purchased for breeding stock or for the dinner table.

A half ton of steaming mad bison is enough to send park wardens scampering. The Waterton bison are normally rounded up in the fall for herd culling, health checks and relocation to winter pasture.

Bugging cottages

Waterton, home to a variety of woodpeckers, was under siege in the spring of 1924 when the birds took a liking to park cottages, then all wooden buildings, inflicting considerable damage to outside walls. By following up the cracks between the shingles, the woodpeckers invariably found insects as the season warmed the wood. In many cases, buildings had to be re-shingled due to the damage.

The problem, while much less severe, reoccurs even today. There's nothing like a gnawing insect—whether it's in a dead tree, a power pole or on a cottage—to attract a feisty and determined woodpecker.

Jim Morrison

A female elk, separated from the herd, is an unusual mid-day sight in Waterton. Elk are most readily observed at dusk and dawn, generally becoming reclusive during the day.

Keeping the count down

While some of the elk (sometimes called wapiti) in Waterton and Glacier are native, the current herds are also the result of introduced animals—29 brought from Yellowstone National Park in 1912 and released near Belton (now West Glacier), Montana.

In 1918, the first of these transplanted animals—the second largest member of the deer family, exceeded in size only by the moose—was spotted in Waterton. The transplants and local animals mixed rapidly, so by 1947 there were more than 1,500 elk wintering in Waterton. A program was started to periodically reduce the herd, which was outpacing the natural food supply.

The first slaughter, in 1947, involved 200 animals. Another whittling of the Waterton herd took place in the 1950s, and another in the 1960s, but public reaction forced the cancellation of the program in 1964. When the herd grew to unmanageable proportions in the 1980s, local ranchers hired area natives, who are exempt from hunting season laws, to whittle the number of elk, which had been raiding their grain crops.

Today, while there are three small herds in Waterton, the largest herd is international in its range, summering near the headwaters of the Belly River in Glacier and combining with the two other herds to winter along the eastern slopes of the mountains within Waterton's boundaries.

A late hunting season for elk adjacent to the park helps keep the herd small while a provincial compensation program is available to ranchers who experience hay loss due to elk.

A good look at the goats

A salt lick frequented by goats was a 1928 feature of the then-newly constructed Carthew Lake trail in Waterton. Located about three miles (4.8 km) up the trail, the salt lick provided a place where tourists could be assured of seeing the ever-illusive goats. Today's park managers would not tolerate such an artificial animal attraction.

Watching the wolves

How attitudes change as time goes by! In October 1933, orders were received in Waterton that all park wardens were to engage in rifle practice with the view to exterminating the wolves that were taking a heavy toll on wildlife every winter.

The animosity that park officials and the public had for wolves as predators of elk, moose and deer, species viewed as photogenic and therefore tourism-friendly, did not begin to change until well into the second half of the 20th century.

In March 1952, a letter writer to the *Hungry Horse News* warned of a rise in "Black Siberian wolves" migrating along the North Fork from Canada, suggesting a bounty was needed to eliminate the predators and worrying that they would seek refuge in Glacier Park. *Hungry Horse News* publisher Mel Ruder did not agree, stating in an editorial that people should recognize the need for wild places with predators, and that those individuals living near the park should accept the danger of wolves no differently than they accept bears.

By the 1990s, there'd been a substantial change in thinking about predators, and the return of wolves in Glacier—from a pack that migrated from Waterton in the early 1980s—was being carefully scrutinized. In April 1992, concern was expressed when seven wolves were reported to have died, bringing the park's population down to 27. The return of wolves to Montana has been on a see-saw, but steadily rising course, ever since, with suggestions from some quarters that the animals can be taken off the protected list.

Cougars become higher profile

Waterton–Glacier is cougar country, but for decades the illusive cats kept to the backcountry and well away from people, a legacy of having been hunted and nearly driven out of the parks in earlier times. By the 1950s, cougars were occasionally seen close to the Waterton townsite, causing concern for the safety of small children.

Ray Djuff collection

Glacier rangers Sousley and Bebee are credited in this 1931 publicity photo for shooting and skinning this cougar. "The beast was preying upon the deer in the park," the caption states, adding: "It will make a nice warm blanket."

In the 1990s, cougars were back in force, showing up in campgrounds and the Waterton townsite. Some said it was because there were more cougars, or more people, or an abundance of cougar food, which potentially includes both people and their pets, as well as deer and sheep. Whatever the reasons, cougar alerts were posted in Waterton after a number of dogs were devoured by the lightning-fast cats.

The only recorded account of a cougar attack in Glacier occurred in July 1990, when a nine-year-old boy was mauled at the Apgar picnic area. He lost the sight in his left eye as a result of the incident.

While cougar attacks on humans have not occurred in Waterton, there have been close encounters. Sightings in Waterton townsite cause tourists in their vehicles to stop, resulting in "cougar jams." Parks Canada took the matter in hand—to the extent possible—by trapping and putting radio collars on a number of cougars one winter.

The following summer, the collared animals were tracked. One warden, noting at least one animal was regularly loitering in the woods behind the back nine of the golf course, speculated the reason was the cougar needed a good laugh at the visiting duffers winging balls into the rough.

While that cougar might have been enjoying himself between feasts of venison or sheep meat, at least one Waterton cottager was not amused when a seasonal warden chased a cougar into her yard, within 20 feet (6 m) of her. Intent on hanging out laundry, the woman was scared silly to see the cougar within pouncing distance. She later said that the radio-collaring program did nothing to help her; it just meant the cat was now dressed for dinner.

Although the radio collaring program did shed some light on cougar habits, it was discontinued as funds ran out and cougar reports became less frequent.

The salamander reawakening

Waterton is the end of the southern range for the long-toed salamander. Their presence was only discovered when road improvements changed their migration route.

Big predators—bears, cougars and wolves—receive a lot of attention in national parks, both from managers and from the public. But from time to time, the lowly amphibian can hold sway, causing people to rethink their actions.

Such was the case in 1990, when Parks Canada rebuilt the road into Waterton, adding curbs and a sidewalk along the section from Linnet Lake to the Akamina Parkway turn off. It was a splendid job, providing a finished look to the road and preventing inadvertent damage to the grassy shoulders.

What park managers did not know was that they had just put up a monumental barrier to the migration of the long-toed salamander which summers in Linnet Lake but spends the winter buried in the woodland above the lake—across the road. Each spring, the nocturnal salamanders scramble down to the lake to lay eggs, when conditions are just right. Each fall, they reverse the route to hibernate. The standard-height curb was insurmountable for the 4- to 6.5-inch-long (10 to 16.5 cm) creatures. So human volunteers were found to go out each night and help the salamanders over the hurdle.

After a season of testing wooden ramps for the salamanders, Parks Canada took a more permanent approach and jack-hammered down the curbs, rounding them down to a more gentle angle to accommodate the reptiles. The discovery of the problem raised so many questions about this animal, studies have been underway off and on ever since.

Toads rule—for a while

In July 2002, a mass migration of boreal toads near Logging Creek forced the temporary closure of a portion of the North Fork Road. The closure was necessary to prevent vehicles from squishing undue numbers of the thousands of juvenile toads spotted crossing the remote dirt road on Glacier's northwest side. It was the second amphibian migration noted in recent times, the previous case happening near Nyack Flats in the early 1990s.

Bull-headed moose

There's not a lot of traffic on the roads into the North Fork area of Glacier, which is just fine for the wildlife.

So when a bulldozer showed up one day for a project in the 1950s, one moose didn't take kindly to the intrusion.

Ranger Harold Estey said it appeared the moose thought the bulldozer was a rival.

"He shook his antlers, pawed the ground, and charged head-on into the 'dozer at full speed. Not once but three times," Estey said.

Finally, the stunned moose staggered off.

"That driver was sure glad to see him go," Estey said.

He took 'em and ran

There is a tale of a visitor to Glacier who lost his car keys while attempting to lure a ground squirrel by dangling them out in front of the critter. The clever squirrel grabbed the keys and ran down a hole, and wouldn't come out again. The keys were never retrieved and a locksmith had to be called to make new car keys. Reportedly, a ranger later cited the man for harassment of wildlife.

A tourist inspects what's left of the abandoned Oil City in Waterton in the late 1920s. Local pioneer John George "Kootenai" Brown learned of the oil seepage on Cameron Creek from Native Americans.

2   Park Lore

Over the decades, many stories have been told about the parks, people, places and events, and many have been nearly lost. Their retelling—even in short form—offers up small slices of history's rich servings that show why Waterton and Glacier are so special.

Taking a pass

Thomas Blakiston (1832–1891) is credited for making the first undisputed visit by a European to what is now Waterton in September 1858. Blakiston was a member of the Palliser Expedition, sent by Britain to find a path through the Rockies for a railway and to determine the suitability of the Prairies for settlement. He was charged with surveying the mountains south of Fort Rocky Mountain House.

Sir Alexander Galt Museum and Archives

Blakiston wasn't particularly thorough, however, as he marked the Crowsnest Pass, just 30 miles (48 km) north of Waterton, on his map but never bothered to explore it. Had Blakiston taken the time to cross Crowsnest Pass, he would have discovered the lowest and best route though the eastern face of the Canadian portion of the Rockies.

Instead, in the early 1880s, the Canadian Pacific Railway would use the treacherous Kicking Horse Pass, near Banff, not realizing the benefit of putting a rail line through the Crowsnest Pass until 1898.

Thomas Blakiston

Hunt for black gold

It is ironic that the first oil wells drilled in Montana and Alberta should each have been drilled in what are now nationally protected areas.

In 1902, the Rocky Mountain Development Company drilled the first producing oil well in Alberta along Cameron Creek in what is now Waterton. In preparation for an influx of workers, Oil City was laid out nearby, but the plans for development were premature. The casing on the discovery well failed, the drilling tools were lost,

Glacier National Park archive

The oil well drilled by the Butte Oil Company at Kintla Lake in what is now Glacier is shown here in 1904, either abandoned or about to be abandoned after it turned out to be not commercially viable.

and work stopped. Many other wells were drilled in the succeeding years, but all were marginal and eventually abandoned.

In 1955, the Waterton Chamber of Commerce tried to interest major oil exploration companies in erecting a marker to commemorate this site. The Historic Sites and Monuments Board of Canada twice declined to recognize the well as being historically significant. Finally, in 1968, after an exhaustive study to determine the exact location, a monument was placed at the well, just off the Akamina Parkway, and it became the first National Historic Site in the park.

Meanwhile, on the west side of Glacier up the North Fork Valley, possibly the least visited area of the park, similar exploration activity was going on. The first oil claims in the state were filed around Kintla Lake in 1892, and the first oil well was drilled in the area in 1901 by the Butte Oil Company. One year later, the Montana Swiftcurrent Oil Company drilled a well near St. Mary Lake, but it showed just 60 barrels a day. Like Waterton, the Glacier oil boom was short-lived. However, scraps of iron pipe and the remains of a huge boiler in shallow water near the Kintla lakeshore can still be seen today.

Trust Hollywood not to let the truth spoil a good story

One of the most colorful women to step foot in what is now Glacier was Libby Smith Collins, the Cattle Queen of Montana. Attracted by the prospects of copper in the 1890s, Collins was said to have spent three summers in the mountains. According to historian Jack Holterman, she had a crew of 18 men working for her. They searched for minerals at the head of Lake McDonald and on Flattop Mountain (6,872 ft, 2,094 m), while she served as cook and foreman.

One day in either 1894 or 1895, Collins, her brother Chan Smith and her mining partner, Frank McPartland, were in a boat on

Lake McDonald when it capsized and McPartland drowned. It has been suggested the trio had been drinking at the time, an argument started and the tragedy followed.

Unsuccessful in finding valuable minerals, Collins returned to her husband and home in Choteau, Montana, moving to California after her husband died.

The Hollywood movie *Cattle Queen of Montana*, starring Barbara Stanwyck (1907–1990) and Ronald Reagan (1911–2004), was filmed in and near Glacier in the 1950s. The film bears little resemblance to Collins' true life adventures, her character or personality.

Averse to change

Support for national parks today ranks high among North Americans—who could possibly be against them? Such was not the case when Montana Senator Thomas Carter (1854–1911) introduced a bill on December 11, 1907, to create Glacier National Park.

The Kalispell *Daily Inter Lake* newspaper, today one of Glacier's foremost supporters, voiced concern that creating a park would ruin the chances of Kalispell being connected to the Canadian Pacific Railway, which was talking about building a spur line down the North Fork from British Columbia.

Kalispell had (recently) been spited when the Great Northern Railway realigned its track, taking Kalispell off the mainline and moving the division point operations to Whitefish. Kalispell hoped the CPR would fill the Great Northern vacuum, but feared a park would take out of production logging and mining lands that would otherwise lure the railway south.

The *Daily Inter Lake* was not alone in its concerns. The *Kalispell Journal* also opposed the removal of harvestable timber from the market; the *Whitefish Pilot* was against the loss of good hunting grounds; and the *Kalispell Bee* wanted previously surveyed land excluded from the park.

Making a mountain out of some Hills

Just how much of a role Great Northern Railway president Louis W. Hill (1872–1948) and his father James Jerome Hill (1838–1916) played in the passing of the legislation creating Glacier National Park is a matter of continuing debate. Some researchers claim the Hills were instrumental in lobbying Washington politicians to get the twice-killed legislation through Congress.

While documentation of any participation by the Hills has not been found, proponents say this is because the Hills worked through surrogates to keep their activities and interests secret. Given the vast volume of papers created by both J.J. Hill and Louis Hill, and still preserved, it would seem odd that evidence of such a major effort has not survived.

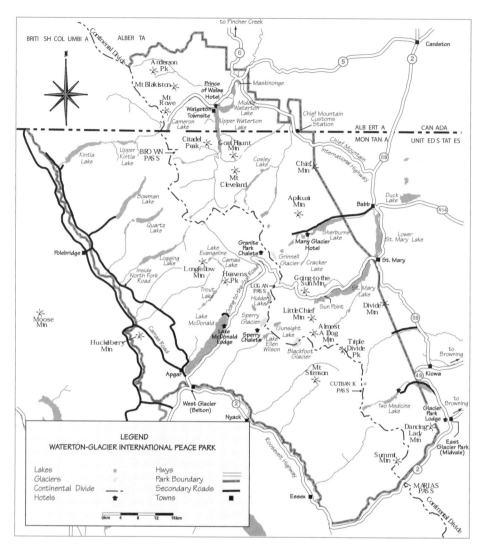

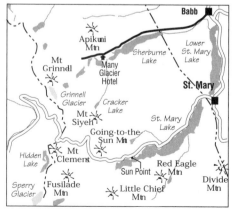

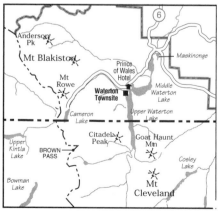

James J. Hill Reference Library

What role Great Northern Railway founder James J. Hill, left, and his son Louis W. Hill, seen here at the Omaha Land Show in 1911, had in the legislation that created Glacier National Park is a matter of debate.

Also, detractors note, when the bill was finally passed and signed in 1910 by President William Howard Taft (1857–1930), the congratulatory letters sent out by Representative Charles Pray (1868–1963) and Senator Thomas Carter did not acknowledge either of the Hills.

Whether the Hills played a part in the legislative creation of Glacier is, in the shadow of time, a moot point. Their railroad, the Great Northern, was the only one to directly serve the park and Glacier was a featured stop on its transcontinental route. Because of his love for the area, Louis Hill quickly became the park's chief booster, and because of its proximity to the rail line, the park received major investment in its developments from Hill's company.

Soon magazine and newspaper writers, encouraged to tour the new park at Great Northern's expense, began touting the idea that the Hills were responsible for it all.

Getting the size just right

Since it was first signed into being by an Order in Council in 1895, Waterton's boundaries have been changed seven times, but not always to make the park larger.

Started as a 54-square mile (140 sq. km) forest reserve, Waterton was proclaimed a Dominion Park and its land reduced in 1911 to 13.5 square miles (35 sq. km) so that the small park staff could effectively manage it. What remained was little more than the slopes of the mountains bordering the west sides of Upper and Middle Waterton Lakes.

Frederick W. Godsal

The reduction in size was a major concern to both the public and park officials because it crippled the park's use as a game preserve. It was believed that hunters walking through such a small park could easily drive game animals out to where they could be conveniently slaughtered.

Adding to the problem was a strip of non-park land two miles wide, between the park and the U.S.–Glacier park border, offering "sportsmen a paradise of game shooting" according to government documents, in effect nullifying the wildlife protection in both parks.

Fears were also strong among some that developers were on the verge of spoiling the mountains.

Making pleas for enlargement of the park were groups such as the Campfire Club of America; individuals like Frederick W. Godsal (1853–1935), a prominent rancher who lived north of the park; bureaucrats like Robert W. Chapman (1868–1920), the 1912 acting superintendent of Glacier; and politicians like Calgary's R.B. Bennett (1870–1947) and others.

R.B. Bennett

After examining all of the arguments, the government of Canada reconsidered and enlarged the park to 423 square miles (1,096 sq. km) in the summer of 1914. The expanded area included the mountains east of the continental divide from the international boundary north to North Kootenay Pass and the Carbondale River, all of Upper Waterton Lake in Canada plus the middle and lower lakes, and a portion of the Belly River Valley. This made Waterton, when combined with Glacier to the south, one of the largest game reserves on the continent.

In 1921, two more changes were made: one, in April to add another one-half square mile, and another, in July, to reduce the park

Sir Alexander Galt Museum and Archives

Ray Djuff collection

to 294 square miles (762 sq. km) by withdrawing the northwestern portion to make administration easier.

In 1930, the park was again reduced, this time to 220 square miles (570 sq. km). Two more reductions, one in 1947, to 204 square miles (528 square km), which removed burned timber land at the southeastern corner of the park, and the last in 1955, to 203 square miles (525 sq. km). The last reduction added 753 acres (305 hectares) to the Blood Indian timber limit along Chief Mountain International Highway.

Last claim to fame

Ora Reeves was the last person to get an original homestead claim in what is now Glacier Park. Reeves filed his claim for a site in the North Fork Valley in August 1910. Although the act establishing the park had been signed in May 1910 and despite government protests, Reeves was granted his claim. In 1912, the 31-year-old Reeves was hired as a seasonal ranger to control predators. Reeves' cabin still stands and is today considered a national historic site.

In Waterton, the last parcel of privately owned land which was subsequently returned to the government of Canada was that purchased by John Lineham (1857–1913) at the turn of the 20th century, when land could be reserved for oil exploration.

Lineham, a former member of the North-West Territories legislative assembly prior to Alberta becoming a province in 1905, lived in Okotoks and purchased about 1,600 acres (647.5 hectares) of land in the Akamina Valley.

John Lineham

His Rocky Mountain Development Company was one of the first to explore the area, bringing in drilling equipment and setting up a camp, with plans for a townsite called Oil City. Neither the oil nor the townsite became a long-term reality.

Designs by a committee of one

Many architects worked on the Swiss-themed designs for the Great Northern hotels and chalets in and around Glacier and Waterton, but the opinion of just one person counted: railway chairman Louis W. Hill, who had the final OK.

Only four of the surviving buildings built between 1912 and 1917 are known to have been designed exclusively by Great Northern architects: the small "dorm" chalet at Granite Park is by Thomas McMahon, while the main chalet at Granite Park is the work of Samuel L. Bartlett (1868–1944), who was also responsible for Glacier Park Lodge and what's now known as the Two Medicine "camp store."

Kirtland Cutter

When the details of a plan didn't suit Hill, he had no compunction about bringing in someone else. Many Glacier Hotel is the work of McMahon, but adapted from the original design of Spokane, Washington, architect Kirtland Cutter (1860–1939). Cutter also created the plan for the dormitory chalet at Sperry.

The original blueprint for the Prince of Wales Hotel was McMahon's, but was radically revised with the help of Beaver Wade Day (1884–1931), employed by the St. Paul, Minnesota, engineering and architecture firm of Toltz King and Day.

The firm of Cutter and Malmgren of Spokane submitted drawings for Belton Chalets, but it is not known which company was awarded the design job.

As for Lake McDonald Lodge, it was only here that Hill's opinion held no sway. The Great Northern bought the hotel in 1930 from Columbia Falls lawyer and businessman John Lewis (1865–1934), who had commissioned Cutter to design the building in 1913.

Who needs horses!

Albert "Death on the Trail" Reynolds (1847–1913) earned his nickname for his disdain for horses and for the stamina he showed in patrolling Glacier's backcountry on foot, averaging 12 miles (19 km) a day on winter outings—no mean feat on snowshoes.

He frequently broke the loneliness of his Goat Haunt posting by making the trip to Waterton to visit John George "Kootenai" Brown, Waterton's forest ranger in charge. It is suggested that the friendship that developed between Reynolds and Brown was Brown's inspiration for suggesting the parks be united, an idea that later became a reality as Waterton–Glacier International Peace Park.

In 1912, Reynolds received a memo from Glacier's superintendent to increase the range of his outings. Despite Reynolds' legendary vigor on the trail, he groused that the request was "a patrol no man can make." Nonetheless, he did try to fulfil the request, but suffered from repeated incidents of frost bite. His feet suffering, he hiked the 15 or so miles (24 km) to Brown's cabin, and was eventually taken to Pincher Creek for treatment. He died there of complications from frost bite at age 65.

Waging a losing battle

A source of frustration for John George "Kootenai" Brown was the disparity between his wage as forest ranger in charge of Waterton, $85 a month, and the pay earned by rangers in Glacier, $100 a month, at a time when the two currencies were very close to par.

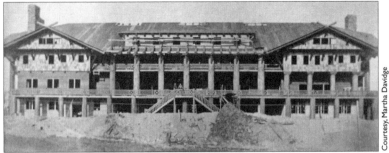

Glacier Park Lodge under construction, spring 1913.

Granite Park Chalets dormitory, 1913.

Numerous architects, both within the Great Northern Railway and from outside the company, were involved in the design of the Waterton and Glacier hotels and chalets, shown here in various stages of construction.

Prince of Wales Hotel, spring 1927.

Sperry Chalets dormitory, 1914.

Many Glacier Hotel is prepared for its July 4, 1915, opening.

Ray Djuff collection

"Kootenai" Brown was 70 when in 1910 he became the first government employee in Waterton, then called Kootenay Lakes Forest Reserve.

In a letter requesting a raise, the 70-year-old Brown stated: "They do not patrol more than I do, and have little or no correspondence to attend to. Nor have they the anxiety and responsibility of spending large sums of government money. More, I have several hundred people to look after in the season. To preserve order, and keep improper persons out, prevent the sale of liquor, gambling etc. etc. And I may say with Truth: and perhaps pardonable pride, that I have done this effectively—I do not ask for or require, an assistant. I have done, and can do, all the work required myself.... I am in the saddle or driving nearly every day. Shoeing and feed cost a great deal."

While a raise was recommended, it never came through and Brown's salary remained the same until he retired in 1914.

The poaching ranger

Glacier National Park archive

Joseph Cosley

Joseph Cosley (1870–1944) was one of Glacier's original rangers, selected in 1910 to patrol and protect the park's Belly River area. Joe Cosley, though, used this isolated region, which he was supposed to be protecting, as his private trapping domain.

Within a year, his superiors were suspicious and for the next three seasons repeatedly sent out rangers to try and catch him in the act. While they failed, reports of Cosley's fur-trading activities in Cardston kept coming in, so he was fired.

Cosley fled to Canada, where he joined the army and fought overseas in the First World War, after which he returned to poaching in Glacier, fleeing across the border whenever the law started to close in on his secret camp.

He was finally nabbed in 1929, put on trial in Belton (now West Glacier), found guilty and fined $100 for having seven traps, three muskrat hides and a beaver carcass in his possession. He claimed he had found the hides and the beaver was his food.

Before the fine could be collected, some sympathetic friends bailed Cosley out of jail and he fled to Canada, picking up a hidden cache of furs to finance his new life across the border. Cosley died of scurvy in 1944. He was found alone in his trapping cabin in northern Alberta.

A reminder of Cosley's time in Glacier and Waterton is still found on the trunks of the trees on which he carved his name.

Dangerous work

Poachers are possibly the worst threat to life Glacier rangers face, and it was a poacher who ultimately caused the death of Theodore W. Barnett in November 1938.

Barnett went through an extended period of recuperation, and was later transferred to Yellowstone National Park. However, colleagues said he never fully recovered from his Glacier bullet wound and died as a result of complications.

A lonely and deadly day

Andrew Bower was the only Waterton warden to die in the line of duty. An eight-year veteran of the Royal Northwest Mounted Police and a sergeant in the First World War, Bower's career as a park warden was exemplary. He was well liked and efficient in his duties, and was even recommended for the post of chief park warden, a promotion he never attained.

He served two stints as a park warden, one from 1918 to 1921 and the last from 1924 until his death in June 1925.

While on a solitary patrol from the Belly River to headquarters, then near the Maskinonge, Bower was thrown from his horse and was apparently knocked unconscious.

He lay in the pouring rain for many hours before he was found. By then medical attention was too late.

He left a wife and five children.

The ranger who got lost in the woods

Thomas Walsh (1859–1933) was quick to press his influence when elected to represent Montana in the U.S. Senate. He and fellow Montana Senator Henry Myers (1862–1943) expected the Department of the Interior to give them authority to appoint Glacier's superintendents on an alternating basis, as well as make other patronage appointments.

The problem was, according to National Park Service boss Horace Albright (1890–1987), some of the choices were less than ideal.

In his memoir, *Creating the National Park Service: The Missing Years*, Albright wrote: "I remember one of Walsh's rangers had to be put on patrol along the railroad tracks to keep him from getting lost, and sometimes another ranger had to be sent to accompany him so he wouldn't get run over by a train."

HICKEN'S FUR BEARING TROUT
Iceberg Lake
Photo by R. E. Marble, Belton, Montana

Ted Marble postcard, Ray Djuff collection

The Hicken fur-bearing trout was a gag that originated in Glacier and has since been copied at other mountain parks where there are ice-cold lakes.

Courtesy, Tony Kastella

Taxidermists Cleve, left, Sumner, center, and Sam Karstetter, at their Whitefish, Montana, shop, created the Hicken fish using a trout and beaver fur. Several of the fur-bearing trout were made at the shop over the years.

The fur-bearing trout

Rocky Mountain lakes are notoriously cold. How cold? So cold there is a long-running gag that a lake in Glacier had spawned a new species of fish: the fur-bearing trout.

The legend of the fur-bearing trout appears to have started with a group of friends from Whitefish during a trip to Glacier. The group included A.S. Frumenti, one of the Karstetter brothers, who operated a taxidermy shop, and Jim Hicken, the chief dispatcher at the Great Northern depot in Whitefish.

The evidence of the new species was there for everyone to see at a 1925 State Firemen's convention at the Lewis (Glacier) Hotel, when the stuffed fish—fur and all—was presented to author and humorist Irving S. Cobb (1876–1944), the featured speaker at the banquet.

It's not known what became of the fur-bearing trout, but a photo of it taken by Ted Marble (1883–1938) was made into a postcard that sold in the thousands to tourists who could prove to their friends back home just how cold the water was in Glacier.

Since the Great Northern considered Glacier "its" park, the fish was attributed to railway employee Hicken, although it was the creation of the Karstetter taxidermy shop.

Mountain retreats

There's nothing like spending time in the mountains to bring high-profile people back down to earth. Over the years, four federal politicians have sought the restorative advantages of quiet cabin ownership in the parks.

Thomas Walsh, a brilliant Helena lawyer and later one of Montana's federal senators, began vacationing at the Geduhn camp on Lake McDonald in 1899. In 1908, he purchased a home site from Frank Geduhn and two years later had a cabin built. Walsh became known in Washington, D.C., for his ability, integrity and industry, and was the leading prosecutor in the Teapot Dome scandal of the early 1920s, which exposed the corrupt practices of the Harding administration. He died the morning he was to have been sworn in as attorney general for the Franklin D. Roosevelt (1882–1945) administration.

Walsh became great friends with another outstanding Montana lawyer-turned-politician, Burton K. Wheeler (1882–1975). Walsh urged the overworked Wheeler to take a vacation, suggesting Glacier as the ideal spot.

Acquiescing, Wheeler thought Glacier to be a paradise and, after several family visits, his wife bought the family a cabin in the same area of Lake McDonald as Walsh. When Wheeler was elected to the U.S. Senate in 1922, both his political and leisure activities were closely tied to his friend Walsh.

Across the border in Canada, where senators are appointed rather than elected, William A. Buchanan (1876–1954) was a long-time devotee of Waterton, having first visited the park around the turn of the 20th century. He purchased a log cabin in the townsite in the 1920s.

Making his mark as the owner of *The Lethbridge Herald*, Buchanan was appointed to the upper chamber in Ottawa in 1925 and was soon known as "the senator

Sir Alexander Galt Museum and Archives

William A. Buchanan

from Waterton." He spent as much time as possible at his summer retreat with family and friends. Back in Ottawa, he was credited with seeing that many park improvements received the necessary financial support from the government. He sponsored the 1932 peace park bill and participated in the dedication ceremony.

When he died in 1954, Buchanan was described by park superintendent J.H. Atkinson, as "the greatest friend Waterton Lakes National Park has had."

The only member of Parliament to own a cabin in Waterton was Ken Hurlburt, whose riding of Lethbridge–Foothills in 1972, when he was first elected, included not only the City of Lethbridge but also a wide area that extended to Waterton.

Hurlburt recalled making an offer on the cabin, having it accepted and taking possession of the place as-is, with "the food in the cupboard and the sheets on the bed." Hurlburt retired from politics in 1979. His family continues to enjoy their Waterton cabin.

Firing the imagination

How attitudes have changed. When the Great Northern Railway was responsible for much of Glacier's tourism, any reference to forest fires in the park was verboten as it was known to cause tourists to cancel reservations.

Updates from railway staff in Glacier about the fire situation in the park were only transmitted to headquarters in St. Paul, Minnesota, by coded telegrams and the words "forest fire" were never to be used. After sensational and inaccurate newspaper reports about a 1926 fire in Glacier, the head of the railway ordered his staff to "see that nothing like this will be repeated," and a complaint was made to the Associated Press.

Today, forest fires are seen as natural and necessary for the environment. In an effort to explain the long-term effects of fire, officials began offering free guided tours after the Moose Mountain fire of 2001.

The tours were so well received by the public that by the spring of 2004, following forest fires in the park the previous season, reservations were required.

It's a situation that would have astonished Great Northern officials.

This pictograph, created by Blood Tribe member Eagle Arrow, once was displayed at the Prince of Wales Hotel.

Ray Djuff

Authentic, to a point

The pictographs painted by Blood and Blackfeet Indians for the Great Northern Railway's hotels in Waterton and Glacier were portrayed as being authentic.

The natives were said to have obtained the colors from natural sources such as vegetables and rocks, and the colors were supposedly applied with a sharp or pointed stick about the size of a pencil.

However, recent studies of the pictographs and discussions with the families of the painters indicate commercial paints were sometimes used, as were stencils for repeated stick figures and brushes for application of the paint.

She aims to please

Julia Wades-in-the-Water, who for many years was one of the Blackfeet who provided demonstrations of native culture at Glacier Park Hotel for tourists, was also a policewoman on the reservation.

Her husband and fellow performer, Chief Wades-in-the-Water (1871–1947), was the police chief.

One magazine article noted that "her reputation as a 'dead shot' may have its contributing influence, but Mrs. Wades-in-the-Water exerts the greatest force in her work with moral suasion."

Ray Djuff collection

Julia Wades-in-the-Water

Follow that road

National Park Service director Stephen Mather (1867–1930) liked to boast that tourists would follow any road into the wilderness, as long as it was paved. Going-to-the-Sun Road was Mather's big test of that theory and it worked beyond his wildest imagination.

When the road opened in 1933, visitation to Glacier jumped to 76,615 from 53,202 the previous year, despite the impact of the Depression on disposable incomes and tourism.

When President Franklin D. Roosevelt toured the road in 1934, visitation jumped again, to 116,965. By 1936, the park counted more than 210,000 visitors annually, nearly quadruple the 1932 tally.

Despite Mather's statement, paving of this road wasn't completed until after the Second World War. However, it was graded and surfaced with a mixed oil-gravel topping, which served to keep dust down.

Going-to-the-Sun Road remains Glacier's premier tourist attraction.

Seen but not seen

The design philosophy for Going-to-the-Sun Road was that it should "lay lightly on the landscape," appearing almost natural. So while bridges might be reinforced with steel and concrete, they were faced with native stone, and timber was used for decorative purposes, to give the structures a rustic look.

This careful attention to color and texture, as well as scale, has resulted in structures that were supposed to be inconspicuous now being admired for their design.

No switchbacks, please

If Lyman B. Sperry (1838–1923), for whom Sperry Glacier is named, had had his way, Going-to-the-Sun Road would have been very different and would have taken another route.

Courtesy, National Park Service

Thomas Vint

Sperry said a trans-mountain road through Glacier should go over Gunsight Pass and "have at least a few tunnels, galleries, terraces, bridges, hairpin turns, and all that sort of thing, to produce the surprises, thrills and joys that tourists seek."

Another early idea for Going-to-the-Sun Road would have done something similar, following Logan Creek, with 15 switchbacks up the cliffs to Logan Pass.

Thomas Vint (1894–1967), an assistant landscape engineer for the National Park Service, railed against that plan, saying it would leave the pristine valley "looking like miners had been in there." Instead, all the switchbacks were eliminated, with a steady incline up the north face of the valley on both sides of Logan Pass, eminently more sensible, safer and tidier.

Ray Djuff collection

The Triple Arches on Going-to-the-Sun Road are triumphs of elegance and engineering, eliminating the need for a large retaining wall.

When's a highway not a highway?

The "highway" description attached to Going-to-the-Sun Highway was replaced by the word "road" in 1956 at the insistence of National Park Service folks in Washington. The idea was to get people to take their time traveling through the national park, and telling them the winding 52-mile (83 km) route over Logan Pass was a "highway" was not the way to do it.

Local Montanans initially balked at the term, thinking that a road was something muddy and dusty, the wrong image they wanted to convey for the Going-to-the-Sun route, which by then had been mostly paved.

Executive drought

There has been a drought of presidential visitors to Glacier ever since Franklin D. Roosevelt's trip through the park in 1934. The nearest any other president came to the park was September 1952, when Harry Truman (1884–1972) made a whistle stop at West Glacier to stump for Democratic presidential nominee Adlai Stevenson (1900–1965). Richard Nixon (1913–1994) was supposed to take a helicopter tour of Glacier in September 1971, but the trip was canceled due to inclement weather.

Prime Minister and the Indian chief

John Diefenbaker (1895–1975) was the first Canadian prime minister to visit Waterton, and is the only Canadian prime minister to have visited Glacier.

Attending Many Glacier Hotel, where he was to be a keynote speaker at the 52nd annual Governors' Conference, Diefenbaker was driven back to Canada on June 27, 1960, and taken to Beebee Flats, just north of the Canada–U.S. border, where he and J. Hugo Aronson (1891–1978), the retiring Montana governor, were inducted into the Kainai Chieftainship, a select organization of the Blood Tribe of the Blackfoot Confederacy. Some 1,500 spectators witnessed the ceremony.

To get to the encampment, Diefenbaker passed within Waterton's boundaries and so his official presence is noted.

Since Diefenbaker did not come to the Waterton townsite, a brief ceremony was held at Chief Mountain border crossing preceding the Beebee Flats event. Diefenbaker was feted by Waterton residents, pioneers, boy scouts and girl guides, and an honor guard of Royal Canadian Mounted Police.

Following the Beebee Flats ceremony, the entourage returned to Many Glacier.

A flying visit

Pierre Elliott Trudeau (1919–2000) was the only Canadian prime minister to spend a night in Waterton and visit the townsite. Arriving by military helicopter on Saturday, July 10, 1971, Trudeau spent most of his time at the Prince of Wales Hotel. He also went to evening mass at Our Lady of Mount Carmel Catholic Church and then made an unannounced tour of the townsite, stopping briefly at Cameron Falls.

Courtesy Vera Quinton

Pierre Trudeau signs autographs after landing at the Prince of Wales Hotel.

During a private meeting with members of the Chamber of Commerce, he was given an honorary perpetual membership certificate, but declined a reception in his honor. He spent the rest of Saturday night and much of Sunday morning in his room. He left by helicopter at about 12:45 p.m. Sunday.

Let's see—two different views

The first "Show Me Day" in Glacier Park was held in 1956. With its objective to promote the park in spring, when few visitors generally come to Glacier, the vast majority of the people who turned up came to watch snow plowing on Going-to-the-Sun Road.

The plowing is still the most popular attraction of the annual events, one of which is usually held on the east side of the park and one on the west side, depending on the weather.

Waterton's Chamber of Commerce held a Show Me Day in June 1962 to give representatives of towns throughout southern Alberta, southeastern British Columbia and northern Montana a look at what the park had to offer to tourists.

Some 75 people attended the event, which paled in comparison to Glacier's more dramatic digging out of its famed trans-mountain road.

People-watching goats

Tourists are often thrilled to see mountain goats at Logan Pass, but few ever wonder why they are there, figuring it just happens to be a regular goat haunt.

In fact, the tourists themselves are the attraction for the goats, or at least their vehicles are. The goats enjoy the sweet taste of anti-freeze that leaks from engines, as well as minerals and salts deposited by vehicle exhausts.

Don't be surprised if you see a park ranger using a baton to chase goats out of the parking lot, as anti-freeze can be deadly to animals, just as it is for people and their pets. However, goats must have a strong constitution as none have been reported becoming ill. Rangers have also tried dousing the anti-freeze with pepper spray to deter the goats.

Don't sweat it

At Waterton's Red Rock Canyon parking lot, bighorn sheep are regulars for much the same reason mountain goats linger at Logan Pass. Early in the season, when visitors' cars still have residual road salt clinging to the surface, sheep eagerly lick parked vehicles giving the cars an odd, spotted appearance.

Later in the season, bike and motorcyclists who park and leave their helmets strapped to their machines may find them wet and well-licked upon their return.

The salt produced by human perspiration is the attraction.

Chris Morrison collection

Dedication of the Waterton portion of the international peace park did not take place until 1936, four years after the Glacier ceremony. The plaque commemorating the event, mounted on a large rock, is still located at the Prince of Wales Hotel, across from the hotel's main doors.

Race to be first

Today, the peace park concept launched in Waterton and Glacier in 1932 is hailed worldwide as a model to be copied. Although not a new idea, fruition of the peace park came about because of a resolution by members of the Rotary Club of Alberta and Montana.

Whether the peace park would be created in 1932 or at some later date was subject, for a time, to speculation, not because of government delays in passing the legislation, but because of organized opposition to the park by those who were in favor of an international peace garden at the border in Manitoba and North Dakota.

This garden had been proposed in 1929, and a bit of jealousy arose because the effort to purchase the land for the garden was by subscription, while the parks were already in the hands of the governments.

Senator Thomas Walsh, himself a landowner in Glacier, helped push the bill through the U.S. Senate after Congressman Scott Leavitt (1879–1966) had guided it through the House of Representatives. President Herbert Hoover (1874–1964) signed the bill on May 3, 1932. The first major hurdle had been leapt.

Even before Hoover made the bill official, Canada's Parliament swung into action, with the minister of the interior introducing the bill in late April.

Although the member of Parliament for Souris, Manitoba, spoke in opposition to the park plan in favor of the peace garden, the bill was passed in Canada on May 24.

Rotarians wasted no time in making arrangements for an elaborate dedication ceremony. The world's first international peace park was dedicated on June 18, 1932 at the Glacier Park Hotel. The International Peace Garden went ahead, as well, and was dedicated on July 14, 1932.

Peace park tribute got licked

When it came to marking the 50th anniversary of Waterton–Glacier International Peace Park, it was a philatelic bust.

In the United States, the postal service overlooked the peace park

Worlds' First International Peace Park
Waterton Lakes National Park, Alberta, Canada
Glacier National Park, Montana, USA

Philatelists were disappointed by the 50th anniversary of Waterton-Glacier peace park. The U.S. envelope above was privately issued with a stamp from a wildlife series. Canada issued a Waterton stamp that makes no mention of the peace park.

and instead issued a stamp commemorating the peace garden on the Manitoba–North Dakota border, which was dedicated the same year, but after Waterton–Glacier.

So when the Glacier Natural History Association produced a commemorative card and envelope to mark the 50th anniversary, it had to use a stamp of a mountain sheep, part of a series on wild animals that had no particular direct tie to the park, other than the fact sheep inhabit Glacier.

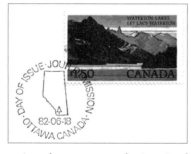

In Canada, a $1.50 definitive stamp for Waterton was issued on the anniversary of the peace park's dedication, June 18, 1982, yet no mention was made of the symbolism in the associated literature. It was the third in a series of national park stamps.

Brent Laycock, a landscape artist who spent much time in the park as a lad, was commissioned by Canada Post to design the stamp. What he came up with was his impression of the Upper Waterton Valley in shades of blue and green.

The depiction of the scene drew the ire of regular Waterton visitors because it failed to accurately portray the mountains. Others were just pleased to have Waterton recognized for the first time on a postage stamp.

A glorious idea, but ...

It may be Waterton–Glacier International Peace Park as far as government officials are concerned, but the Great Northern Railway shunned the name as too long and awkward, and for subordinating Glacier as its primary focus.

The railway would never use it in its advertising, preferring shorter, simpler phrases such as "Glorious Glacier." When Waterton was mentioned in advertisements or on brochures, it was almost always second or in smaller print. Even when the accompanying illustration featured the Canadian park, the ads were still titled "Glorious Glacier."

Today, Glacier Park, Inc., which operates the hotels formerly owned by Great Northern, sometimes reverses the name of the parks to Glacier–Waterton on its advertising material.

The G-Man's phobia

J. Edgar Hoover (1895–1972), head of the Federal Bureau of Investigation, briefly visited Glacier and Waterton in 1938 as part of a cross-country journey. Hoover was driven from Glacier to Waterton over the Chief Mountain International Highway. While in Waterton, he took a cruise down Waterton Lake on the *Motor Vessel International*. That same afternoon, he returned to Glacier.

J. Edgar Hoover

This one-day excursion involved crossing the Canada–U.S. border four times. This was extremely unusual for Hoover, who, according to a biographer, had a deep distrust of all foreigners.

Except for this and one or two other one-day excursions across the Canada–U.S. or the Mexico–U.S. borders, Hoover never traveled outside the United States.

The first X-File

Was there an ulterior motive to J. Edgar Hoover's visit to Glacier? If you're a fan of the television show *The X-Files*, you might believe so.

Episode 19, "Shapes," in the first season of *The X-Files* was about an incident at the fictional Two Medicine Ranch near Browning, Montana, in which the rancher shoots what he believes to be a beast, but it turns out to be a Native American.

During the episode, FBI agent Mulder (David Duchovny) tells his partner, Scully (Gillian Anderson) about the case: "A true piece of history, Scully. The very first X-File, initiated by J. Edgar Hoover himself.... During World War II, a series of murders occurred in and around the northwest, seven here in Browning alone.... In 1946, police cornered what they believed to be such an animal in a cabin in Glacier National Park. They shot it, but when they went in to retrieve the carcass, they found only the body of Richard Watkins."

Clearing the trail for others

The gender revolution and the equal opportunity legislation it helped foster first really made an impact on Glacier in 1972, when Sandi Nelson headed the first women's trail crew.

The other members included Merita Dablow, Janice Bonham and Connie Jo Isdahl.

The base wage for the trail crew was $3.14 an hour.

That summer, the park also hired its first female seasonal ranger since the Second World War. She was Elizabeth Sullivan, who was assigned to the west entrance of the park.

Women at the top

Women have come late to the top ranks of national parks management.

When Josie Weninger became superintendent of Waterton in September 1997, she was the first Metis woman ever appointed to head a national park in Canada. Her tenure was short-lived; she transferred to duties in the Calgary regional office late in 1998.

Suzanne Lewis was the first woman appointed superintendent of Glacier. She took over in March 2000. In 2002, she was appointed superintendent of Yellowstone.

William R. Logan was an Indian agent before becoming Glacier's first superintendent.

Let's keep it uniform

When Glacier was created in 1910, there was no National Park Service, and ranger uniforms varied from park to park. Glacier's first superintendent, William R. Logan (1856–1912), placed an order with Parker, Bridget & Co. in Washington, D.C., to supply uniforms for his rangers. At $15, the uniform consisted of "one Norfolk jacket, one wool shirt, one pair riding trousers, one pair leggings, and one felt camping hat after the Stetson style."

After examining the dark olive green uniform, the Department of the Interior, which had been under pressure to standardize the dress of park staff across the country, issued a letter sanctioning, but not requiring, the Glacier uniform be used throughout the park system.

There's no life like it

Today, we tend to see park superintendents as career public servants, but that wasn't the case in earlier times.

Glacier's first superintendent, William R. Logan, was a soldier, rising to the rank of major prior to his appointment. He started as a scout and fought in the so-called Indian wars, in the Sioux campaign, under Generals John Gibbon and A.H. Terry. He went into private enterprise for a number of years and then accepted an appointment as a United States Indian agent at Browning, Montana, which led to a number of supervisory jobs on Indian reservations, his last being Fort Belknap.

Eivind Scoyen

Eivind T. Scoyen, superintendent of Glacier from 1931 to 1938, served in the U.S. navy during the First World War and became a ranger in Yellowstone after his discharge. Scoyen was at Zion–Bryce Canyon before taking up duties in Glacier in 1930.

John George "Kootenai" Brown, Waterton's forest ranger in charge, today's equivalent of park superintendent, was commissioned as an ensign in the 8th Regiment of Foot in England in 1857. He served for three years in the British military, including a stint in India, before heading to Canada, where he worked for the colonial government of British Columbia in 1865 as a police constable. He was involved in several private enterprises and in civil service jobs in both the U.S. and Canada before taking his last job in Waterton. He retired in 1914 and died in 1916.

Permanent understudy

Henry Hutchings (1887–1955) was the understudy for the superintendent's job in Glacier longer than possibly any other second in command: nearly two decades. Starting with the park's first superintendent, William R. Logan, Hutchings would serve as an administrative aide to five successors, through to Charles Kraebel, 1924–27, and numerous acting superintendents.

Henry Hutchings

Three times Hutchings himself served as the acting superintendent until a new boss could be found. Hutchings never was appointed to the park's top job.

Explosive personality

For years, the explanation given for National Park Service director Stephen Mather blowing up the sawmill at Many Glacier in 1925 was because he was angry that Great Northern officials had ignored requests to remove the unsightly building.

In fact, Great Northern had a permit to keep the building and had not been ordered to remove it.

Glacier National Park archive

Stephen Mather

Rather, Mather was mentally unstable, suffering from bipolar disorder, or manic depression as it was then known. He went through bouts of the illness during his public service career, the first occasion prompting Horace Albright to become the de facto head of the department for two years, 1917–19, because Mather was so ill.

From eyewitness accounts and statements taken at the time of the incident at Many Glacier, Mather was again going through another bout of stress-induced depression and suffering from periods of schizophrenia. Four years later, Mather would resign his position as head of the park service due to illness, and would die a year later, in 1930.

Mather's illness was covered up until Albright wrote an account of the time, *Creating the National Park Service: The Missing Years*. Even then, the manuscript wasn't released by Albright's daughter until 1999, 12 years after her father's death.

Beds for bridge

Chief Mountain border crossing has been a vital road link between the two parks since the Chief Mountain International Highway was opened in 1936. The border port was opened on May 20, operating out of a tent, and was the highest, by elevation above sea level, customs office in Canada.

Sir Alexander Galt Museum and Archives

Canada's Chief Mountain customs and immigration office and residence was opened in 1937 and served until 1951, when it was replaced.

When visiting officials arrived to pick out the site for the new customs office, it was pouring rain and the road was a sea of mud, preventing travel. Forced to turn back, the men sought accommodation with Waterton warden Bert Barnes at the Belly River warden station.

Barnes had been posted at this station since 1928 on a year-round basis and it was one of the most remote in the park. He and his wife often went for long stretches without visitors. So when the customs men requested accommodation for a few days, one of the first questions Barnes asked was: "Can you play bridge?" Acknowledging that they did, the group spent hours into successive nights playing bridge and waiting for the rain to stop.

It was not until the beginning of the 1937 season that the new Canadian customs building, a log structure for both office and residence, was finished by Waterton builders Erik Hagglund and Carl Carlson.

The U.S. Customs office was operated out of temporary quarters until a new station was finished for the 1939 season.

The lakeshore trail, one of the first in Waterton, connects to Goat Haunt in Glacier. Today, horses are restricted from crossing the international boundary unless they have the necessary veterinary certifications.

3   On the Trail

Only a small percentage of park visitors ever enter the backcountry, but for those who do, the journey itself, either afoot or on horseback, becomes the thing that makes memories. Whether the destination is a high altitude lake to catch trout or a backcountry campsite, whether the outing is a day trip or an overnighter, speed is seldom a consideration. The sights, smells and sounds of time on the trail become the essence of adventure.

Waterton's trails slow to be developed

A good network of hiking trails in Waterton was a long time coming. Although the park was established in 1895, it was not until 1911 that even the first trail, from Cameron Falls to the international boundary, was built.

The need for good roads and bridges to bring tourists into the park competed financially with backcountry trail building, and when Canada became significantly involved in the First World War, funds and manpower for park improvements dried up.

Beginning in 1920, visitation soared, due in part to development in the townsite and to more people owning cars. This spurred the federal government to devote more resources to park improvements.

Backcountry trails served two purposes: increased visitor access and improved routes for park employees involved in fire protection, fish stocking or wildlife patrols.

In the 1920s, trails were built to Bertha Lake, Lineham Creek, Sage Pass and South Kootenay Pass, and fish stocking began. At the end of 1927, Waterton's own fish hatchery was completed to end reliance on other sources of fish for the park waters and area streams.

In the 1930s, more trails were completed, including one to Blakiston Falls, Crypt Lake and Lost Lake, and one around Bertha Lake. Kitchen shelters were constructed at many of these locations to encourage overnight camping.

Today Waterton has about 120 miles (193 km) of trails, making its back country the most developed of the Canadian mountain parks of its size.

Chris Morrison

Glacier's popular Highline Trail from Logan Pass to Granite Park Chalets is gouged out of sheer cliffs in places, and offers some spectacular mountain scenery, flora and fauna.

The squeaky wheel

Had it not been for Louis W. Hill, head of the Great Northern Railway, Glacier's system of trails might not have been developed quite as quickly as it was. Hill had a penchant for quality and adamantly expressed his opinions of trails, usually based on his personal observations during visits, to those who could make things happen.

In a 1923 tirade to superintendent J. Ross Eakin (1879–1946), for example, Hill listed a number of long-established trails that were now "not passable," "neglected" or "not in condition to travel" and "disgraceful." He also called for new trails and detailed how they should be built.

While the railway company itself was only marginally involved in trail construction—it built the Mount Henry trail from Glacier Park Hotel to Two Medicine Chalets in 1913—Hill said he felt his firm's investment in the park justified his demands. And demand he did.

Over a period of about 20 years, Hill sent letter after letter criticizing, cajoling, threatening and warning that trails must be built or improved and be well-maintained because "the tourist spends only a few hours on roads and several days on trails."

As it was in the beginning and continues to be today, there was never enough money, people or time to do everything that needed to be done. But Hill's nagging eventually paid off. Congress gradually increased appropriations, and by the time Hill retired as chairman of the railway in 1929, trails in Glacier had been substantially improved.

Chief among mountains

Although not the highest peak in the area, Chief Mountain (9,080 ft, 2,767 m), due to its isolation from other mountains and prominence when viewed from the prairie, has attracted the attention of hikers and climbers from earliest times.

One of the more notable legends about the mountain has to do with a young Flathead native who climbed its summit on a "vision quest." In a vision quest, a native person goes to an inspirational site and fasts over several days, chanting songs and hoping to commune with the spirits, through a vision, who will decide his destiny.

As the legend goes, the spirit of the mountain tried to drive the Flathead youth off, but after four days, gave up and made peace, giving the young man powerful "medicine" that made him a renowned warrior. It is said the Flathead left behind on the mountain a bison skull, which he had used as a pillow during his quest.

The legend gained authenticity when in 1892 Henry L. Stimson, later Secretary of State under President Hoover and Secretary of War under President Roosevelt, hiked to the summit of Chief Mountain, where his guide discovered a weathered bison skull.

"It was certainly one of the very oldest I have ever seen," Stimson wrote of the bison skull in a later account of the hike. "We left the skull where it had been found. Much as we should have treasured it as a token of the day, the devotion of the old warrior who had brought it was an influence quite sufficient to protect this memorial of his visit."

Ray Djuff collection

Courtesy, Richard Schwab

When Eric Schwab, 18, right, reached the summit of Chief Mountain on August 3, 1976, accompanied by his father, uncle, cousin and a friend, he discovered remnants of a bison skull that may confirm a native legend.

Joining Stimson (1867–1950) on the climb were Dr. Walter James of New York and Blackfeet guide William Kipp; it was the first climb of Chief Mountain recorded in modern times.

In 1976, Eric Schwab of Santa Ana, California, found two very old bison teeth and a few deteriorated bone fragments that may have been the same items found by Stimson. Schwab also discovered a register that had been placed at the summit in 1896 by a border survey party. He left the skull fragments there, just as Stimson had.

Chris Morrison

Mount Cleveland, at left, is Glacier's highest, but is best seen from Waterton. Melting snow on Cleveland's north face marks summer's progress.

Reaching for the top

It might be the view, it might be the challenge or it might just be that reaching the top of many mountains is so physically demanding that the joy is in the achievement.

Even from the early days of the parks, visitors have sought to get to the top of the peaks. One of the first scrambles up Glacier's tallest was recorded in 1914, when a group of American and Canadian friends climbed Mount Cleveland (10,466 ft, 3,190 m) and claimed bragging rights for their achievement.

To confirm claims were valid, the practice of placing hiking registers at mountain summits was begun in both Waterton and Glacier, and even today no climb is considered complete without everyone in the party making an entry.

On Mount Cleveland there were two climbing registers, one placed there in 1920 by three members of the Nature Study Club of Indiana and another, in a weather-proof lead container, carried up by a special committee of the Sierra Alpine Club of California in 1924.

Since the best route up Mount Cleveland is via the broken cliffs and shale side of the southwest face, it is a long, hot and arduous climb that is not to everyone's physical abilities.

Ode to a mountain

"To the God of the open air we dedicate this mountain summit. To us has been given the rare privilege of its attainment. Splendid and inspiring is the reward of the toilsome ascent! Its rugged course most trying was, but now triumphant visions greet us everywhere, symbolizing the blessings to the steadfast traveler along life's trail.

"The flame we here do kindle typifies the awakening of the inert dead into flaming life, effulgent and eternal. Its smoke, rising far beyond our reach and ken, wafts upward the spirit of our aspiration toward the beneficent and Infinite One, whose presence and power we acknowledge with grateful hearts."

This dedication was usually read by Dr. Frank B. Wynn, president of the Nature Study Club of Indiana, whose members came to Glacier from 1919 to 1922 to hike and climb peaks. Once at the top, they would light a small fire with twigs they'd brought and give the blessing. They also placed registers in flat metal boxes on many peaks, including Chief Mountain, Going-to-the-Sun Mountain (9,642 ft, 2,939 m), Mount Gould (9,553 ft, 2,912 m) and Mount Jackson (10,052 ft, 3,064 m). Until the 1960s, the boxes and registers remained, but have all since disappeared.

Dr. Wynn died near the top of Mount Siyeh (10,014 ft, 3,052 m) on July 27, 1922.

They were tramping, but weren't tramps

Before it was called hiking, walking Waterton and Glacier's trails was more commonly known as "tramping." The idea was to cover distances and not resort to using built facilities for accommodations, but instead camp along the way, in the manner of hobos, or tramps.

One of the earliest organized groups of "trampers" in Glacier was the Seattle

This brochure featuring the Seattle Mountaineers promoted "tramping," or hiking as we now know it, a popular pastime prior to the First World War.

Mountaineers, whose 115 members arrived in 1914 for two weeks of hiking and climbing. These trampers, though, did periodically avail themselves of the Great Northern's accommodations (their room costs may have been underwritten by the railway). They went from Two Medicine to Red Eagle Pass, cross-country to Gunsight Lake, then over Piegan Pass and Swiftcurrent Pass to Waterton. They then hiked back to Lake McDonald.

The story of their adventures, *With the "Mountaineers" in Glacier National Park*, proved a valuable advertising tool for Great Northern to attract like-minded visitors to the park.

The Seattle Mountaineers would return to Glacier again in 1934 and 1952.

Group hiking—by the hundreds

The Sierra Club of California held its summer outing in Glacier in July 1924. For three weeks 200-plus club members traveled through the north section of the park, hiking and climbing.

The majority hiked from Belton to the head of the Upper Waterton Lake in stretches of 12 to 14 miles (19 to 23 km) a day. They set up hundreds of pup tents on the lakeshore, spent the night and climbed Mount Cleveland, their ultimate objective.

So appealing were the parks that other Sierra Club members returned in 1937, 1954, 1955 and 1956, bringing with them a highly organized routine.

On the 1954 trip, 170 members, ranging in age from children to grandparents, hiked from Many Glacier to Waterton and back, covering between 50 and 60 miles (80 to 100 km) in 10 days. Organized as a military body, the hikers each carried a bedroll and personal equipment amounting to 30 pounds (14 kg). A commissary group of 25, whose expenses were paid by the club, was responsible for setting up camps and doing most of the camp work. Members of the club assisted by gathering firewood and doing other camp jobs. Cooks were hired to prepare the food for the entire group.

At the peak of his form

Ray Djuff collection

Norman Clyde

Among Glacier climbers, Norman Clyde (1885–1972) is a legend. The school teacher from Independence, California, came to the park in 1923 and spent a month and a half on the trails.

In that time, he climbed 38 peaks (some say 42 peaks), at least 10 of which were first ascents.

On top of that, Clyde eschewed the bus service offered by Glacier Park Transportation Company, walking everywhere.

Clyde returned the following summer to continue his climbing, though at a less hectic pace. In two years, he had 50 summits to his credit, a record which many in the Glacier Mountaineering Society strive to achieve—over decades.

Glacier would be but a side trip for Clyde, more popularly linked with the Sierras. He wrote many books and articles on his decades of climbing in the California mountains, where a peak is named for him.

Alone at the top

Rolf Engel, originally from Bavaria, is believed to have been the first person to climb Mount Cleveland alone, a practice frowned on by experienced park people.

Engel took two days to complete his journey in July 1953. On the first day, he climbed to the timberline, reaching the summit late the next afternoon. Prunes and chocolate bars, traditional foods of Bavarian climbers, made up his meals.

Engel worked as night watch relief in East Glacier Park during the summer and attended the University of Washington. His family had emigrated from Germany to Seattle in 1947.

Don't try to keep up

With modern, lightweight equipment, some of today's hikers think nothing of covering 20 miles (32 km) or more in a day. They'd certainly find a kindred spirit in Albert "Death on the Trail" Reynolds, one of Glacier's first rangers.

C.D. O'Neil, a pioneer lumberman in the Flathead Valley, told of an incident between Dr. Lyman Sperry and Reynolds that's but one example of how the latter earned his nickname.

Dr. Lyman Sperry

Sperry was with a group from Oberlin College when they met Reynolds on the trail in the mid-afternoon. They had given up trying to make it to the top of a near-by mountain, as it was farther than they could comfortably do that day. Instead, Sperry said they'd climb it the next day, when they had more time.

Reynolds, however, said he'd climb it that afternoon and promptly disappeared, turning up in Sperry's camp that evening, saying when they went up the next day, the party would find a piece of paper with everyone's name on it.

When they reached the summit the next day, "sure enough, and to their surprise, they found the note with their names on it—plus a notation of their approximate heights and weights," O'Neil said.

Albert "Death on the Trail" Reynolds

Speed demons

In the 1910s and 1920s, when saddle horse trips were considered the way to see Waterton and Glacier, a tour of the parks could easily last a week or more. Environmentalist and outdoor enthusiast John Muir (1838–1914) recommended that visitors to Glacier "give a month at least to this precious reserve."

While the park remains, as Muir said, "the best care-killing scenery on the continent," some of today's hikers are taking it in at a much less leisurely pace than did visitors of yesteryear.

Where a trip from Logan Pass to Goat Haunt might have taken three days by horse, with stops at Granite Park and Fifty Mountain, ranger Kyle Johnson, Glacier's wilderness manager, says it's now often done in a day.

"Twenty-plus mile trips aren't that unheard of anymore," Johnson told the Kalispell *Daily Inter Lake* in 2004.

"I know a lot of people who don't go overnight in Glacier backcountry," he said. "They like to go light and go fast."

Better hiking shoes, lighter equipment and wildlife fears while camping are cited as some of the reasons for the growing long-distance day hiking trend.

Chris Morrison, The Lethbridge Herald

Bud Larson, left, and Mike Hicken climbed the parks' two highest peaks, Cleveland and Waterton, within 24 hours, a rare feat they both agreed they'd never attempt again.

Two mountains in one day

Reaching the summit of either Mount Cleveland or Mount Blakiston (9,547 ft, 2,910 m), respectively Glacier and Waterton's tallest peaks, is an admirable achievement claimed by only a select few, but climbing both mountains in the same day is an incredible accomplishment.

Not only did Bud Larson, 25, and Mike Hicken, 26, both of Alberta, reach the top of the two mountains in one day in August 1994, they took a video camera with them to document their climbs. The men set out from Waterton in a private boat at 5:30 a.m., reaching the starting point for the hike up Mount Cleveland at 6 a.m. Five and a half hours later, moving at full speed, they reached the summit.

Descent was by a different route, which appeared from the summit looking down to be shorter but, in fact, was fraught with errors, not the least of which was crashing through skin-tearing brush.

"There's no quick way down unless you fall," Hicken said later. A normal round trip hike up and down Mount Cleveland takes two days.

Met at the lakeshore by a Waterton cottager with a boat who had learned of the challenge, the men were rushed to the Waterton townsite, where they jumped in a car and zipped to the Lineham trail head to begin the Blakiston portion of the adventure.

By 8:15 p.m. they had topped Mount Blakiston and about an hour later, when they had returned to the trail head, they had a small crowd of admirers and friends waiting for them.

Copycats

During the mid-1920s, the Park Saddle Horse Company hired climbing guides, who were stationed at Many Glacier Hotel, to cater to the growing popularity of rock climbing.

Hans Reiss (1885–1968), the brother of artist Winold Reiss (1886–1953) and an artist/sculptor in his own right, was one of the guides. Another was Leo Seethaler, who in 1928 guided groups at Grinnell Glacier. Seethaler once climbed the huge rock chimney in the dining room of Many Glacier Hotel to show off his ability and drum up business.

The hiring of Reiss and Seethaler came at the same time rival Canadian Pacific Railway brought in Swiss mountain guides at its Banff Springs Hotel. The loss of tourism during the Depression ended the hiring of European guides in Glacier.

The taming of the steed

One of the challenges of the Park Saddle Horse Company was overcoming the fear of dudes about riding and traveling long distances on a saddle horse over Glacier's mountain trails. Most tourists to the

Ray Djuff collection

The caption for this photo from a 1930s Great Northern Railway brochure had this advice for dudes wary of riding on Glacier's mountain trails: "The guide is a sage counselor in matters pertaining to horsemanship."

park, frequently easterners, had not ridden a horse before or had limited experience around them.

When the Depression hit and ridership fell—from a high of 9,700 people in 1926, or 26 percent of all Glacier visitors, to 1,800 in 1932, or 3.5 percent of park visitors—saddle horse company owner George W. Noffsinger (1883–1947) tried advertising the fact that his horses were now gentler.

This was achieved, Noffsinger claimed, by breeding the plains broncos with Arabian stallions. He said it "solved the problem of taking the shimmying buck and kick out of the western pony."

Ridership did increase, but not enough to see the Park Saddle Horse Company survive past the Second World War.

Laying it on—thick

How gullible are tourists? Very, if you'd asked Glacier dude wrangler James Whilt (1878–1967) during his hey-days as a guide in the 1920s and 1930s. Whilt, like other wranglers, was renowned for stringing dudes (tourists) along with outrageous stories that usually contained enough of a kernel of truth to merit attention, until disbelief kicked in. Here is an example:

"There was a time when dude wranglers used long horses in the park—three saddles to a horse. But the park trail-makers put in the switchbacks on the trails, and the long horses could not get their hind legs around the corners. So the horse company had to get shorter horses."

* * *

"Right up there, folks," the dude wrangler told his party of tourists, "is where an Indian jumped off a cliff to three thousand feet below."

"Oh, mercy!" said one of the women. "Was the poor fellow killed?"

"Killed?!" replied the wrangler. "No, no! Why, he had on his light fall suit!"

* * *

"Oh, you poor man! Did you get your finger cut off?" asked the sympathetic lady, noticing that one of the guide's fingers was missing.

"Oh, no, lady!" the guide replied. "It just got worn down from pointing at mountains all day."

Bourbon—on the rocks

Hoke Smith, Great Northern's Glacier publicity agent in the 1910s and 1920s, had an incredible imagination and was given to telling tall tales about his time on park trails. One such story concerned a secret outcropping that served up ice-cold bourbon that was 4,000 years old.

As Smith described it, the area that is now the national park was once home to "a most thriving and prosperous people who raised great quantities of corn." An earthquake tossed the cornfields into the air and then "dropped down great fissures in the ground, and three or four mountain ranges piled on top of them." A hot-water geyser "flowed through the buried corn, distilling the grain and turning it to whisky," which seeped out "a cute little spring."

During the dry years of Prohibition, the tale no doubt took on added significance with one man vowing to find the spring and stake a claim on it.

Beware the Wimpuss

Another of Hoke Smith's hoary stories concerned the secretive but lively Glacier wimpuss. "A wimpuss grows about as big as a hoogle-bug, but it has a long tail like a collywop and has wings like a bearcat. It lives in the top of high trees, whence it flies down to attack defenseless travelers."

MAKING THE WIMPUSSES LAUGH

This cartoon suggests one way to handle Glacier's elusive, and fictional, wimpuss.

However, Smith would tell listeners, "no harm is to be feared from the wimpuss if you know what to do when you see one comin'," after which followed a convoluted story about subduing the creatures by setting a trap with cheese by a waterfall and tying its tail in a double bow-knot.

During the early years of Great Northern's involvement in Glacier Park, staff regaled guests and visitors with stories about wimpusses, fired on no doubt by hotel company officials who published a newsletter for its workers called "The Wimpuss." It also helped that someone commissioned two wimpusses from a taxidermist. They were displayed at hotels in the chain for some time.

Warren Hanna (1898–1987), a transportation agent at Many Glacier Hotel about the time of the First World War, described the exhibit as "part fish and part bird, with an odd cranium like that of a monkey surmounting its body."

These Eagle Scouts came from troops across the U.S. Northwest in 1929 to work on the trail from Red Eagle Landing on St. Mary Lake to the upper end of the lake.

Doing their good deed

If one good turn deserves another, the Eagle Scouts of Montana, Washington, Oregon and Idaho got their just desserts for the trail work they did in Glacier. Starting in 1925, the scouts built and improved trails in the park with the full approval of Stephen Mather (1867–1930), then director of the National Park Service.

For 10 days at a time during the summers of 1925 and 1927–1932, the scouts labored with picks, shovels, mattocks, crosscut saws, crowbars and brush hooks. They cut timber, built bridges, moved rocks and leveled the soil for park trails along the shore of St. Mary Lake from Red Eagle landing and in the Two Medicine area.

Their only expense was for rail transportation home. Tools, equipment, supplies and a cook were furnished by the National Park Service.

The boys, ages 14 to 19, having accomplished their good deeds, returned husky, clean and healthy-looking when they came out of the mountains.

Over this hill and that

The Thursday Over-the-Hill Gang is a group of friends, who have been hiking and climbing Glacier peaks each Thursday during the summer since 1976.

The median age of the hikers is 65. As older members retire, it is often their children who join the hikes. It's calculated that each member of "the Gang" will hike about 350 miles (564 km) a season, climbing 100,000 vertical feet (30,480 m) doing so.

The origin of the Gang was the Thursday Mountain Club, consisting of mostly Kalispell-area seniors with an insatiable appetite for hiking and mountain scrambling. Some of the original members included Harry Isch, Ivan O'Neill, Spencer Ryder, Dr. Harry Gibson and Ambrose Measure.

The exploits of club members gained wider prominence when journalist George Ostrom joined the ranks, recounting exploits and tidbits in his newspaper columns and in his commentaries on the KOFI radio station in Kalispell, Montana.

Ruhle rules

For decades, the bible for Glacier hikers was park naturalist George C. Ruhle's *Guide to Glacier*, favored for its thorough description of trails and the conditions hikers could expect, as well as for valuable information for the motorist.

Ruhle (1900–1994), who held a PhD in nuclear physics and taught at the universities of Oklahoma, California and Illinois, was appointed Glacier's first permanent naturalist in 1929 and spent 12 years in the park. To obtain trail mileage for his book, he pushed a cyclometer attached to a bicycle wheel all over the park's nearly 1,000 miles (1,610 km) of trails.

Glacier National Park archive

Dr. George C. Ruhle

Ruhle produced his *Guide to Glacier* in 1949, with revised editions published in 1954, 1957 and 1963. Ironically, Ruhle was working at another national park, at Crater Lake, when *Guide to Glacier* came out.

Prior to Ruhle's publication, hikers relied on a guide produced in 1924 (and updated in 1930) by Dr. Morton J. Elrod. While comprehensive for its time, Elrod's *Guide to and Book of Information of Glacier National Park* was outdated by the 1940s.

Ruhle returned to Glacier and produced an updated version of his guide in 1972 called *The Roads and Trails of Waterton–Glacier National Parks*, which amazed readers by proving to be even better than his first thorough work.

Where goats dare not tread

Numerous hiking guidebooks have been produced since George Ruhle's last work. For those of a more serious bent, J. Gordon Edwards' *A Climber's Guide to Glacier National Park* is a must-have, featuring not only climbs, but detailed descriptions of all the goat trails and other lesser-known paths. It was first released in 1976 and has been updated at least three times since.

Courtesy, Rolf Larson

J. Gordon Edwards

Gordon Edwards' interest in Glacier began in the late 1940s when he became a seasonal ranger-naturalist in the park. His unconventional routes, particularly along goat paths, have now become famous: Iceberg Notch, Ptarmigan Traverse and the Red Gap Traverse. Gordon pioneered the routes to more than 70 peaks in Glacier.

His wife, Alice, is no slouch either, climbing many of the peaks with him, including six of those in the park that are over 10,000 feet (3,048 m). At the turn of the century, the two, both octogenarians, were still scrambling about in the park, with a next generation of the family often leading the way.

Gordon Edwards was an entomologist at California's San Jose State University and was known to stop mid-climb to collect a rare bug or two. His collection is now housed in the Gordon Edwards Museum of Entomology at the university.

Edwards, known as the patron saint of climbing in Glacier, died in the summer of 2004 at age 85 while hiking with Alice on Divide Mountain (8,665 ft, 2,641 m), just outside the park.

Getting a leg up

One-legged taxidermist Clyde Cobb of Kalispell climbed to the summit of Going-to-the-Sun Mountain (9,642 ft, 2,939 m) during the summer of 1926 along with friend Edward Clysdale, taking a little over seven hours to reach the top from Going-to-the-Sun Chalets (the chalets, located at Sun Point on St. Mary Lake, were torn down in the late 1940s).

While Cobb usually wore an artificial limb with a shoe (his leg was amputated below the knee), for his treks in the park he used a peg. He said it worked fine, except on loose rock or shale, when he'd tie a large piece of leather over the end to prevent it from slipping.

In his brother's footsteps

Jim Kanzler overcame incredible odds and a family jinx when he, Terry Kennedy and Steve Jackson became the first to climb the north face of Mount Cleveland in September 1976.

Kanzler's brother, Jerry, died in an avalanche trying to do the same climb in December 1969.

The foreboding north face of 10,466-foot-high (3,190 m) Cleveland was not climbed again until August 1991, when Kenny Kasselder, 24, and Mark Brown, 23, both of Whitefish, managed the feat. It took them 15 hours of climbing, 10 pitches or sections of roped climbing, and a bivouac midway.

Mysterious disappearances

There have been several mysterious disappearances of hikers in Glacier. One of the first, which prompted considerable media attention, was in August 1924 when brothers Joseph Whitehead, 29, and William Whitehead, 22, both of Chicago, vanished while hiking between Granite Park and the Lewis Hotel (now Lake McDonald Lodge).

Despite considerable effort, the involvement of the Federal Bureau of Investigation and the offer of reward money, the Whiteheads were never found.

Ten years later, in August 1934, Dr. Frederick H. Lumley, 27, an assistant professor at Ohio State University, set out alone from Goat Haunt camp at the south end of Upper Waterton Lake to hike to the Waterton townsite and was never seen again. An extensive search, which included experienced backcountry men and the use of tracking dogs, failed to turn up even the smallest item belonging to Lumley. Neither the FBI nor the Royal Canadian Mounted Police were able to solve the disappearance and the reward money for Lumley's return went unclaimed.

$1,700.00 REWARD

For

JOSEPH and WILLIAM WHITEHEAD

Brothers disappeared Sunday, August 24, on the trail between Granite Park Chalets and the Lewis Hotel in Glacier National Park, Montana.

JOSEPH H. WHITEHEAD

WILLIAM A. WHITEHEAD

Age 29.
Height, 5 ft. 11 in.
Weight, 175 lbs.
Gray eyes.
Dark brown hair.
Ruddy complexion.
Wore glasses with dark rims.

Age, 22.
Height, 5 ft. 11½ in.
Weight, 155 lbs.
Brown eyes.
Dark brown hair.
Dark complexion.
Wore glasses with dark rims.

Both wore hiking clothes: gray knickers, gray wool shirts, high, tan laced hiking shoes, soft felt hats. Carried light packs. Both wore sweaters: one gray, the other tan.

Sons of Mrs. Dora B. Whitehead, 3040 Warren Avenue, Chicago.

Notify: Charles J. Kraebel, Supt. Glacier National Park, Belton, Montana.

Glacier National Park archive

This reward poster was issued in 1924 after the Whitehead brothers went missing.

In July 1963, David Paul Wilson, 20, a summer employee with the National Park Service, disappeared after signing the climbing register on Going-to-the-Sun Mountain. Neither Glacier Park staff nor the FBI turned up a single clue to Wilson's disappearance.

Gone without a trace

The case of Larry T. Kimble continues to puzzle Glacier officials. Kimble, 40, disappeared from his home in Dorr, Michigan, in the spring of 2003. His 1998 GMC truck was found in a parking area for the Rocky Point trailhead on the Inside North Fork Road in Glacier on June 16, 2003. Kimble had been in or around Glacier since at least May 29, the date on a park entrance receipt found in the truck.

Divers checked the water of Lake McDonald off Rocky Point, search dogs were brought in and underwater cameras were used, all to no avail. The search was postponed that summer after several massive forest fires swept through the western parts of Glacier.

In June 2004, five dog teams were deployed, utilizing animals that specialize in cadaver recovery, but no clues about Kimble were found.

The matter remains an unsolved missing person case.

The mysterious camper

The last evidence officials have of Patrick T. Whalen alive is on November 3, 2000, when his Toyota pickup hit a deer on Highway 89 near Kiowa Junction. The truck was found abandoned on the road, but there was no sign of Whalen.

In May 2001, Glacier rangers on a patrol of the Cut Bank Valley found an illicit camp that Whalen, 33, of Cleveland, Ohio, had used the previous fall, but no evidence that he'd been there since.

A two-day search of the area with dogs found no further signs of Whalen, who family members said had been showing signs of paranoia prior to disappearing. There have been no signs of him since.

Horses were never like this

The first motorized trail ride to make it through the Akamina Pass was staged as a protest, or "drive in," from Polebridge, Montana, to Cameron Lake in early September 1969, at a time when a "sit in" was the way to make a statement.

Sponsored by the Waterton Chamber of Commerce to draw attention to a long sought after highway through the pass to link Glacier and Waterton, the ride was open to all comers with four-wheel-drive vehicles. According to Chamber president Emanuel Cohen, two-wheel drive vehicles would not be able to maneuver many of the 15 stream crossings along the 22-mile (35 km) route. Some 28 vehicles carrying 80 people from Alberta and Montana participated and good weather contributed to successful completion of the trip.

The motorized trail rides, dubbed The Kishinena Caravan, were repeated in 1970 and 1971, but despite public discussions that went on for years, the road was never built, in large measure because of the refusal of British Columbia.

With the turn of the 21st century, federal–provincial government discussions were reopened. This time the goal was not to build the road but rather to extend Waterton Lakes National Park westward to incorporate British Columbia's Akamina–Kishinena Provincial Park. Talks continue.

The ring bearer

Mark Wolodkewitsch and his girlfriend Treena Hutchins of Des Moines, Iowa, were looking for a pebble keepsake at Sunrift Gorge, along Going-to-the-Sun Road, in August 2002 when Wolodkewitsch said: "Come up and see this rock I found."

Wolodkewitsch opened a green box containing a ring, intending to pop the question to Hutchins, when the ring "sprung out of the box. We watched it hit a rock and fall into the gorge. We were stunned."

They spent two days hunting for the ring and when they couldn't find it, turned to the park authorities for help. Charles Farmer, a park ranger, agreed to don his wetsuit and snorkel and, after repeated dives, found it, wedged between two boulders in a deep part of the gorge.

"He came back up and was holding the ring in both hands," Hutchins said. "He handed me the ring, I put it on my finger and I started screaming."

Seat of the pants hiking

Chicago resident John Mauff (1912–2004) hiked Glacier's trails nearly every summer from 1946 to 2000, but even he was caught short a few times despite his vast experience in the park.

During the summer of 1958, Mauff was hiking up Mount Helen (8,538 ft, 2,602 m) when clouds suddenly rolled in, quickly followed by sunset and darkness. Unable to see the headwall and a 1,500-foot (450 m) sheer drop ahead and without a trail to follow, Mauff descended by the "seat of the pants" method. He reached the bottom of the headwall safely and then waded along the shore of Upper Two Medicine Lake to the trail.

Mauff, a member of the Glacier Mountaineering Society, said it was the first time climbing in the park that he'd been caught by night.

Vice-Presidential visit to Glacier

When the vice-president of the United States comes to visit, success is all in the details, lots and lots of details.

Having already geared up for the 50th anniversary ceremonies of the Going-to-the-Sun Road and the arrival of Secretary of the Interior James G. Watt in July 1983, the park staff was in action mode when it was announced that Vice-President George Herbert Walker Bush and his wife, Barbara, planned to be in Glacier August 6–8.

The trip was the suggestion of Derrick Crandell, president of the American Recreation Coalition, a non-profit group involved in partnerships to enhance outdoor recreational opportunities. The visit would provide Bush with a taste of a national park experience.

Chris Morrison collection

To Chris Morrison, best wishes,

Barbara Bush   George Bush

Barbara and George Bush sent this photo to the author after learning she had, some years later, used the same tent they did while visiting Glacier.

An advance team including members of Bush's staff, White House communications agency staff and the Secret Service arrived in the park a month before to spend three days scouting the facilities.

Every detail was attended to, including the assignment of four navy frogmen to patrol Lake McDonald near Fish Creek Campground, where the vice-president would be staying.

Twelve members of the national parks special events team, additional Secret Service men, Glacier rangers and intelligence security were also at the ready.

The Coleman Company, makers of outdoor equipment, arrived with a caravan, including a semi-trailer loaded with 24 lanterns, 12 coolers, eight tents, 35 sleeping bags, 12 day packs, four canoes, eight pop-up trailers and the largest Coleman cook stove in the world, featuring two large grills atop 20 burners.

Other suppliers provided self-inflating air mattresses, 20 day packs, three motor boats ranging from 17 to 21 feet (5.1 to 6.3 m) long, a 22-foot (6.6 m) recreational vehicle for the Secret Service command post and a 28-foot (8.4 m) fifth-wheel trailer with shower facilities.

Prior to the arrival of Bush and his wife, all of the equipment was set up, tested and retested.

The next morning after breakfast, Bush and a small group were driven to Logan Pass, where they then hiked into Hidden Lake to fish. They later greeted visitors and posed for photos at the Logan Pass visitor center. Barbara Bush stayed behind in the camp and later attended church services at the Fish Creek Amphitheater and took a walk on the Rocky Point Nature Trail, along Lake McDonald.

Swimming and boating followed in the afternoon.

The next morning, after a 40-minute news conference and photo session, the couple was driven to Glacier International Airport in Kalispell, where they left on Air Force 2 for Casper, Wyoming.

This photograph of a Blackfeet camp by St. Mary Lake was one of many staged to create the impression the natives were "Glacier's" Indians.

You weren't the first

As you walk the trails of Glacier and Waterton parks, it's relatively easy to think of the First Nations people who may have tread on some of the same paths. Long before the Native Americans, however, the foothills and valleys of Glacier and Waterton were home to the Clovis people.

Evidence of their treks some 10,000 years ago in and around the parks is found in the distinctive tools, such as rock net weights and spear points, they left behind at camp sites. In a 1998 survey of Glacier, University of Calgary archeologist Dr. Brian Reeves identified 450 possible sites related to the Clovis people.

Know your audience

Doug Follett, a seasonal ranger-naturalist in Glacier and former teacher from Whitefish, Montana, has acquired an incredible amount of knowledge in four decades of working in and living near the park. His ranger talks and guided hikes, while folksy, can be spellbinding, not to mention authoritative.

Early in his career as a summer ranger, though, there were slip-ups.

Follett recalls that he had trouble remembering the names of all the wildflowers in Glacier, so when someone would ask about a particular flower, Follett would identify it as a "mouse-ear chickweed." After pointing out a number of different variations, a woman asked Follett where he got his information and he replied from a certain book.

"That's impossible," the lady said.

"Why?" asked Follett.

"Because I'm the author of that book," the lady replied.

For the rest of the walk, the woman "assisted" Follett with his flower identification skills.

Preparation—Don't leave home without it

Park visitors who venture into the backcountry unprepared and encounter trouble often find the mountains an unforgiving, foreboding place. Take the case of University of Calgary students Norman Ferguson, 25, and Joan Fulton, 22, who decided to take a day hike in June 1975 without benefit of proper footwear, adequate clothing or food, and without checking conditions or the weather forecast.

They set out on a Sunday afternoon walk from Cameron Lake on the 2.5 mile (4 km) trail toward Summit Lake and were caught by a blizzard. They became lost when they were disoriented by the falling snow.

A search was launched Monday, when park officials were alerted by friends that the two were missing. Twelve men, including Canadian wardens, U.S. rangers and the Royal Canadian Mounted Police, using a search dog and a helicopter, combed the area.

An SOS the students made from pine bows was spotted from the air on Wednesday afternoon. They were rescued two miles (3.2 km) south of the Canada–U.S. border, in the North Lakes region of Glacier, miles from where they had set out.

Fulton, who lost her tennis shoes during the ordeal while tramping through the heavy wet snow, suffered only exposure and frostbite. Ferguson was checked but not admitted to hospital. Waterton superintendent Tom Smith labeled the incident a "near tragedy."

Know your limits

Knowing your limits can be a life saver on a seemingly innocent hike.

When two New Jersey university students set out on a stroll over a mountain ridge in Waterton's Red Rock Canyon area in June 1980, they walked into nothing but trouble.

The two men, looking for a remote campsite, had begun following a well-used sheep trail to cross a steep hillside when suddenly they realized the climb was more than they had bargained for—they were above a cliff with a 197-foot (63 m) drop.

Panicked and afraid to move, for five hours they called for help.

Eventually two other hikers at Goat Lake heard them and summoned help. Three wardens made their way to the stranded men and eased them down to safety.

Two lost hikers ended up here, at Lake Nooney in the northern section of Glacier, after becoming disoriented in a June snow storm. They mistook Nooney for Cameron Lake.

Chris Morrison

"They just about kissed us," said warden Max Winkler, who took part in the rescue.

Peace park hike a long tradition

The first regularly scheduled international peace park group hikes were begun in late June 1978. Led by naturalists from both Waterton and Glacier, the day-long Saturday hikes have become a mainstay of peace park interpretation.

The hikes begin in Waterton heading south on the lakeshore trail, with a brief hands-across-the-border ceremony at the international boundary, and continue to Goat Haunt for the boat ride back to Waterton.

The peace park hike format grew to include an interpretative presentation in the Falls Theatre the night before, so hikers could have a better understanding of the significance of the joining of these two parks.

Chris Morrison

An impromptu hands-across-the-border ceremony at the international boundary on the shore of Upper Waterton Lake is a routine part of the peace park hike.

The hikes continued until the summer of 2002, when they were suspended for a time while the U.S. and Canada unraveled a sticky matter related to unmanned border crossings following the terrorist attacks the preceding September.

In the summer of 2004, the peace park hike was increased to twice a week, Wednesdays and Saturdays, to accommodate growing interest in this one major guided hike through both parks.

Bear, let go of my hand

Anyone who spends any time on the trails of Waterton and Glacier will inevitably come back with a bear story, usually a sighting—and hopefully from afar. For former Glacier seasonal ranger-naturalist J. Gordon Edwards, the experience on July 24, 1972, was up-close and much too personal.

The encounter happened near Morning Eagle Falls, near Grinnell Lake, while Edwards was hiking by himself. The "yip, yip" of two bear cubs, followed by the bawling of a sow grizzly abruptly ended the idyllic sojourn.

The sow leaped through the thick brush after Edwards, a rock and ice climber who said he instinctively held up his ice axe for protection. The bear ran into the point of the axe and fell, off balance, rolling a short way down the hill. The bear quickly righted herself and came at Edwards again, this time knocking the axe from his hand as she leapt at him. After a moment's confusion, Edwards found himself face-to-face with his left hand in the sow's mouth.

Edwards said he dropped to his knees and tried to get his hand out, talking gently to the bear and patting it on the head. The bear finally let go and, with a last bawl at Edwards, rejoined her cubs.

While Edward's hand was bloodied and required 15 stitches, there was no permanent damage.

Water is biggest park hazard

The chief cause of accidental deaths in Waterton and Glacier is not attacks by wild animals, but mishaps involving water.

While there are many stories of near-drownings in both parks, what seemed like a good idea at the time—forming a human chain to cross a stream—nearly resulted in a group disaster in July 1950.

Five girls, three of whom were members of the Prince of Wales Hotel staff and acquainted with the potential dangers of the park, were heading to Glacier along the lakeshore trail when they discovered the bridge over Boundary Creek had been washed away by spring flooding.

Undaunted, they tied their shoes together and put them around their necks before forming a chain to cross the swift-flowing, icy stream. They had nearly reached the far side when one of the girls slipped and was carried downstream toward the lake. Only grabbing onto a log jam allowed her to clamber to safety.

Another girl, who could not swim, was also washed downstream, and popped to the surface face down. She was pulled to safety, but lost her shoes, making the hike over the next four miles (6.4 km) to Goat Haunt an unforgettable ordeal.

Water hazards are plentiful in the parks, even at seemingly innocuous mountain lakes such as Kootenai Lake in Glacier.

Where there's a will, there's a way

Packing a horse takes skill, ingenuity and sometimes determination, depending on the load.

In the summer of 1949, when Waterton dance hall owner/operator Pat Maclean decided he wanted his 12-foot (3.65 m) canoe taken to Bertha Lake, reached only by a 3.65 mile (5.8 km) trail from the

Ray Djuff collection

As if to prove naysayers wrong, a person was photographed plying a boat on Bertha Lake. The craft was likely packed up on horseback.

townsite, some said it couldn't be done. But horseman Slim Walker thought otherwise.

The skilled packer not only loaded the boat on a horse, he made near record time getting to Bertha Lake and back to the townsite again: two-and-a-half hours flat.

When Maclean had time to try his fishing luck in the well-stocked lake that summer, he was able do so from the comfort of his own canoe rather than hiking around the lake.

Lack of a ski lift wouldn't stop them

For a number of years, Waterton residents hosted a downhill ski competition in June at the south end of Cameron Lake.

The events, for both men and women, were unusual because of the time of year and the fact that participants had to take a boat to the base of the slope and scramble up on foot carrying their skis because there were no lift facilities. Skiers from many parts of Western Canada attended the annual ski meet and many more came to watch.

Conditions at Cameron Lake sometimes remained favorable for skiing well into August for those who just wanted to give the activity a try. When they got tired of skiing, they could drop down to the lakeshore and cast a fly.

He got both photos and plaster

When Frank Royal (1909–1975), chief of the National Film Board of Canada's photo service, came to Waterton in 1950, he got more than photos to take back to Ottawa.

He got a plaster cast for his leg after his horse stumbled and fell on the Crypt Lake Trail, sending Royal crashing into a rock wall. Interviewed after he returned from the hospital, Royal said he was thankful the horse had not fallen the other way.

"If he had, they would be scraping me off the bottom of the canyon."

Stubborn as a mule

One of the oddest sights on Glacier trails in the 1950s was Grandma Walker, a.k.a. Mrs. T.O. Court of Oregon, and her burro, Uranium. Grandma Walker, dressed as a pioneer, led Uranium on a 100-plus-mile (160 km) hiking trek through the park, the burro carrying her tent and supplies.

All went fine until they came to a part of a trail on a steep slope where water cascaded across the track in a small falls. Uranium refused to continue, braying loudly at the prospect of crossing the stream.

According to one version of the story, a group of hikers came along and, with much pushing, prodding and arm and hand waving, the burro made a giant leap over the creek and ended up hauling Grandma Walker down the trail.

In another version, the group of hikers, primarily students working in the park for the summer, ended up carrying the beast across the stream.

Naked musicians

Gunsight Lake is in one of the less-traveled parts of Glacier, and that may have accounted for what longtime park visitor John Mauff encountered while hiking near there with a friend in 1947.

"To somewhat my surprise, lying atop (a large rock) were two youngish individuals, sunbathing ... *au naturel*," Mauff recalled. "We stopped and chatted and exchanged names and from where we and they came."

It was only later, upon reflection, that Mauff realized the two were noted musicians, pianist Leonid Hambro of Chicago and violinist Robert Mann, an instructor at the Juilliard School of Music in New York City and founder of the Juilliard Quartet.

Mauff, who was a proficient pianist in his own right, said "it gave me a thrill to have this chance meeting under such circumstances," adding, "I never met either one again."

This still from the 1920 movie *Bob Hampton of Placer* was taken near Glacier, one of the earliest films to utilize park scenery. The cast included James Kirkwood, Wesley Barry, Marjorie Daw and Noah Beery.

4 Movies, Stars and VIPs

When you've got scenery as spectacular as that in Waterton and Glacier, it's only natural that Hollywood would tap it. The parks have been the backdrop for several dozen movies, with accompanying stars. But Hollywood stars aren't the only celebrities attracted to the parks. Over the years, Waterton and Glacier have been visited by innumerable prominent people.

Movies and stars

There are several lists of movies, both big screen and made-for-TV, that have been filmed either in the parks or using the Rockies of Waterton and Glacier as backdrops. Here's a compilation of that information, in order of the year of release:

2003 – *Hidalgo* (St. Mary area)
2002 – *Spirit: Stallion of the Cimarron* (Glacier; animated)
2000 – *Big Eden* (West Glacier area)
1998 – *What Dreams May Come* (Glacier)
1997 – *Excess Baggage* (Waterton)
1994 – *Forrest Gump* (Glacier)
1994 – *The River Wild* (Glacier)
1993 – *Beethoven's 2nd* (Glacier)
1993 – *Samurai Cowboy* (Waterton)
1986 – *Amy Grant: Heading Home for the Holidays—NBC Christmas Special* (Glacier)
1981 – *Continental Divide* (Glacier)
1980 – *Heaven's Gate* (Glacier)
1980 – *The Shining* (Glacier)
1978 – *The Snow War* (Glacier)
1960 – *All the Young Men* (St. Mary area)
1954 – *Dangerous Mission* (Glacier)
1954 – *Cattle Queen of Montana* (East Glacier area)
1953 – *Powder River* (Glacier)
1931 – *Private Lives* (Glacier)
1922 – *Bob Hampton of Placer* (Glacier, Blackfeet reservation)

Courtesy, United Artists

The cast of *Heaven's Gate* poses in the film for an itinerant photographer on a set constructed at Two Medicine Lake in Glacier in 1979. The film was a colossal failure.

Box-office flops

Almost without exception, movies filmed in Waterton and Glacier have been unremarkable, making little lasting impression other than on studio budgets.

The exceptions are mostly movies where the park has served as a minor or obscure backdrop, such as *The Shining* and *Forrest Gump*. In both cases, filming was by second units and no stars were involved.

Heaven's Gate (1980), starring Kris Kristofferson and Jeff Bridges, probably tops the list for flops, based on budget, location and length.

Directed by Michael Cimino, *Heaven's Gate* is about a range war in Wyoming and ran an incredible five hours.

Part of the filming was done at Two Medicine Lake, where an entire town was built on the lake shore in the spring of 1979.

Cimino ran afoul of park officials when a cow was butchered in the park and the remains were not cleaned up.

Rangers feared the remains would draw bears just coming out of hibernation and the filmmaker was kicked out of the park.

The United Artists' release turned out to be a dud at the box office, garnering poor reviews and hardly any return on the $36-million-plus investment, contributing to the movie studio's bankruptcy and eventual purchase by MGM in 1981.

The Shining

Despite popular belief, Many Glacier Hotel was not the setting for Stephen King's haunting book *The Shining*, and neither the movie nor TV series was filmed there.

The exteriors and interiors of the TV version were shot at The Stanley, the impressive, real-life Colorado hotel that inspired The Overlook Hotel in Stephen King's book.

The confusion probably stems from the opening aerial scenes of the Stanley Kubrick film showing a mountain road. These scenes were shot in Glacier and include the Logan Pass Visitor Center, implying the scene was physically related while in fact it was hundreds of miles away.

Stanley Kubrick (1928–1999) almost didn't choose Glacier for those second-unit scenes (filmed without any of the stars) that set the ominous mood during Jack Nicholson's drive up to the hotel in *The Shining*.

The crew doing the test filming reported to Kubrick that the area "wasn't interesting."

However, when Kubrick saw the test shots, he said, "We were staggered," and he hired a new crew to take what he described as "some of the most beautiful mountain helicopter shots I've ever seen."

Who was that bearded man?

In the movie *Forrest Gump*, star Tom Hanks runs back and forth across America after the death of his mother, played by Sally Field, in a marathon of grief.

One of the marathon scenes shows Hank's Forrest Gump character jogging across a bridge with Glacier's mountains as a backdrop.

While you're supposed to believe that it is Tom Hanks in makeup, with a long beard and uncut hair, the runner is in fact Tom's younger brother, Jim, who stood in for the Oscar winner in many of the running scenes.

Stars trek into Waterton

The cast of *Pioneer Woman*, a made-for-television movie broadcast on ABC, created quite a stir among tourists and townsfolk alike in Waterton in the fall of 1973.

Joanna Pettet

William Shatner, of *Star Trek* fame, a nine-year-old Helen Hunt, later to star in the TV hit *Mad About You*, David Janssen (1931–1980), star of the hit TV show *The Fugitive*, Joanna Pettet and Russell Baer, plus a crew of about 50 people, stayed at various motels and cabins and frequented local restaurants during production.

The show, about 1867 Wyoming homesteaders, was filmed on the Palmer Ranch, adjacent to the eastern boundary of the park.

Scene stealers

The scenery approaching Waterton and Glacier from the east, with mountains rising abruptly from the prairie, is apparently a perfect backdrop for film and, as a result, the areas adjacent to the parks have frequently been featured in movies.

In 2002, it proved just right for the Touchstone Pictures movie *Hidalgo*, about long-distance race horse rider Frank Hopkins (played by Viggo Mortensen) and his steed, Hidalgo.

With his film crew based on the Blackfeet reservation, director Joe Johnston found plenty of horses for a stampede—750—claimed to be the largest stampede ever recorded. He also cast about 100 Blackfeet to play roles in a re-creation of Buffalo Bill's Wild West Show. For scenery there was Divide Mountain (8,665 ft, 2,641 m), which "rises like a behemoth in the background of *Hidalgo*'s final sequence," according to a report in the *Great Falls Tribune*.

There's no place like 'homeland'

Some of the spectacular mountain and lake scenery in the 2002 animated movie *Spirit: Stallion of the Cimarron* is based on scenes in Glacier Park.

Production designer Kathy Altieri was with a group of artists the DreamWorks Pictures studio brought to Glacier for a whirlwind tour to gain inspiration for the backgrounds used in *Spirit*.

"It was just as fresh and pretty as any place I'd ever been," Altieri would later remark of the trip to Glacier.

Glacier Park's mountains are used as the basis for *Spirit*'s "homeland," featured in the opening, early and final sequences of the movie.

This cover of the media kit for the animated movie *Spirit: Stallion of the Cimarron* features some of the scenery artists created based on a tour of Glacier.

Ray Djuff collection

You can't stay here

The making of *Samurai Cowboy*, (Robert Conrad, Hiromi Go, Catherine Mary Stewart and Matt McCoy) filmed in and around Waterton in the fall of 1993, created quite a stir—but not just because it was a movie in the making. Some of the film's cast and crew wanted to stay in the townsite and sought cabins to rent. Renting private cabins without written permission from the park superintendent is forbidden under the terms of land leases, but this didn't stop a number of cabin owners from doing so anyway.

Obviously angered by this violation, the superintendent sent a letter to all cabin owners advising them this transgression would not be allowed, even though only a few cabins had been rented and even then only for a short time. The non-offending cabin owners were left scratching their heads over the whole matter.

Meanwhile, some businesses in Waterton were used in sets, with new signage applied. The Royal Canadian Mounted Police office was one such "conversion." The building became a real estate office in the film, which centers on a Japanese businessman who buys a ranch to fulfil his dream of becoming a cowboy.

Reagan does laundry duty

During the filming of *Cattle Queen of Montana* in 1953 with Barbara Stanwyck (1907–1990), co-star Ronald Reagan (1911–2004) stayed at the St. Mary Lodge, operated by Hugh Black (1902–1983) and his family. When he wasn't required for filming, Reagan enjoyed fishing, with Hugh Black sometimes acting as his guide.

On a couple of occasions when Black wasn't available, his teenage son Roscoe filled in, providing the manpower at the oars of a boat on St. Mary Lake.

Hugh Black's wife, Margaret, remembers an instance when Reagan wanted to go fishing and only Roscoe was around to take him, though Roscoe couldn't go until he finished collecting the laundry from guest rooms.

Ronald Reagan signs an autograph for fan Rita Mercier of Montreal while en route to London in 1948. Reagan starred in *Cattle Queen of Montana*, filmed near Glacier.

Margaret Black says she still laughs at the image of a Hollywood actor, future governor of California and future president of the United States scampering up and down the hallways and around the cabins of the St. Mary Lodge complex helping Roscoe finish his laundry collection so they could go fishing.

Movie Mountain

Although similar in appearance, that's not one of Glacier's peaks in the Paramount movie studio logo.

87

"That's a myth," said Jack Potter, the assistant chief of science and natural resources management for Glacier, when asked about it by *Hungry Horse News* in 2001. "I think that's just people passing down some sort of folklore."

The rock that composes mountains in Glacier is actually the wrong type to be the Paramount logo, experts have noted. While Glacier's mountains are composed of sedimentary rock, the Paramount peak appears more "granitic."

A spokesperson for Paramount Motion Pictures told the newspaper that the famous movie logo is half a model of the Matterhorn in Switzerland and half artist's rendition. The myth, however, is still being passed to visitors by some Glacier tour bus drivers.

No room to film

That's the Prince of Wales Hotel, all right, featured prominently in the 1997 movie *Excess Baggage* starring Alicia Silverstone, but the interior shots are not the hotel's rooms.

Although plausible looking, if you've never been inside the Prince of Wales Hotel, the interior views of a hotel room and lounge for the movie were taken elsewhere.

Guest rooms in the Prince of Wales Hotel are too small and dark for film purposes, with an average size of just 12 by 17 feet (3.6 by 5.1 m), not including the bathroom, and dark wainscoting that runs up the walls to about five feet.

But where's Glacier?

One of the great disappointments for Great Northern Railway chairman Louis W. Hill (1872–1948) was the 1922 movie *Bob Hampton of Placer*.

Movie producer Marshal Neilan (1891–1958) had approached railway baron Hill the previous year about getting Great Northern's co-operation to use Blackfeet for what was to be a personal retelling of the events leading up to the Custer massacre.

Hill was keen on the advertising value in promoting Glacier and "Glacier's Indians" and arranged to have Great Northern officials co-operate with Neilan and have Blackfeet from the reservation appear in the movie.

When Great Northern president Ralph Budd (1879–1962) saw the movie while in Washington, D.C., he wrote Hill and said, "I found it delightful entertainment," "the scenes are beautifully staged, but there is no mention whatever of Glacier National Park."

A title credit read, "Indians and authentic locations obtained courtesy of Louis J. Hill [sic] Great Northern Railway Company."

There is "absolutely nothing to indicate this picture was not taken on the Custer Battlefield," Budd wrote.

Not even Hollywood could change the weather

Columbia Pictures chose St. Mary, adjacent to the eastern boundary of Glacier, for some of the location shooting of *All the Young Men*, about the struggle between race and merit among a group of Marines in the Korean War.

The tiny tourist town became a cauldron of activity as semi-trucks full of equipment pulled in and the crew scurried to start work in October 1959, while the media flocked in to do interviews.

Hugh Black

The cast was a mix of Hollywood long timers and newcomers. Alan Ladd (1913–1964), star of numerous films including the now-classic *Shane*, was featured along with then-television notable Sidney Poitier, world heavyweight boxer Ingemar Johansson, singer James Darren and comedian Mort Shal.

Local Blackfeet Indians were hired to play the part of North Korean soldiers, not untypical of Hollywood's racial stretches.

When snow and fog moved in to spoil the shooting, some of the actors took trail rides while others gave newspaper interviews and signed autographs.

The ever-accommodating Hugh Black, owner of St. Mary Lodge, arranged for Johansson's horseback outing to include a Swedish-speaking female trail guide and went out of his way to introduce the stars to an eager young visitor.

Scene setter

The painted scenery in the Hollywood movie *North West Mounted Police* may be vaguely familiar to fans of Glacier, since artist Joe De Yong used Charlie Russell (1864–1926) paintings of Glacier in the production designs for the 1940 film.

De Yong (1894–1975) was working as a technical adviser to silent era cowboy star Tom Mix when he contracted spinal meningitis and suffered permanent hearing loss.

During his recuperation, De Yong wrote to Russell for advice on a career as an artist.

De Yong would eventually live with the Russells, spending time learning from Charlie during summers at Bull Head Lodge in Glacier and acting as caretaker of the building in the winter.

In 1936, Hollywood rediscovered De Yong, and he became a historical adviser and costume artist for *The Plainsman*, starring Gary Cooper (1901–1961). De Yong designed many of the Blackfeet costumes worn in the movie. He ended up working on 21 major movies, including *Union Pacific*, *The Virginian*, *Red River* and *Shane*.

Although the studio had planned to film *North West Mounted Police* in Canada, it ended up being made on a Hollywood backlot.

Changes were bigger than the film

The RKO production *Dangerous Mission*, originally titled "The Glacier Story," was to have been filmed entirely in Glacier during July 1952, but was canceled due to production difficulties. The operation was revived in May 1953 and eventually started in late July after casting problems were resolved.

Hearing that a movie was being made in Glacier, seven Prince of Wales Hotel employees hitch-hiked to Lake McDonald on their day off to watch the stars on location. Piper Laurie, Victor Mature (1915–1999), Vincent Price (1911–1993) and William Bendix (1906–1964) were hospitable enough to talk to the seven young people, giving them plenty to share with friends when they returned to Waterton.

Although the National Park Service was to have had some say in the final story line, so many changes were made on a daily basis that very little advice or control could be exerted in trying to keep to park service objectives.

The plot involves a woman who witnesses a mob killing, then flees to Montana to work in a gift shop at a resort hotel in a national park. A hitman tracks her down to keep her from testifying while a cop tries to protect her.

Ray Djuff collection

Victor Mature

Toothbrush the final straw

The cast of *Dangerous Mission* may have been Hollywood stars, but some still had to share bedrooms and bathrooms during the filming of the movie in Glacier.

Walter Reed (1916–2001) said he and Dennis Weaver, who played forest rangers in the movie, shared a bedroom. In the next room, linked by a passageway with a bathroom, was Victor Mature.

"(Mature) didn't have a shower or bathtub," Reed recalled later in an interview with Herb Fagen. "I told him I'd leave the door unlocked from our side, and when he wanted to take a shower he could go in there. Well. Soon he was not only showering, he was using my razor.

"I said: Victor, when you get to my toothbrush I'm going to close the door and lock it!"

Clint made bartender's day

It wasn't quite the standoff between the cop and the criminal in the movie *Dirty Harry* in which the main character utters the famous line, "Go ahead, make my day," but for a few seconds it was just as tense. The showdown was between Clint Eastwood (a.k.a. Dirty Harry) and Ray Djuff, Prince of Wales Hotel bartender.

Eastwood, on a break in filming *Thunderbolt and Lightfoot* in Montana in 1973, came into the Prince of Wales Hotel bar accompanied by a woman carrying a young child. While children can accompany parents into a bar in Montana, Alberta law prohibits it, and the bartender was faced with the delicate task of explaining the situation to the tall, imposing Eastwood.

Fortunately, the star took it well and his companion waited in the lobby while Eastwood enjoyed a beer. The woman then traded places with him and he looked after the child while she had a drink.

Interestingly, no one in the Windsor Lounge dared approach Eastwood to say hello or ask for an autograph. But when his companion came in, a few people sidled up to ask if that was Eastwood she was with. They then went out in the lobby to pass on the news to friends and discreetly point out the celebrity.

Ray Djuff collection

Actress Linda Blair herds mustangs in the Crowsnest Pass, north of Waterton, in 1978 for a forgettable movie originally called *Wild Horse Hank*. It was later renamed *Hard Ride to Rantan*. Blair stayed in Waterton during part of the filming.

Out in the cold

Linda Blair didn't exactly enjoy all of her stint during the filming of *Wild Horse Hank* in September 1978 in Lundbreck, Alberta, about 45 miles (72 km) northwest of Waterton. Soon after arriving, Blair, better known for her role as the possessed child in *The Exorcist*, came down with a nasty flu or cold and was bedridden in a Waterton hotel room for part of a week. It probably didn't help that the weather was miserable, rainy and overcast for some of the time.

She might have wanted to stay in bed and forget the film, about a university student who saves 30 wild horses from ranchers who want to kill them. The movie was renamed *Hard Ride to Rantan* and quickly disappeared after its run on television.

... and VIPs

Were you expecting company?

John George "Kootenai" Brown (1839–1916) and his family had the Waterton area pretty much to themselves when they moved to

Ray Djuff collection

Alexander Stavely Hill

the region in 1878. Neighbors were few and far between, except for infrequent visitors and Native Americans with whom Brown traded. So it must have been a surprise in September 1883 when British Member of Parliament and lawyer Alexander Stavely Hill (1825–1905) showed up on Brown's doorstep with Lord Lanthom.

Hill and Lanthom were prospecting for opportunities to invest in large-scale cattle ranching, which was just taking off in Alberta. They called on Brown to provide guiding services for a hunting trip into the mountains.

Hill described Brown, who would become the first forest ranger in charge of Waterton, as "a wild Indian looking fellow, in a Slouch hat and curiously constructed garments and moccasins.... He had seen something of service with the British army, but with his long dark hair and moccasins had not much of the European remaining about his appearance."

Brown didn't record his reaction to Hill and Lanthom.

Feeding the ego

MANY LAUGHS
FOR MANY DAYS

IRVIN S· COBB

Chris Morrison collection

Irvin Cobb was a humorist and radio celebrity.

Humorist Irvin Cobb (1876–1944), after an evening's entertainment in 1925 at the Glacier (Lewis) Hotel, now Lake McDonald Lodge, with western artist Charlie Russell, commented: "This, to my way of thinking, is one of the best mountain hotels in the whole world. It has every imaginable convenience, including my books on sale in the lobby."

Royal visitors

No public money was spent on Crown Prince Olav (1903–1991) and Crown Princess Martha (1901–1954) of Norway during their May–June 1939 visit to Montana and three-day stay in Glacier. With 15,000 state residents born in Scandinavia, local cultural organizations had no problem raising the necessary funds to sponsor the trip. Along with the prince and princess, there was a sizable retinue that included: Maj. and Mrs. Nicolai Ostgaard, friends of the prince and princess, two servants, two maids, the prince's personal secretary, Norway's ambassador to the U.S., an adjutant, a first secretary from the embassy, an official photographer, a State Department official, a representative of the Norwegian press and another from the Norwegian–American press.

The party was housed at Two Medicine Chalets for the duration of their stay. Their visit of Glacier included a stop at Many Glacier, a trip over Going-to-the-Sun Road and tea with the park superintendent, Donald Libby (1882–1959), and his wife.

The Prince of Wales Hotel was readied for this royal visit, which was to have included Waterton, but those plans were canceled at the last minute, much to the disappointment of town residents.

Tomer Hileman postcard, Ray Djuff collection

In his book *Home Country*, Ernie Pyle, left, called Glacier "my favorite of all the national parks," and recounted his trek to Waterton and a memorable stay at Granite Park Chalets.

Ernie Pyle gets soaked

Granite Park Chalets are rustic and remote, reached by hiking six or more miles (10 km) from the nearest road. Today, the chalets are a hikers shelter, where guests must pack in all their needs, including food, water and overnight gear.

In earlier times, guests could expect to be pampered. So when author and syndicated newspaper columnist Ernest T. "Ernie" Pyle (1900–1945) showed up and said he wanted a bath, waitress/maid Patty Whitwell flinched only momentarily.

While the chalets have limited running water, outhouses and no private baths in the rooms, Whitwell knew how to make do.

She hauled out an old tin washtub, took it to Ernie Pyle's room and began boiling water on the kitchen stove. She made trip after trip to his room with porcelain jugs of hot water until the tub was full. It was the first time any of the staff could remember having fulfilled such a request.

Chris Morrison collection

Lady and Lord Willingdon cruised on the then-new *Motor Vessel International* while visiting Waterton. At right is Canon S.H. Middleton.

Vice-regal visitors

Through the years, three governors general have visited Waterton, each marveling at the mountain beauty and each being given the VIP treatment that protocol demands for a vice-regal official (the monarch's official representative in Canada).

The first to visit was Lord Willingdon (1866–1941) in July 1928, who, along with his wife, took a trip on the new excursion boat *Motor Vessel International.*

Lord Willingdon was so taken with Waterton, he consented to becoming honorary president of the Rocky Mountains Club, a newly formed local organization. "As long as I don't have to climb a mountain," he said.

Sir John Buchan, also known as Lord Tweedsmuir (1875–1940), was also said to have been very impressed with the park when he arrived on September 9, 1936.

Buchan toured the Prince of Wales Hotel, which had reopened that summer after three years of Depression-forced closure, and was driven through the town. He, too, took a lake cruise on the *Motor Vessel International*, showing great interest in learning more about the park wildlife after spotting a bear during the cruise.

Ray Djuff collection

Viscount Alexander

In August 1951, Viscount Alexander of Tunis (1891–1969) checked into the Prince of Wales Hotel with his two sons, Brian, 12, and Shane, 16, and their tutor, J.R. Heald. They then headed to Carthew Lake for an all-day fishing trip, where they filled their creels. That evening, they had dinner with Senator William Buchanan (1876–1954), a long-time Waterton supporter. Their stay at the Prince of Wales Hotel made Viscount Alexander the first vice-regal visitor to stay overnight in the park. He left the next day.

Just being neighborly

Although Albertans had nothing to do with a July 1953 addition of 10,000 acres (4,050 hectares) to Glacier, Alberta Premier Ernest C. Manning (1908–1996) and Waterton superintendent James H. Atkinson were invited to take part in the dedication ceremony as an act of inter-park goodwill.

The addition of the state-owned North Fork forest land on the west side of Glacier was the culmination of a land trade that was several years in the making. In return, the state of Montana received about 200,000 acres (80,935 hectares) of federal grazing land in the eastern part of the state.

The trade was part of a continuing policy by the National Park Service to consolidate its holdings and reduce state and private ownership of land within the park.

Appropriately, Secretary of the Interior Douglas McKay (1893–1959) gave the principal dedication speech at the ceremony, held at McDonald Meadows near West Glacier. The program continued with a visit to the newly completed Hungry Horse Dam and dinner at Glacier Park Hotel.

The noble persona

Blackfeet Chief Two Guns White Calf (1872–1934) seldom spoke English in public, at least when tourists, guests or dignitaries were within earshot. The chief, who worked extensively with the Great Northern Railway to publicize Glacier and was a fixture at Glacier Park Lodge entertaining guests, would speak the Blackfeet language at public events or use Indian sign language, with fellow tribesman Richard Sanderville (1873–1951) often acting as translator.

Richard Sanderville, left, acts as interpreter for Blackfeet Chief Two Guns White Calf as he addresses the crowd at Logan Pass in July 1933 for the ceremony opening Going-to-the-Sun Road.

White Calf was perfectly capable of speaking English, and fluently. The use of a translator was meant to maintain a mystique about the railway's foremost Glacier spokesman.

95

Riding the rails, Rockefeller style

Each summer, John D. Rockefeller (1839–1937), "a committed conservationist," would travel the West to learn about the national parks and talk to the park superintendents.

In 1926, Rockefeller took the whole family, traveling "in a private Pullman railway car, the Boston, which was usually reserved for the chairman of the New York Central Rail Road.

"We left the car on sidings at various points along the way and visited national parks and other sites of interest by automobile," son David Rockefeller recalls in his autobiography.

For the Glacier portion of the tour, the Pullman was parked on a siding at Midvale (East Glacier Park) while the family was chauffeured through the park in a private car provided by the Glacier Park Transportation Company.

One of the stops was the art gallery of sculptor John L. Clarke (1881–1970) in Midvale, where the family picked up Clarke carvings as mementos of the Glacier visit. They still have them.

Rockefeller, his sons and a small party returned to Glacier in 1930, took in the North Circle Tour by horseback, and arrived in Waterton aboard the *Motor Vessel International* from Goat Haunt. Both Glacier and Waterton concessioners were advised to give no publicity to the visitors' arrival and word of their presence only reached *The Lethbridge Herald* when a fellow boat passenger reported it.

The missing element

Natural beauty abounds in Glacier, but for years Great Northern Railway chairman Louis W. Hill harbored the idea that there was something missing that would be a surefire way to get VIPs to the park: a health spa, such as the Canadian Pacific Railway had in the "Banff springs" and the Union Pacific Railway had in Yellowstone.

So when a sulphur spring was discovered in the Belly River area in 1919, Hill was thrilled and turned to his friend and family physician, Dr. Charles Mayo (1873–1951) of the Mayo Clinic in Rochester, Minnesota, for advice.

"It is really quite a discovery and maybe it will smell enough to rival some of the stink holes in Yellowstone," Mayo replied, only half joking.

Hill had samples of the water tested by several labs for its "medicinal qualities and chemical content," but the reports were conflicting and inconclusive. Hill's vision of a spa in Glacier would never be.

Catering to the elite

One of the ways Louis W. Hill hoped to build business in Waterton and Glacier was by catering to the wealthy, whether it was inviting a select few for subsidized or complimentary tours of the parks or ensuring those who booked vacations were properly looked after. In both cases, the hope was that word of mouth advertising among the rich would ensure future, well-heeled visitors.

As a result, Hill expected to be informed by his Glacier Park Hotel Company staff of any booking by prominent people, and lists were routinely provided, such as this partial rundown from 1920:

- Stephen A Baker, president of the Bank of Manhattan
- H.M. Blackmer, Midwest Oil
- R.W. Steward, Standard Oil
- Prof. John G. Jacks, Harvard University
- H.P. Kelsey, president of the Appalachian Club
- Gen. Robert E. Wood, Montgomery Ward
- Charles Bell, president of American Security and Trust Co.

For certain people, Hill would personally escort the tour. For others, he provided a letter of introduction to be handed to each hotel and chalet manager.

Do you have a job for my son?

One of the hazards Louis W. Hill faced as a result of catering to the well-known and wealthy was having to field favors of employment at his Glacier hotels.

Such a request came from C.E. Patterson of General Electric Company in New York, asking if there was a position for his son Roger at a Glacier hotel for the summer of 1922.

Howard Noble, head of the Glacier Park Hotel Company, suggested the job of porter at Going-to-the-Sun Chalets. Noble explained to Hill that the work involved handling guests' luggage, carrying wood for the fireplaces, and keeping the lobby and men's toilets neat and clean. "It requires no special ability except that of being obliging and accommodating to the guests and doing the work cheerfully and conscientiously."

James J. Hill Reference Library

Hill, noting the reference to keeping the toilets clean, asked Noble to find something else for the lad.

Louis W. Hill

Instead, Roger was offered the job of groundskeeper at Glacier Park Hotel at a wage of $50 a month, minus the $33 cost of his train ticket to the park. His fare home would be covered by the railway, if he completed his contract.

Pouty guest

When word came to staff at Granite Park Chalets that Gloria Vanderbilt would be a guest, they were excited, recalled Millie Perkins of St. Paul, Minnesota, who worked with her mother, Ema Gunn Perkins (1886–1962), manager of the chalets in the 1930s and 1940s.

Courtesy, Millie Perkins

Ema Gunn Perkins

"Everyone was glued to the kitchen window as the party dismounted," Perkins recalled. "There was one lady quite appropriately dressed in riding pants and boots, and another in blue jeans and long, dark uncombed hair. Of course, we had pegged the Fifth Avenue attire to be Gloria...."

It was her maid. "(Vanderbilt) was wearing the jeans and as you know, went on to market them at quite a great price," Perkins says.

Perkins added that Vanderbilt did not seem happy to be on the trail or with any aspect of the trip: "No hikes, no food, no laughter. Just a sullen lady dragging on cigarettes and drinking black coffee. She didn't like our food nor the people who served it.... They departed the next day."

Big entry, big exit

Two of the most flamboyant guests to show up in Glacier were Hopalong Cassidy (1895–1972) and his wife Tripalong, actress Grace Bradley (1913–1972).

Hopalong (a.k.a. William Boyd) arrived at Many Glacier Hotel in the early 1950s in a big convertible decorated in a style befitting a Hollywood cowboy legend, with cowhide upholstery and six-shooters fashioned into door handles. Both were outfitted in cowboy costumes.

Their departure was just as memorable, as they personally presented silver spur pendants to the female hotel employees in the lobby and cufflinks to the men.

Reluctant swimmer

A swim made by Eleanor Roosevelt (1884–1962) in the ice-cold Two Medicine Lake during a visit in the company of President Franklin D. Roosevelt (1882–1945) and the couple's three sons to Glacier in August 1934 has been cited as evidence of her strong constitution and outdoors nature.

Mrs. Roosevelt's dip in the lake, however, was not her idea.

Glacier National Park archive

President Franklin Delano Roosevelt takes in Glacier's sites from a seat in a Cadillac touring car.

In her biography, she tells how she and sons James (1907–1991) and Franklin Jr. (1914–1988) made the plunge: "the boys decided that they were going to swim in the lake ... and induced me to go with them. As I stood hesitating and wondering whether I could bear the icy water, one of the boys gave me a push and I found myself gasping and swimming back as quickly as possible." Meanwhile, the third son, John (1916–1981), was taken for a short fishing trip by assistant chief ranger, Arthur R. Best.

Eleanor and Franklin Roosevelt wave to admirers from a Great Northern Railway train. FDR, who was confined to a wheelchair due to polio, usually relied on one of his sons, and leg braces, to help steady him when standing for such events.

Flawless day in the park

Franklin D. Roosevelt's visit to Glacier went like clockwork, with only minor modifications to the itinerary. The efficiency and apparent smoothness of the one-day event in August 1934 took the co-operation and assistance of many more people than the public was aware.

The Great Northern Railway, which took the president to and from the park, ran a track tester train minutes ahead of the presidential train to guard against an unforeseen mechanical crisis as well as cranks, criminals and conspirators.

The railway's Many Glacier Hotel and Two Medicine Chalets took special care in preparing facilities and staff for the meals and other needs of the 80-plus party.

Glacier Park Transport Company, the tour bus concessioner, arranged for the spit and polish of 14 cars and provided the drivers to ferry the guests and news reporters.

A government pilot car was driven ahead of the fleet, while a government truck and two Montana state patrol cars covered the rear to prevent a break in the official cavalcade.

Side roads to Many Glacier and Two Medicine had been oiled and repaired by highway crews; tunnels on the Going-to-the-Sun Road were guarded for 24 hours prior to the presidential trip, as were the vehicles and the rooms which were to be used during the visit.

The Blackfeet Indians and members of the Civilian Conservation Corps, who performed at various ceremonies, the Kalispell National Guard, the Flathead and Glacier country sheriffs, and U.S. Customs Service all played their part in the success of the visit.

The park staff also ensured the presidential visit went off without a hitch when faced with last-minute itinerary changes such as the cancellation of the stop at Going-to-the-Sun Chalets, cancellation of the overnight stay at Two Medicine Chalets, and inclusion of a late evening drive to East Glacier.

The bashful spectator

When Franklin and Eleanor Roosevelt came through St. Mary on their 1934 tour of Glacier, Karola Miener (nee Mankenberg) was waiting at the side of the road. She was a student at Winold Reiss' art school and was standing with Reiss and some Blackfeet natives.

Eleanor's car stopped and Riess approached it. Miener said she "was supposed to get [an] autograph for the school but I was bashful" and missed the chance.

"I later wrote to Mrs. Roosevelt and told her that I had been afraid to come to the car."

Mrs. Roosevelt replied, on White House stationery, that "I read [your letter] with much interest [and] ... am enclosing an autographed card for your book, with my best wishes."

Table for four

How do you get a table at a busy restaurant? If you're First Lady Laura Bush on a visit to Glacier in July 2004, you get a little help from your friends: some burly Secret Service agents.

Bush came to Glacier with three childhood friends to hike and do a little fundraising for the National Park Service's Junior Ranger Program and the National Parks Foundation.

News reports indicate the agents at first politely tried to get two tables in a specific spot in the Park Café in St. Mary, without say-

Colleen Perret, left, Prince of Wales Hotel manager, was host to First Lady Laura Bush and her friends in July 2004. In the background is a relief map of the two parks, an original hotel fixture.

ing they were for Laura Bush and her friends. When café manager Kathryn Hiestand balked, as it was busy at the time, the Secret Service agents took Hiestand outside and explained who they were trying to get the tables for and the fact the Bush party would be there very soon. Empty tables were quickly found and breakfast was served—promptly.

The Bush group spent one night in Glacier at the Many Glacier Hotel, where the party dined along with other guests. The next morning, they headed for Waterton, where they stayed at the Prince of Wales Hotel, slipping into town without any of the locals being aware.

According to Prince of Wales Hotel manager Colleen Perret, the visit went extremely smoothly, thanks in part to the advance work of the Secret Service. The party left Canada as quietly as it had come, with no news coverage and no publicity.

Turning the table on fame

During the 1960 Governors' Conference at Many Glacier Hotel, a tall, dark stranger ambled into the kitchen. The staff were amazed at his gall, as the hotel's kitchen was the domain of the feared Minnie Rhody, whom even hotel manager Ian B. Tippett dared not cross. The stranger headed to Rhody's elevated and glass-enclosed office

101

at the end of the kitchen, and staff watched dumfounded as she followed the stranger out to a balcony, where someone took their picture.

They later learned that the stranger was television reporter Edward R. Murrow (1908–1965), who was covering the governors' conference. He had asked to have his picture taken with Mrs. Rhody, who had been a cook at Murrow's college fraternity house. This was their first meeting since those days.

The wrangling skills used daily by Park Saddle Horse Company guides were sometimes featured in mini-rodeo demonstrations for select Great Northern Railway guests.

Rich but penniless

In 1918, wranglers at Many Glacier Hotel put on an impromptu bucking bronc riding display at the corral for a group of distinguished guests, including Great Northern Railway chairman Louis W. Hill and U.S. Treasury Secretary William Gibbs McAdoo (1863–1941).

"Several riders acquitted themselves well at the exhibition," recalled Warren Hanna, the hotel's transportation agent, so "I passed a four-quart hat among the crowd for their benefit."

Hanna said he was amused that when the hat reached Hill, Hill had no money and had to accept $5 from his wife to contribute. Likewise, McAdoo had to borrow funds from a friend.

"It was interesting that neither the railroad king nor the Treasury Secretary was able to produce any ready cash," Hanna said.

Unsung hero

Many dignitaries or VIPS who visit Waterton and Glacier prefer to keep a low-profile, with no publicity. So when a personality does arrive, it can be a shock for hotel staff.

Such was the case for Richard Rohleder, a bellhop at Many Glacier Hotel just after the Second World War. Responding to a call of "Front" from the desk clerk, Rohleder took the keys, looked at them, then grabbed the baggage of a "very nice, but non-descript gentleman and his wife" to lead them to their rooms.

Richard Rohleder

At the room, Rohleder opened the door, put down the bags, opened the window to let in fresh air and then reached into his pocket for a piece of paper with the name of the guest so he could depart with a personal greeting: "Have a nice stay ... Admiral Raymond Spruance."

Rohleder, who had finished naval officer training and received his commission in 1946, said he "immediately snapped to attention" in the presence of Spruance (1886–1969), the hero of the 1942 Battle of Midway.

Photographer Roland Reed imagined himself the next Edward Curtis and staged many recreations of Blackfeet life in the days before contact with white settlers. These photos were used by the Great Northern Railway.

5   What's in a Name

Naming mountains and other natural features has been a time-honored tradition in the parks, reflecting history, cultural heritage or distinctive geological characteristics. What follows is a look at some prominent and off-beat names among the hundreds bestowed in the two parks.

Before the white man

Maps can give the impression that the names of geographic features are static and unchanging, and for almost 100 years in Waterton and Glacier they have been. But today's names are really only those of the latest occupiers of the land.

Before European explorers and settlers, natives had their own names for features in the parks. Mount Rockwell (9,272 ft, 2,826 m), at Two Medicine Lake, for instance, was called Rising Bull Mountain by the Blackfeet.

The Great Northern Railway liked to promote a connection between the Blackfeet, whose reservation abuts Glacier, and the park as a way to induce travelers to visit the region. Names such as Going-to-the-Sun Mountain (9,642 ft, 2,939 m) played to the romantic visions of eastern tourists about Native Americans and the wilderness. But in doing so, the railway helped overshadow names given to the peaks and valleys by other tribes with links to the region.

The Kootenai had occupied the Waterton and Glacier region for hundreds of years before the Blackfeet, who only arrived around 1650 as they migrated south from Canada and, through constant warfare, displaced the Kootenai to the western side of the Continental Divide.

A number of names of features in Glacier have thus gone through at least three recorded changes. Heavens Peak (8,987 ft, 2,739 m), named by prospector "Dutch" Louie Meyer, was called Where God Lives Mountain by the Blackfeet and, before that, Red Bird by the Kootenai.

Today, only a few Kootenai names survive, such as Akamina in Waterton, which means valley or bench land; Kishinena, adjoining Waterton, coming from the Kootenai word for balsam or white fir; and Kishenehn in Glacier, usually meaning "no good."

Indian names, courtesy of others

That so many place names in Glacier are linked to the Blackfeet has less to do with the tribe than it does with other interveners. The Blackfeet were primarily a plains tribe and only occasionally ventured into the Rockies.

However, sympathetic explorers, such as magazine editor-publisher George Bird Grinnell (1849–1938), named landmarks for the Blackfeet—in Grinnell's case, Blackfoot Glacier and Little Dog Mountain (8,610 ft, 2,624 m).

But it was a lobbying effort backed by the Great Northern Railway to "Indianize" the names of Glacier landmarks that had the most impact.

In April 1915, the railway sent a delegation of Blackfeet chiefs, Bird Rattler, Curly Bear and Wolf Plume, to visit Stephen Mather (1867–1930) at the Department of the Interior in Washington, D.C., to protest the use of white men's names.

That summer, the railway organized a tour of the park with nine Blackfeet elders and their families hosted by author James Willard Schultz (1859–1947). In the resulting book, *Blackfeet Tales of Glacier Park*, Schultz reports the indignation of Yellow Wolf at the loss of earlier place names: "Not satisfied with taking our mountains, the whites even take away the ancient names we have given them!"

Writer Mary Roberts Rinehart (1876–1958) was also in Glacier that summer. In her book *Through Glacier Park in 1915*, she wrote: "One by one, the historic names of peaks, lakes, and rivers of Glacier

Blackfeet chiefs Bird Rattler, from left, Curly Bear and Wolf Plume appeal to Stephen Mather, seated, at the Department of the Interior in Washington, D.C., in April 1916 to restore native names to Glacier landmarks.

Park are being replaced by names of obscure Government officials, professors in small universities, unimportant people who go out there to the West and memorialize themselves on Government maps."

Schultz, in collaboration with Takes-Gun-First and Curly Bear, came up with suggestions for Blackfeet names for Glacier landmarks. Schultz chronicled the effort and reasons for the name changes in his book *Signposts of Adventure* (1926).

These members of the British boundary commission, along with their U.S. counterparts, ensured the border was officially located and marked.

Since they drew the map, they got to make the labels

Three major survey parties worked to mark the boundary between the United States and Canada, leaving behind reminders of their presence along the 49th parallel. The separate American and British expeditions mapped the boundary from the Pacific to Waterton–Glacier, arriving in 1860 and 1861 respectively, and a joint American–British survey plotted the boundary from the Great Lakes to the Rockies, arriving in the region in August 1874.

A number of mountains, mostly in Waterton, still bear the names of some members of the three survey parties: Mount Richards (7,926 ft, 2,416 m), Mount Bauerman (7,904 ft, 2,409 m), Mount Galwey (7,703 ft, 2,348 m), Mount Rowe (8,025 ft, 2,446 m) and Mount Boswell (8,002 ft, 2,439 m).

Cameron Lake, creek and falls, and Rowe Lakes, also reflect survey member names.

In Glacier, Mount Custer (8,883 ft, 2,708 m) and Mount Campbell (8,245 ft, 2,513 m) are linked to survey members, but the origin of the Custer designation is disputed.

Glacier's Lake Wurdeman and Lake Nooney were also named for survey members.

Named for the name-givers

U.S. Senator Thomas H. Carter (1854–1911) of Montana is said to have named Glacier National Park, and a mountain and a glacier are named for Carter.

Explorer Thomas Blakiston (1832–1891) suggested the name Waterton when he explored the area in 1858 for the Palliser Expedition. Oddly, his report does not specify who Waterton was, but it is widely believed to be the Englishman Charles Waterton (1782–1865), a fellow ornithologist whom Blakiston admired.

In recognition of his explorations, the tallest peak in Waterton was later named for Blakiston, but it is not clear who chose the name.

Charles Waterton

First hired men

The first superintendent of Glacier, William R. Logan (1856–1912), is commemorated in the names Logan Pass, creek, glacier and mountain, but, oddly, the only geographical name honoring Waterton's forest ranger in charge, John George "Kootenai" Brown (1839–1916), is Brown Pass, which is in the northern section of Glacier.

North of the 49th

While tipping our hats to the efforts of pioneers like Albert "Death on the Trail" Reynolds and John George "Kootenai" Brown, who were among the first to suggest the removal of artificial boundaries in the parks, and to the Rotarians who brought the "peace park movement" to the attention of legislators for the greater good of world peace and natural harmony, here's a north–south, Waterton–Glacier look at geographic names.

Let's get it right

As early as 1926, *The Lethbridge Herald* implored readers to stop calling the park Waterton Lakes, its colloquial name.

Since many people outside the region were not aware that Waterton was a national park, one editorial suggested it be consistently called Waterton National Park and a month later a columnist from Waterton said, "We believe this could be improved upon by adding the word 'lakes,' calling it "The Waterton Lakes National Park."

The official name had been determined 15 years earlier when a federal Order-in-Council decided the name would be Waterton Lakes National Park.

Courtesy, Parks Canada

Today, most people in the region simply refer to the place as Waterton and, except for official internal park documents, it is seldom referred to by its initials, WLNP.

The townsite, which is a center for visitor services, is known by Canada Post as Waterton Park and has its own postal code, T0K 2M0. The post office named the townsite on June 15, 1917.

The name for the townsite created problems in the past when hunters near the park border confused the name of the townsite with the name of the park and inadvertently shot wildlife within the national park thinking the actual borders were several miles distant.

Just one politician

Buchanan ridge and mountain (7,903 ft, 2,409 m), in Waterton's Akamina Valley, were named for William A. Buchanan, a Canadian senator, long-time Waterton cabin owner, park supporter and owner of *The Lethbridge Herald*. Previously, the mountain was known as Cameron or Cameronian Mountain, after a member of one of the Boundary Commission members.

The name change was suggested shortly after Buchanan's death in 1954, but was not made official until 1971. It is the only mountain in the park named for a politician.

First World War left its mark

The names of a number of Waterton landmarks are associated with the First World War, a reflection of its impact on society at the time.

Vimy Peak (7,805 ft, 2,379 m) is named after Vimy Ridge in France, where Canadian troops, fighting for the first time together and under Canadian command, broke the stalemate on the Western Front in April 1917 to take key high ground.

Mount Alderson (8,832 ft, 2,692 m) was named for Lt.-Gen. E.A.H. Alderson (1859–1927), who commanded the Canadian Expeditionary Force from 1915 to 1916.

Mount Carthew (8,650 ft, 2636 m), Carthew Creek and Carthew Lakes honor a young surveyor, William Morden Carthew, who was an assistant to dominion land surveyor R.W. Cautley, climbing the mountain later named for him to set a signal for his colleague. Carthew was killed in France in 1916. The name was made official in 1971.

The Dardenelles, a short waterway linking Middle and Lower Waterton Lakes, marks a disastrous Allied naval campaign against Turkey in 1915.

Lt.-Gen. E.A.H. Alderson

The Bosporus, also known as the Narrows, is a strip of land between Upper and Middle Waterton lakes. It is named after the strait joining the Sea of Marmara and the Black Sea in Turkey, and is associated with the same 1915 battle.

Avion Ridge was named for Avion, France, which was captured by Canadian troops in 1917.

Ever-changing names

Bertha Peak (8,005 ft, 2,440 m), lake and falls were said to have been named after an early resident of the park. While some said Bertha was a bootlegger, others claimed she was a counterfeiter, a friend of a local resident, a niece of a Pincher Creek postmaster or even a girlfriend of Glacier ranger-turned-poacher Joe Cosley (1870–1943). No one bothered to record her last name.

Before about 1910, Bertha Lake was known as Spirit Lake. The name Mount Bertha was first used on a map in 1914.

In 1940, Ottawa officials considered changing the name of the falls, located about two miles (3 km) from the townsite trailhead, to Grey Mare's Tail Falls because of its resemblance to a waterfall by the same name in Scotland, said to be one of the most breathtaking in that country.

C.K. LeCapelain, then park superintendent, cautioned that the falls would probably always be known locally as Bertha because "… the old name sticks and is the only one recognized by local people."

In most cases, however, LeCapelain was wrong. While Blakiston Brook is locally known as Pass Creek, many other names have been changed over the years with few people now recalling the original ones. Sheep Mountain became Vimy Peak, the First Narrows became the Bosporus, the Second Narrows the Dardenelles, Blue Lake lost out to Crandell Lake, and the Pimple became the Bear's Hump.

Young campers from the city

Sampson Basin is not marked on topographical maps, but for more than three decades it was a popular destination for the thousands of youngsters who attended the YMCA's Camp Inuspi in Waterton.

Located in a small cirque at the head of Sofa Creek, just east of Crypt Lake, Sampson Basin got its name shortly after the camp opened in 1934. It was named for Jim Sampson of Lethbridge, who was the Y's physical director and the first camp director. Sampson did much to organize Camp Inuspi, which was located on the south shore of Lower Waterton Lake. He led campers on hikes and the basin named for him became a favorite destination.

Inuspi, a native word for "long hair," was the name given to John George "Kootenai" Brown, forest ranger in charge of Waterton. By taking the name Inuspi for the camp, the YMCA helped to honor Brown in a manner that was more appropriate than any other attempted in the park.

The camp served southern Alberta boys and girls until 1969. The lease for the land was sold back to the government in 1971.

Oil legacy lives on

Mount Crandell (7,802 ft, 2,378 m) was named for Edward Henry Crandell (1859–1944), president of the company that drilled the original oil discovery well in Waterton. Crandell, who died in 1944, had lived in Calgary since 1899 and had little or no contact with the park after oil production petered out.

The discovery well, the first in Western Canada, was drilled in the Akamina Valley close to what is now known as Cameron Creek. At the time, it was known as Oil Creek. The Akamina Valley was also home to the short-lived Oil City.

The five Lineham lakes and creek were also named for an oil-man. John Lineham (1857–1913), of Calgary and Okotoks, Alberta, was a major player in the search for oil in the park. Originally from England, Lineham became a member of the Territorial Legislative Assembly in 1888 and was also involved in raising cattle and horses, as well as harvesting timber and searching for oil.

Ray Djuff collection

This 1920s view of the Waterton registration office near Linnet Lake prominently features the Bear's Hump, once called the Pimple, a part of Crandell Mountain.

A bear with a pimple

Mount Crandell was for many years known locally as Black Bear Mountain or Bear Mountain.

Only one portion of Mount Crandell has retained an association with its original name. The Bear's Hump, a popular view point over-looking Waterton townsite and the lakes, is a short but steep hike from the visitor information centre. In the 1920s, before a trail was built to the top of the Bear's Hump, it was known as the Pimple.

111

The mountain's name was revived in 2004 when the El Cortez Motel in Waterton was sold and renamed Bear Mountain Motel. The mountain dominates the scenery from the registration area.

The big four lakes

At one time, the four large adjoining lakes in Waterton were known as Upper Waterton, Lower Waterton, Knight's Lake and the Maskinonge.

In 1969, the Canadian Permanent Committee on Geographical Names made two official name changes that still confuse long-time area residents: Lower Waterton Lake was renamed Middle Waterton Lake and Knight's Lake became Lower Waterton Lake.

Popular warden turned superintendent

Knight's Lake was named for one of the park's most popular officials. Herbert Knight (1885–1962) was Waterton's chief park warden starting in 1919, a position which called for his living in the Cedar Cabin on the west shore of what became known as Knight's Lake (now Lower Waterton Lake).

He did double duty, also serving as acting superintendent during the winter months from 1925 to 1930, and was appointed superintendent full-time in 1932.

The Cedar Cabin continued to be occupied by various park wardens until 1951, when a new warden house was built in the townsite. The Cedar Cabin was later torn down.

To this day, the section of the entry road above the place where the cabin stood is known locally as Knight's Hill.

Wrong bird

Linnet Lake, just north of the Prince of Wales Hotel, was named for a finch that does not live in Canada, *Carduelis cannabina*.

While no one seems to know who named the lake or when, the bird's flight pattern is very similar to native birds of the area which frequent the tiny lake's environment.

South of the border

Schultz and Grinnell put names on many

Author James Willard Schultz and one of his publishers, George Bird Grinnell, stand out when it comes to having given Glacier landmarks the most and longest enduring names. Schultz's influence helped name 15 landmarks, while Grinnell holds the record with 28.

Schultz has been credited for naming:
- Almost-a-Dog Mountain (8,922 ft, 2,719 m)
- Going-to-the-Sun Mountain
- Heavy Runner (8,016 ft, 2,443 m)
- Loneman Mountain (7,181 ft, 2,189 m)
- Old Sun Glacier
- Piegan Mountain (9,220 ft, 2,810 m), falls, glacier and pass
- Red Eagle Mountain (8,881 ft, 2,707 m), creek, glacier, lake and pass
- Singleshot Mountain (7,926 ft, 2,416 m)

Grinnell can take credit for:
- Blackfoot Glacier
- Mount Cleveland (10,466 ft, 3,190 m)
- Fusillade Mountain (8,750 ft, 2,667 m)
- Mount Gould (9,553 ft, 2,912 m)
- Gunsight Pass, mountain (9,258 ft, 2,258 m) and lake
- Jackson Mountain (10,052 ft, 3,064 m)
- Little Chief Mountain (9,541 ft, 2,908)
- Little Dog Mountain (8,610 ft, 2,624 m)
- Norris Mountain (8,882 ft, 2,707 m)
- Otokomi Mountain (7,935 ft, 2,418 m) and lake
- Reynolds Mountain (9,125 ft, 2,781 m)
- Seward Mountain (8,917 ft, 2,718 m)
- Mount Siyeh (10,014 ft, 3,052 m), Siyeh Creek, glacier and pass
- Mount Stimson (10,142 ft, 3,091 m)
- Swiftcurrent Creek, falls, glacier, lake, mountain (8,436 ft, 2,572 m), pass and ridge
- Mount Wilbur (9,321 ft, 2,841 m) and Wilbur Creek

As well, both men have landmarks named for them. In Schultz's case, it's Apikuni Mountain (9,068 ft, 2,764 m), creek and falls, after the Blackfeet name Schultz took while living with the tribe. Grinnell has a namesake glacier, falls and peak (8,851 ft, 2,698 m).

Neither Schultz nor Grinnell were worried about trampling local traditional names when they chose to christen landmarks.

In Schultz's case, some of the native names have no direct association with the park. For instance, Almost-a-Dog was one of the few survivors of the so-called Baker Massacre of 1870, while Heavy Runner died in the attack.

George Bird Grinnell

Grinnell's familiarity with firearms and hunting was evident in many of the names associated with him, such as Gunsight and Fusillade, as well as places named after hunting partners, such

113

as: William H. Seward III, grandson of Lincoln's secretary of state; George H. Gould, a banker from Santa Barbara, California; and Henry L. Stimson (1867–1950), a prominent New York lawyer.

Glacier's Running Eagle Falls was once called Trick Falls because of a geological feature that has a hidden waterfall under the main fall that's only visible when flow rates are low. The phenomenon was featured in a *Ripley's Believe It or Not!* article.

Running Eagle

One of the Blackfeet names lost and now restored to a Glacier landmark is Running Eagle Falls, near Two Medicine Lake.

Running Eagle, also known as Pitamakin, was a Blackfeet woman whose parents died when she was a teen. Rather than be taken in by relatives, she kept her orphaned siblings together as a family, heading the household. According to author James Willard Schultz, who was told the story by Tail-Feathers-Coming-over-the-Hill, when she was 20, Weasel Woman demanded to go along on a raid on a Flathead camp.

Weasel Woman's daring on that and subsequent raids earned her the name Pitimakan and the right to go on a vision quest, a custom that is usually reserved for men. For the site of her vision quest, she chose the falls near Two Medicine Lake.

Until recently it was called Trick Falls, a name a Great Northern official is believed to have coined to describe its curious geological feature: when the water level of Two Medicine Creek drops later in the season, a tunnel cut in the rock reveals a second waterfall under the main falls.

The falls were renamed in July 1981 due largely to lobbying by the James Willard Schultz Society.

Squaw is no longer politically correct

Two sites in Glacier have recently been given new native names. It happened after the state legislature passed Bill 412 in 1999, introduced by Democrat Carol Juneau of Browning, Montana. They were originally named Squaw Mountain and Old Squaw.

"Squaw is a real hurtful word and a derogatory word," Juneau said. "It never meant anything nice. I always viewed it as somebody trying to belittle me, or somebody trying to make fun of me.... But as a younger person, you don't have the power to make a change; you don't have the power to influence."

That was until she was elected to the Montana legislature and introduced Bill 412 to remove the word squaw from every one of 76 geographic sites in Montana.

In Glacier, Squaw Mountain is now Dancing Lady Mountain (7,695 ft, 2,346 m) and Old Squaw, a formation in front of Dancing Lady Mountain, is Stands Alone Woman.

Would you repeat that, please?

Sometimes names happen by accident, as was the case with Appistoki Peak (8,164 ft, 2,489 m).

R.T. Evans, a topographer who worked on an early map of Glacier, asked his Indian guide what the Blackfeet word was for "looking over something."

The guide misunderstood and said "Appistoki," the Indian god who looks over everything and everyone.

Or could you spell it for me?

Cosley Lake, in the northeastern section of Glacier, was, for many years, known as Crossley Lake and was the site of a tent camp operated by the Park Saddle Horse Company that provided shelter and meals to trail riders and hikers.

Cosley Lake, once the site of a tent camp, was for 40 years incorrectly known as Crossley Lake.

The last of the mountain men, Joseph Cosley (1870–1944) was a Glacier ranger who became a poacher and had a cabin in the area. The lake's name was misspelled as Crossley on maps and was known as such until it was corrected after the Second World War.

Whose mountain is it anyway?

Chief Mountain (9,080 ft, 2,767 m) has had a variety of names over the years. When Hudson's Bay Company explorer/fur trader Peter Fidler (1769–1822) saw it in 1792, it was known as "King's Mountain." Meriwether Lewis (1774–1809) apparently saw the peak in 1806 on his trip up the Marias River and marked it "Tower Mountain." The present name comes from the Blackfeet designation of "Old Chief" or "Mountain-of-the-Chief."

While the entire mountain lies in the U.S., part of it is in Glacier and part of it is on the Blackfeet reservation. However, the best view of this impressive mountain, which resembles a chief's head in profile looking at the sky, can be had from Alberta. Several businesses just north of the border have attached the name Chief Mountain to theirs, and locals in towns close to the border where the view is best consider the mountain part of Canada.

Shifting names

The Mount Stimson (10,142 ft, 3,091 m) we know today was originally called Mount James.

The mountain that George Bird Grinnell picked to honor Henry L. Stimson is the present-day Mount Logan (9,239 ft, 2,816 m). It is suspected that cartographers working with material from the U.S. Geological Survey of the early 20th century switched the names.

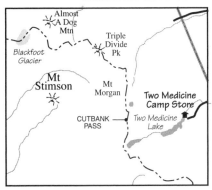

Stimson was an up-and-coming Republican lawyer with a fascination for adventure and the outdoors when he visited the Glacier region in the 1890s. He was Secretary of War under President William Taft (1857–1930) and, later, Secretary of State under Herbert Hoover (1874–1964). Despite their political differences, President Franklin D. Roosevelt, a Democrat, picked Stimson as his Secretary of War. Stimson was the president's chief adviser on atomic policy and, although he had doubts, recommended to President Harry S Truman (1884–1972) the bombings of Hiroshima and Nagasaki.

During his 1890s visits to Glacier, Stimson made several first ascents, including Chief Mountain, Blackfoot Mountain (9,597 ft, 2,925 m) and Little Chief Mountain.

One of Stimson's guides on his 1894 ascent of Little Chief Mountain with George Bird Grinnell was William Jackson, who had been a scout under Maj. Marcus Reno's command at the Battle of the Little Big Horn in 1876.

Also present for the climb and acting as a guide was James Willard Schultz, who wrote the 1927 book, *William Jackson, Indian*

Scout. His True Story, Told by His Friend, James Willard Schultz. The work first appeared as a four-part series in 1926 in the magazine, *The American Boy.*

Cracker Lake is a popular hiking and riding destination from Many Glacier Hotel. It was also the site of several mines. The boom was short-lived and the mines were abandoned before the creation of the park.

Like a trail of crumbs

Cracker Lake, about seven miles (11 km) south of Many Glacier Hotel and one of the bluest-colored lakes in Glacier (the result of glacial "flour") gets its name from soda crackers.

In L.C. Emmons' version of the name, he and St. Mary-area resident Hank Norris were searching for lead and copper and "stopped for our lunch of crackers and cheese, of which we had brought enough for two meals. Intending to return that evening to eat what remained, we cached it on a flat rock, putting a second rock on top...."

A variation of that tale has prospectors in the area when it was still part of the Blackfeet reservation and off limits to exploration. Trying to keep their activities hidden from the natives, the explorers said they were just passing through and were up near the lake to get crackers they'd cached there.

Miners would eventually get their way when the "ceded strip," what is now the eastern portion of Glacier, was purchased from the Blackfeet and opened to the public in April 1898.

Cracker Lake copper mine was the biggest and most productive during the short-lived mining boom in the Glacier area. The mine extended some 1,300 feet (396 m) into the mountainside. A road from Swiftcurrent Valley was built to the site at a reported cost of $5,000, and a concentrator was brought from Coeur d'Alene, Idaho. Some of the abandoned mine equipment can still be seen there today.

Courtesy, Martha Davidge

Curious tourists examine some of the equipment left when mining was abandoned near Cracker Lake.

Wynn's last climb

Wynn Mountain (8,404 ft, 2,561 m) was named for Dr. Frank B. Wynn, who led members of the Nature Study Club of Indiana on hiking and climbing expeditions to Glacier between 1919 and 1922. The group took with it flat metal boxes containing registers that were left at the top of each mountain when members climbed.

Dr. Wynn died near the top of Mount Siyeh on a hike July 27, 1922, and that year Point Mountain was renamed in his honor.

Gone but not forgotten

Mount Altyn (7,947 ft, 2,422 m) was named for David Greenwood Altyn, a financial backer of the Cracker Lake mine.

Except, it's not the original Mount Altyn. The original Mount Altyn is now called Mount Wynn, named for Dr. Francis B. Wynn. As George Bird Grinnell had previously named the original Mount Altyn Point Mountain, topographers transferred the name Mount Altyn to the present peak.

Altyn was also the name of the boom town near the head of Sherburne Lake that was the supply centre for miners who rushed into the area to stake their claims. At its height in 1900, Altyn had a population of 1,000, a hotel built by Sam Somes, several saloons, one operated by William and Dan Haggerty, stores, a newspaper (the *Swift Current Courier*) and a connection to the outside world by way of a stage line to Browning, Montana, started by Joe Kipp.

The boom was short-lived as the mines weren't economical; by 1902 it is said only a few diehards remained in Altyn. Remnants of the town were still visible in the 1930s.

Minnesota Historical Society

Tourists appear to link hands as they prepare to venture out on Sperry Glacier. The glacier is named for Dr. Lyman Sperry, an instructor at Carleton College in Minnesota.

Sperry's "find"

Sperry Glacier and Sperry Chalets are named for Dr. Lyman B. Sperry (1838–1923), a geologist and instructor at Carleton College in Northfield, Minnesota.

Although the glacier is named for Sperry, he did not in fact "find" it. The block of ice and snow had been spotted in 1894 by Charles Howe, an early settler in the Lake McDonald area, from the summit of Mount Brown (8,565 ft, 2,610 m).

Howe told Sperry, the "gentleman explorer," of the find the next year and that prompted Sperry to search the Avalanche Lake Valley and eventually set foot on what would become his namesake glacier.

While the chalets and glacier have the same name, indicating proximity, it is about a four-mile (6.4 km) hike from the chalets to the glacier.

Going-to-the-Sun sounded good

There are several native legends regarding Going-to-the-Sun Mountain (9,642 ft, 2,939 m).

The truth, however, may be a lot less exotic.

Author James Willard Schultz once wrote: "I, myself, named Going to the Sun Mountain [sic]; simply because of its imposing uplift into the blue. There is no Indian legend in connection with its name."

This is not improbable, as Schultz was known to play fast and loose with history and events, and many of his tales about the Blackfeet must be taken for what they are, fiction based on elements of fact—sometimes more, sometimes less.

Ray Djuff collection

Going-to-the-Sun Mountain, seen here rising from St. Mary Lake, is a lyrical name that intrigues visitors. Legends about the name's origin abound.

In the oral tradition of present-day Blackfeet, however, the name originates with a legend about the ubiquitous and scared Napi, who was said to have been sent to teach natives the life skills they would need to survive. When Napi climbed this mountain and vanished into the sun, it was given its name.

Money counts

Baring Creek, near Sun Point, gets its name from two Baring brothers, members of the London banking family. They were guided on a hunting trip into the Glacier area in the 1880s by Joe Kipp and James Willard Schultz.

The Barings Bank, acting as financial representatives for the United States' government in Europe, helped Thomas Jefferson raise the cash ($15 million, about four cents an acre) for the Louisiana Purchase in 1803, and funded America's budding entrepreneurs prior to the Civil War. It also participated in the financing of the Panama Canal and the campaign to oust Napoleon Bonaparte.

The prestigious family company, founded in 1762, collapsed in 1995 after being bankrupted by rogue trader Nick Leeson. ING Group bought the firm, once valued in the billions, for a single British pound.

Poetic lake name

Evangeline Lake may have been named by members of R.H. Sargent's U.S. Geographical Survey party, which mapped much of the Glacier area between 1900 and 1904. The lake takes its name from the narrative poem written by Henry Wadsworth Longfellow (1807–1882), who also penned *Hiawatha*.

Evangeline (1847) is a story about two young lovers who were separated by the Acadian deportations of 1755. In the poem, Evangeline searches fruitlessly for years for Gabriel, finally giving up and becoming a Sister of Mercy in Philadelphia. After dedicating her life to the service of others, she then discovers Gabriel, destitute and near death.

The poem became the basis for an opera, two movies (1919 and 1929), a Bourbon Street burlesque show, creation of The Evangeline Girls group in the 1920s, and a renewed interest in the history of Acadians, with several families claiming members to have been the real-life inspiration for Evangeline.

It's a measure of this epic tale's popularity that not only is the lake named after the poem's heroine, but Sargent also named a nearby peak in Glacier after the poet. Longfellow Peak (8,904 ft, 2,714 m) can easily be seen from Waterton, providing a visual, if distant, backstop to the Upper Lake.

A beautiful lake by any name

It may never be known who named the St. Mary lakes. James Willard Schultz claimed they were christened by Father Pierre-Jean DeSmet (1801–1873) during his 1845 visit to the Glacier area in search of Hugh Monroe (ca.1798–1892), a trapper and area resident. However, DeSmet makes no mention of this in his journals.

In fact, scholars can only surmise that DeSmet visited the Glacier area, as he mentions wandering for weeks through "a labyrinth of narrow valleys" looking for Monroe, but never clearly identifies the location of those "narrow valleys."

Father Pierre DeSmet

Chris Morrison collection

Others claim Monroe was so overcome by the beauty of the lakes when he first arrived that he erected a cross on the shores of the lower lake and named it after the Virgin Mary.

The origin of the name St. Mary Lake, seen here in a 1920s publicity photo featuring the *Motor Vessel St. Mary*, cannot be definitively fixed. Most scholars credit it to Jesuit priest Pierre DeSmet, who was in the area in 1845, but even that claim takes some imagination.

When James Doty, searching for the elusive Marias Pass for Gov. Isaac Stevens (1818–1862) of the Washington Territory, camped by the lakes, he called the upper one Bow Lake and the lower one Chief Mountain Lake. The first time the lakes were recorded as St. Mary was by the International Boundary Commission, about 1870. The name has since stuck.

Large honor for a short visit

Although Lt. George Patrick Ahern (1859–1942) was only in Glacier little more than a month during the summer of 1890, charting the last blocks of unmapped territory, his legacy abounds.

Ahern Creek, Ahern Glacier, Ahern Pass and Ahern Peak (8,749 ft, 2,422 m) are all named for the explorer, who has more citations in the park than any other individual.

Interestingly, none of the other 10 or so people who accompanied Ahern on the expedition was similarly blessed by having a geographical feature named after him.

Ahern Pass is no great tribute, as it is considered forbidding to traverse, and it wasn't until 1913, when R.H. Sargent of the U.S. Geological Survey went over it, that a second crossing was recorded.

The Ptarmigan Tunnel was built to overcome that geological obstacle.

Man on a mission

Louis W. Hill (1872–1948), head of the Great Northern Railway, has been called the "godfather of Glacier" for his interest in having the area designated a national park, developing tourist facilities, and promoting the park as a travel destination—yet no natural feature bears his name.

Hill took an active interest not only in the facilities the railway built and their operation, but also in park maintenance and operations. After visiting the park each summer, he would never hesitate to call deficiencies to the attention of officials locally and nationally, and demand improvements.

Both nationally influential and personally knowledgeable about Glacier, Hill brought many of the day's movers and shakers to the park to enjoy its splendors, and he missed few opportunities to promote the park.

Some say the real tribute to Hill is the park itself.

Once Lethbridge's city clerk, Donald Duff was also an engineer and survey-
or who played a key role in the building of the Chief Mountain International
Highway, linking Waterton and Glacier.

6 Connections

Waterton and Glacier parks, joined by geography and geology, have a human history that is sometimes intertwined without consideration for the international boundary that separates them. Other times, the history is tied with the world outside, long before the parks were established or since. These lingering connections have left footprints throughout history.

Close call with Custer

George Bird Grinnell (1849–1938), dubbed the "father of conservation" in the United States and the person most responsible for the creation of Glacier as a national park, can thank George Armstrong Custer (1839–1876) for igniting his interest in nature. It was sparked when Grinnell accompanied Custer on an 1874 expedition to the Black Hills of South Dakota as the expedition's naturalist.

Grinnell was busy at Yale University's Peabody Museum and had to turn down an invitation from Custer when offered the opportunity to go on his fateful campaign to the Big Horn Mountains in 1876.

Local engineer got the jobs

Scottish born Donald A. Duff (1879–1945), whose pioneering family moved to Lethbridge, Alberta, in 1885, was a civil engineer and surveyor for the Canadian portion of Chief Mountain International Highway.

As homesteaders, the Duff family was one of the first to run large cattle herds in southern Alberta. In the early 1900s, the Duff homestead was annexed by the City of Lethbridge and became known as the Duff Addition.

After becoming an engineer, Donald Duff helped build railroads on both sides of the border and later established a surveying and engineering firm in Lethbridge.

In what he thought was a temporary career move, Duff was appointed Lethbridge city clerk in 1917 and remained in that post until the end of 1930.

He then returned to surveying and engineering work, and in 1932 was hired to work on Waterton's new road linking Glacier. It was completed in 1936.

With the outbreak of hostilities in Europe and until his death, Duff helped in the engineering of airports in southern Alberta built for the British Commonwealth Air Training Plan.

In his own write

Canadian Governor General John Buchan (1875–1940), who visited Waterton in 1936, was more than the King's representative to the country and a much welcomed visitor. He was a well-known novelist.

The year before his Waterton visit, Buchan's *The Thirty Nine Steps* was made into a movie directed by Alfred Hitchcock (1899–1980), staring Robert Donat (1905–1958) and Madeleine Carroll (1906–1987).

This black and white film of espionage and murder has been described as "one of the best films Hitchcock ... ever made, filled with action, humor and suspense."

Building ideas

The Rocky Mountains Club, organized in Waterton in 1926 by local stone mason and builder Walter "Waddy" Foster, was a naturalists' club, hikers' organization and precursor to the peace park movement rolled into one. Foster hoped the club "would promote united development of the two parks."

Foster was eager to build a headquarters for the club and had already laid the foundations for what he hoped would become the gathering place for members. The building, which still stands opposite the marina in Waterton and is known as the Captain's Cabin or Cliff Hummel House, was to be the home of a nature library, map collections, pictures and "other objects suitable for a park museum."

Tentative plans also called for the club to publish illustrated articles and maps, providing funds could be obtained.

Within two years, excellent progress was reported on the club's activities: It had distributed advertising material and membership buttons, created bylaws, and conducted a number of day and overnight trips for members.

In June 1928, Stephen Mather (1867–1930), director of the U.S. National Park Service, agreed to serve as honorary president and Senator William A. Buchanan (1876–1954) of Lethbridge was appointed his Canadian counterpart, while Foster and a group of local residents carried the load of actual club operation.

The Depression stole Foster's dream. He was forced to sell the clubhouse as his resources dwindled. The club also suffered from amalgamation woes when members agreed to include branches for the Rod and Gun Club, and golf, tennis and boating clubs.

Ever higher profile honorary presidents, Louis W. Hill (1872–1948) and Governor General Viscount Willingdon (1866–1941), were selected and interest continued in view of the fact that Waterton had no park staff to lead hikes or deal with natural history.

With the deepening of the Depression, however, the club faded from active service after the 1932 season. Its legacy lives, however, with the on-going presence of the peace park designation, the park's own interpretive programs and the work of the Waterton Natural History Association.

Colorado hero a Montana pioneer

The pioneering work in tourist transportation that Roe Emery (1875–1953) did in Glacier would ultimately also benefit Colorado.

Emery, a Montana-born entrepreneur, was one of the two principles behind the creation of Glacier's "red bus" system of transporting tourists between hotels. Emery, along with Walter White, vice-president of the White Motor Company, introduced their buses to the park in 1914, creating a reliable way to ferry tourists from place to place.

Emery and White used the knowledge gained in Glacier about scheduling and the placement of hotels to undertake a similar venture in Colorado's Rocky Mountain National Park in 1916.

Emery and White's Rocky Mountain Motor Company created the breath-taking Circle Tour, a three-day bus trip centered in Rocky Mountain National Park. The buses would take tourists from railheads in Denver, Greeley and Lyons to his Estes Park Chalet, cross the "Top of the World" Road to Grand Lake Lodge, which Emery owned, and then over

Roe Emery, left, head of the Glacier Park Transportation Company, sends a group off from Glacier Park Hotel in 1916. Underwritten by the White Motor Company, the transport company used its vehicles exclusively.

Berthoud Pass to the Hot Springs Hotel, also owned by Emery.

Emery and his family operated this mini-tourism empire until 1953, long after he'd turned over control of his Glacier operations, in

127

1927, to Howard Hays Sr. (1883–1969) of Riverside, California.

For his efforts, Emery was hailed as "the father of Colorado tourism."

Glacier National Park archive

This Model 706 bus, seen here on August 15, 1938, on Going-to-the-Sun Road, was made by the White Motor Company of Cleveland, Ohio. The buses are still on the road today.

Sewing up the tour bus business

The red buses that shuttle tourists between Glacier and Waterton are now as much a fixture as the land itself. They've been in service since the mid-1930s, making the buses the longest in continuous use in North America.

The buses were built by the White Motor Company of Cleveland, Ohio. The White name should ring a bell with anyone familiar with sewing machines.

The White Sewing Machine Company was founded in 1876 by Thomas H. White (1836–1914). White's sons, Walter (1876–1929) and Rollin (1872–1949), persuaded their father to start building motor vehicles, resulting in the White Steam Car.

The White Motor Company became a separate entity in November 1906, and soon was also producing trucks, then buses.

Car production halted in 1918.

In 1915, Walter White took an equity stake in the newly formed Glacier Park Transportation Company to get the exclusive contract for his buses to be on the road in the park. The White Motor Company, however, had to compete in 1935 against Ford, REO and General Motors for the contract to supply updated buses. The 1930s White Model 706 buses still ply the roads of Waterton and Glacier today.

While the White company continues to make sewing machines, the White nameplate for trucks disappeared in 1995, following a corporate takeover by Volvo.

Blakiston the birdman

If you're looking for the grave of English adventurer Lt. Thomas Blakiston (1832–1891), the first European to explore the area now encompassing Waterton, in September 1858, you'll have to go to Columbus, Ohio.

After completing his work with the Palliser Expedition and its exploration of Western Canada, Blakiston was promoted to captain and his regiment was sent to China. There, he organized an expedition up the Yangtze River, going further than any European before him.

In 1861, Blakiston moved to Hakodate, Japan, and entered the lumber and transportation business, continued his study of birds in the northern part of the country, and became renowned as an outstanding naturalist. A number of species of birds are named for him, including Blakiston's fish owl (*Ketupa blakistoni*).

After 23 years in Japan, Blakiston moved to the United States in 1884. Now divorced, at the age of 52 he married the eldest sister of Edwin Dunn, an American businessman he met in Japan. Blakiston died of pneumonia in San Diego, California in 1891. His widow undertook his burial in her own home town of Columbus, Ohio.

Birds of a feather

George Bird Grinnell is hailed for his singular devotion to having the Glacier area eventually set aside as a national park. It was by no means the first crusade for Grinnell, who was the editor and publisher of *Forest and Stream*.

In 1886, alarmed by the use of bird feathers on women's hats and the impact of that fashion on bird populations, Grinnell announced in *Forest and Stream* the founding of the Audubon Society, dedicated to saving birds. The following year, with Theodore "Teddy" Roosevelt (1858–1919), he also founded the Boone and Crockett Club. He had met Roosevelt in 1885 and given him a report on the slaughter of big game in the West.

The Boone and Crockett Club was founded to promote "fair hunting" and to push for legislation to promote conservation.

The excursion boat *DeSmet* was built by Capt. William Swanson, who rides in the bow, while truck owner and driver Jack Keller navigates to Lake McDonald. It is still in use.

Little house on the prairie

Pioneer Jesuit priest Father Pierre Jean DeSmet (1801–1873), who traveled extensively on both sides of the Rockies and the international border beginning in the 1840s taking religion to Indians, had a remarkable reputation for parlaying peace between natives and whites. He also became renowned for his missionary work.

Well known among Glacier luminaries such as Hugh Monroe (1799–1892) and James Willard Schultz (1859–1947), and a regular visitor to the Glacier area, DeSmet was constantly on the go. In the final 50 years of his life, it is said he covered some 180,000 miles (288,000 km).

It was appropriate that the excursion boat *DeSmet*, which plies Glacier's Lake McDonald every day in the summer, was named for this man. DeSmet took travel seriously and his last official act was to christen a steamboat named for him in St. Louis, Missouri.

The DeSmet name should also ring a bell for fans of Laura Ingalls Wilder's *Little House on the Prairie* books. Wilder (1867–1957) set five of her eight stories in De Smet, South Dakota: *By the Shores of Silver Lake, The Long Winter, Little Town on the Prairie, These Happy Golden Years, The First Four Years* and *On The Way Home*. The De Smet cemetery was the final resting place for several members of the Ingalls family.

The 20-Cent Workers

The Government of Canada saw its Depression-era relief camps program as an opportunity to kill two birds with one stone: put men to work and make much needed improvements to park facilities at little expense. The legacy of that work is still evident today.

In January 1931, Ottawa announced it had earmarked a total of $33,000 for winter relief camps in three national parks, of which $2,000 would be set aside for Waterton. The rest went to Banff and Jasper.

Unlike the Civilian Conservation Corps in the U.S., the Canadian relief camp wages were significantly lower—initially only 20 cents a day plus room and board. In the U.S., workers received $1 a day plus room and board. Later, wages in Canada were moderately increased, but never matched those in the U.S. Even at that, camp positions in Waterton, always limited, were highly sought after as its reputation grew for relatively good living conditions and good and plentiful food.

Gradually, more money was allocated for Waterton's relief camp works, and a number of major projects were completed: townsite curbs and flagstone walks, additions to campground facilities, bridges, a new gate house and expansion of the park's golf course. But it was the building of the roads, including portions of the Akamina Parkway and all of the Canadian section of the Chief Mountain International Highway, billed as "the park to park link," that was the pride of the workers and is most appreciated by visitors to this day.

A Glacier Park Transport Company driver stops at an overlook on the American side of Chief Mountain Highway to describe the mountain's storied past.

Ray Djuff collection

Short visit, long legacy

Lt. George Patrick Ahern (1859–1942) led an expedition through what is now Glacier Park in August 1890, charting the last blocks of unmapped territory. His legacy remains in the names Ahern Creek, Ahern Glacier, Ahern Pass and Ahern Peak.

Ahern's greater legacy was later in life. Taking courses at Yale law school while still in the army, Ahern developed an interest in forestry and its uses in national defense, writing a thesis entitled, "The Necessity for Forestry Legislation." He was one of the chief proponents of establishing forestry preserves in the Bitterroot and Gallatin areas of Montana. This pitted Ahern against the state's powerful mining and forestry developers (which would see him denied the superintendency of Yellowstone).

He founded the Montana Forestry Association and established the Bureau of Forestry for the Philippine government.

During the Spanish–American War, he received the Silver Star for bravery under fire while serving in Cuba. He would later serve as Secretary of the War College in Washington, D.C., and then in the Veteran's Bureau.

Right place, wrong theory

The distinct U-shaped valleys of Waterton and Glacier parks are clear evidence of the handiwork of glaciers. Our understanding of geology and the effects of glaciation are thanks, in part, to Raphael Pumpelly.

Pumpelly (1837–1923) is usually listed in Glacier history books as one of a succession of 19th-century explorers who came through the region. Pumpelly undertook two summer expeditions (1882 and '83), under the auspices of the Northern Transcontinental Survey, to collect information on the topographical and economic features of the Dakotas, Montana and Washington.

Pumpelly, an early scholar on glaciation, was eminently qualified for the task of recording the region's topography.

He believed that the erosive power of glaciers was not sufficient to explain the deep, U-shaped valleys. He came up with a theory of "secular disintegration," where, over eons, continental rocks slowly decayed, forming loose material that was later easily eroded by glaciers. The scraped out material, Pumpelly said, would later be deposited in the ocean or distributed as loess (or dust) by the winds.

The theory was ultimately disproved, but played a key role in early discussions on glaciation and the development of modern theories and understanding of the effects of the ice ages.

On top of the world

The locating in 1889 of Marias Pass by John F. Stevens (1853–1943) was a turning point in the development of northwestern Montana and, ultimately, what would become Glacier. Had the Great Northern Railway been forced to go further south to find a suitable pass through the Rocky Mountain front, the benefits of the railway's arrival would have been delayed for possibly a decade or more.

The person who ensured the public understood the importance of Stevens' trailblazing was Grace H. Flandrau (1889–1971), author of *The Story of Marias Pass*.

Flandrau was a relatively well-known author of books and articles when she penned the piece in 1925 for the Great Northern, which the railway hoped to capitalize on to get its story heard. She was a member of Minnesota's literary elite and an acquaintance of F. Scott Fitzgerald (1896–1940), who wrote *The Great Gatsby* among other works, and his wife, Zelda Fitzgerald (1900–1948). Flandrau's love story-novel, *Being Respectable*, was made into a 1924 silent film.

The name Flandrau may have more than a passing meaning to anyone who has lived in or visited Tucson, Arizona. She bequeathed the funds used to build the Grace H. Flandrau Planetarium, renamed the Flandrau Science Center and Planetarium in 1991.

Ties that bind

Glacier Park, post-revolution Russian railways, the Panama Canal and the Spokane, Portland & Seattle Railway have one thing in common: John F. Stevens.

Ray Djuff collection

John F. Stevens

Stevens, whose locating of Marias Pass in 1889 was a boon for the Great Northern Railway and the development of the Glacier area, played a critical role in the building of the Panama Canal. As chief engineer of the Isthmian Canal Commission, it was Stevens who lobbied for the canal to be built using locks, rather than at sea-level, saving substantial construction cost and effort. He also set up the earth-moving and railway infrastructure that got the bogged down construction project moving after years of slow and no progress. Stevens quit the project in 1907, satisfied that the job could be completed without him. It was opened in 1914.

Stevens would return to the Great Northern fold in 1909 to oversee construction of the Spokane, Portland & Seattle Railway. He chose as his chief engineer Ralph Budd (1879–1962), who would later become president of the Great Northern. After the Russian Revolution of 1917, Stevens helped rehabilitate the crippled railways of the new Soviet Union.

Tale of the Indian head nickel

Blackfeet Chief Two Guns (John) White Calf (1872–1934) will probably be forever linked with the Indian head/buffalo nickel, despite the fact the image on the coin is not actually his.

When the coin was issued in February 1913, Great Northern officials immediately saw the resemblance. With the Glacier Park Hotel just about to open, it was a not-to-be-missed publicity opportunity.

Some 1.2 billion of the nickels were minted through to 1938, with Great Northern public relations folks all the time encouraging tourists to come to Glacier Park to see Two Guns White Calf,

Tomer Hileman postcard, Ray Djuff collection

Chief Two Guns White Calf

Ray Djuff collection

The bison on the reverse of the Indian head-buffalo nickel was modeled on one at New York's Central Park Zoo, an animal said to have been born in captivity.

the supposed model for the coin. The designer of the nickel, James Earle Fraser (1876–1953), refuted the railway's claims to no avail, even though he reportedly had a form letter printed stating Two Guns White Calf was not one of his three models; that in actuality he had used Cheyenne Chief Two Moons (1847–1917), Iroquois Chief John Big Tree (1865–1967) and Sioux Chief Iron Tail (1857–1955).

When Two Guns White Calf died in 1934, news releases told of the death of Glacier Park's "Nickel" Indian—and the legend persists.

Flip side of the coin

The model for the animal on the Indian head/buffalo nickel was Black Diamond, a bison at New York's Central Park Zoo. Then a resident of that city, artist James Earle Fraser used Black Diamond because he was the only living bison at hand.

The 1,500-pound bull, said to have been captive born and donated by the Barnum & Bailey circus, was not an easy study for Fraser.

Black Diamond often stood staring at the artist and Fraser reportedly had to get a zoo worker to distract the animal so he could get a good profile while he modeled in clay.

The nickel had been a boon for the Great Northern in its promotion of Glacier, but the director at the New York zoo thought Black Diamond was a poor example of the species and the coin's image "a sad failure," as the bison's head drooped as if in despair.

Despite the misgivings, Black Diamond became a celebrity. A few years later, Black Diamond's time was considered up and he was sold to a meat-packing plant.

There was an attempt by some in the public to save the beast, but it failed.

The meat packer was quick to cash in on the publicity, selling Black Diamond steaks while they lasted.

Building a reputation by design

The design of the beautiful and now restored Davenport Hotel in Spokane, Washington, would result in its architect getting several projects in Glacier Park.

The $2-million Davenport Hotel, built in 1912–13, was the brainchild of successful Spokane restaurateur Louis M. Davenport (1868–1951), and was backed by the financial might of newspaper magnate William H. Cowles, Great Northern Railway founder James J. Hill (1838–1916) and Hill's his son, Louis W. Hill. Their idea was to create in Spokane, on the Great Northern's mainline between Chicago and Seattle, a northwest version of New York's famed Waldorf Astoria.

The architect was Spokane's Kirtland Cutter (1860–1939) of the firm Cutter and Malmgren. The attention Cutter garnered from this masterful project contributed to the firm's growing reputation, which had previously included the design of influential businessman Charles Conrad's mansion in Kalispell.

In 1913, John Lewis (1865–1934) chose Cutter and Malmgren to design his hotel on Lake McDonald, today known as Lake McDonald Lodge. Louis W. Hill also contracted Cutter to draft the plans for Many Glacier Hotel and the dormitory for Sperry Chalets in Glacier, although he rejected Cutter's plan for Many Glacier.

Blackfeet Indians, here identified as Glacier National Park Indians, visited the unfinished Davenport Hotel while attending a pow-wow in Spokane, Washington.

A rising son

When Louis Hill Jr. (1902–1995), son of Great Northern chairman Louis W. Hill, was 12 years old, he was made an honorary member of the Blackfeet tribe. The induction ceremony in Glacier was performed by Chief Three Bears. The younger Hill was given the name Ot Que Kaitsup Imo, or Little Yellow Pinto Pony Rider.

The ceremony left the nugget of an idea with the young lad about bridging cultural gaps. In the 1950s, Louis Hill Jr. arranged a meeting with President Dwight D. Eisenhower (1890–1969). Hill, who had at Yale developed what would become a lifelong interest in Japan and Japanese culture, suggested to Eisenhower the need for person-to-person diplomacy to rebuild relations with Japan in the wake of the Second World War.

Hill's idea was to establish a "sister city" relationship between St. Paul, Minnesota, and Nagasaki. It was the first sister city link of its kind in the United States—one that would be copied across the country and around the world.

In 1987, Louis Jr. was awarded the Order of the Rising Sun with Golden Rosettes medal for his work in international relations.

Wright on

The George Wright Society is dedicated to protection and management of U.S. natural parks and reserves through research and education. It was named for George Melendez Wright (1904–1936), the first chief of the wildlife division for the National Park Service.

Wright's field notes from his 1931 trips to Kintla Lake, Cracker Lake, Ptarmigan Lake and Red Eagle Lake are still studied by naturalists for the bountiful information they contain.

Over the rainbow

For a period in the 1920s, the prestigious Culver Military Academy in Indiana had an independent offshoot at Bowman Lake in Glacier known as Skyland Camps.

Privately set up in 1922 by Col. L.R. Gignilliat, superintendent of Culver, the camp, on the west side of the park in the North Fork region, consisted of six five-room cabins and a mess hall, called Rainbow Lodge. It was constructed by Capt. J. William Swanson (1883–1971), boat builder and tour boat operator on Glacier's Two Medicine and Swiftcurrent Lakes.

Subsequent branch camps were situated at Upper and Lower Kintla Lakes. They became the only operation in Glacier to operate as both a boys' camp and a tourist facility. The cabins were to be available to cadets from Culver (at $50 a week, all costs, including horse and boat rentals) and, at alternate times, to the public ($4.50 per day or $28 per week for room and board, and horse and boat rentals; guides extra).

While the Great Northern's hotel company had first right to setting up facilities in the area, the North Fork was considered so remote the railway subsidiary wasn't worried about competition.

A financial and operational fiasco, the Skyland Camps facility remained until 1940, although it only operated intermittently after 1926. All the facilities, except for the Rainbow Lodge, were dismantled. The lodge is now used as the Bowman Lake Ranger Station.

There's no place like two homes

Butterfly Lodge in Greer, Arizona, was home away from home for James Willard Schultz, author of *Blackfeet Tales of Glacier National Park* and other books on the Blackfeet, and his son, Hart Merriam, a.k.a. Lone Wolf (1882–1970).

The lodge was built in 1913 as a mountain retreat where Schultz could write during a period away from his beloved Montana, Glacier and the Blackfeet Indians with whom he'd spent decades living as a brother. Schultz would later develop the habit of returning to Glacier each summer, from wherever he called home.

Butterfly Lodge was eventually taken over by Shultz's son, Lone Wolf (1882–1970) and his wife, Naoma Tracy. A native of Montana, Lone Wolf, like his father, could not shake his ties to Glacier. Also like his father, he got in the habit of returning every summer, usually to St. Mary, where he would live in a teepee or cabin and spend time creating his now highly collectible paintings and sketches.

Butterfly Lodge was listed in the national Register of Historic Places in 1992. In 1994, it was turned over to the Forest Service to be restored and operated as a museum to recognize the famous father and son.

Try picturing this

Winold Reiss (1886–1953) is renowned for his colorful portraits of Alberta and Montana natives, commissioned by the Great Northern to promote tourism to Waterton and Glacier parks. But Reiss' artistic interests went well beyond spending time in Waterton and Glacier to indulge his fascination for Native Americans.

He designed many of New York's great eateries, such as the Restaurant Crillon and the Longchamps chain. As well, he designed the interior of the Tavern Club in Chicago. Probably his best known public space is Cincinnati's Union Terminal.

Some of the 20-foot (6 m) square Union Terminal murals were moved to the Greater Cincinnati/Northern Kentucky International Airport. The Union Terminal became a shopping center in the 1980s and in 1990 was turned into the Cincinnati Museum Center, where the murals can still be seen.

Reiss' futuristic murals from the Longchamps restaurants are now in the lobby of New York's Shoreham Hotel.

Lone Eagle swoops over Glacier

After making history for being the first person to fly solo across the Atlantic in May 1927, Charles Lindbergh (1902–1974) went on a 20,000 mile (32,180 km), 82-stop cross-continental tour of the United States for the "promotion of Aeronautics." Sponsored by the Daniel Guggenheim Foundation, the trip was to promote the safety and durability of modern aircraft for civil aviation.

Lindbergh did not stop near Glacier Park, but he did fly over it. Several aerial shots were included in a record of his flight in the January 1928 edition of *National Geographic*.

Donald Keyhoe (1897–1988), who accompanied Lindbergh on this trip, subsequently writing an account called *Flying with Lindbergh*, noted the Glacier fly-over: "With evident delight Lindbergh was soon realizing his long cherished ambition to explore the famous park...."

Keyhoe wrote: "Tilting the silver-winged *Spirit of St. Louis*, he slid down toward a glacier-carved bowl where white snow patches glistened as though in defiance to the sun ... in a flowered valley where a tiny lake lay prisoner. Across its turquoise surface he skimmed like a dragonfly while a phantom plane gave chase in the mirrored water beneath. Nestling at the farther end of the lake was a rustic chalet from which a canoe was slowly gliding. With paddles transfixed in mid air, the occupants stared upward at this strange intruder. Then a quick, impassioned welcome as perhaps they recognized the famous NX-211 that had already thrilled countless thousands."

High noon for guest ranch

Chris Morrison collection

Montana-born actor Gary Cooper in costume for one of his early Hollywood western roles.

In the late 1920s, retired Montana Supreme Court justice Charles H. Cooper (1865–1946), father of the then silver-screen newcomer Gary Cooper (1901–1961), approached Great Northern executive Louis W. Hill about establishing dude ranches under the name of the Gary Cooper Dude Ranches, with one near Glacier.

Charles Cooper hinted that the Paramount motion picture studio was considering a film about Montana historical events starring Gary Cooper. He noted that it might be based on the Lewis and Clark expedition, and that it would create "an intense desire to see the route of Lewis and Clark."

Leveraging the initial interest expressed by the Great Northern's competitors near Yellowstone and the worldwide publicity movie studios gave to their players and picture sets, Charles Cooper told

Hill such a dude camp would "add very materially to your summer business." Without coming right out and saying so, Cooper was looking for Great Northern's backing.

Cooper failed to persuade the railway to back the ranch and he went ahead on his own with a 7,000-acre (2,835-hectare) spread along the Taylor's Fork of the Gallatin River, south of Great Falls, Montana, and far from Glacier National Park. Known as the Gary Cooper Guest Ranch (Seven Bar Nine) it opened in 1930 and was advertised erroneously as the actor's birthplace. With accommodation for guests in a large ranch house and a number of rustic guest and tent houses, the ranch offered "all the thrilling activities of an old time western cattle ranch." The Gary Cooper Guest Ranch did not last out the Depression.

However, two of the cabins from the ranch are once again being used for guests. The cabins are on the ranch of Pat Pauli, who has opened them to tourists.

So close, yet so far

A long-held dream of Dr. George Ruhle (1900–1994), Glacier's chief naturalist through the 1930s, was to set up a museum in the park, one that would, among other things, focus on the ties with the Blackfeet.

Such a museum would be built, but not in the park and not with Ruhle as its boss.

Richard Sanderville (1873–1951), a prominent Blackfeet leader, led a delegation of natives and whites that persuaded Secretary of the Interior Harold Ickes (1874–1952) to fund the building of a museum and to locate it at Browning, Montana, headquarters for the Blackfeet tribe, 13 miles (21 km) east of Glacier.

The Museum of the Plains Indian, costing some $150,000, opened in June 29, 1941, headed by John C. Ewers (1909–1997), a Yale graduate whose master's thesis was published in 1939 as his first book, *Plains Indian Painting: A Description of an Aboriginal American Art.*

Ewers built the collection from nothing. He and his staff gathered specimens and artifacts and built display cases from scratch. Great Northern and its one-time chairman Louis W. Hill both donated many artifacts that had become part of their corporate and personal collections.

"One of the functions of the museum is to provide a marketing center for craft products of the Indians," Ewers noted.

Ewers left Browning in 1944 to join the navy, serving two years. He would continue his research into the Blackfeet and other native tribes for the rest of his life, publishing innumerable articles and becoming the senior ethnologist emeritus of the Smithsonian Institution.

Ruhle's other parks

Fans of Glacier tend to think of Dr. George Ruhle, the park's chief naturalist from 1929 to 1940, as "their" Ruhle, particularly for his *Guide to Glacier*, published in 1949. This book became the bible for generations of hikers and visitors.

But Glacier was just one of many stops on Ruhle's long career with the National Park Service. He served in Yosemite, Yellowstone, Crater Lake, Great Smokey Mountains, Hawaii Volcanoes and Haleakala national parks, writing guide books on Crater Lake and Haleakala, and setting up a museum at Hawaii.

Following Ruhle's work assessing the park systems in Thailand and Indonesia in the 1950s, he persuaded the National Park Service to found the Division of International Co-operation, which he headed until 1965.

He would travel the world in the next three decades, sharing his knowledge about national parks and their operations.

Ain't no mountain high enough

Visitors to Glacier can thank the U.S. Army's 10th Mountain Division for training at least two people who found careers serving the public in the park.

The 10th Mountain Division was created during the Second World War in response to lessons learned from the annihilation of two Russian tank divisions in Finland by soldiers on skis. United States military commanders decided they needed mountain troops and set up the beginnings of the 10th at Camp Hale, Colorado, recruiting anyone with mountain and skiing experience.

Bob Frauson and Ross Luding (1911–1979) were two who served with the 10th Mountain Division, which saw combat in Italy in 1945.

After the war, Frauson transferred his military mountaineering skills to civilian life by joining the National Park Service and later working as a ranger in Glacier for 20 years.

Luding took over operation of Granite and Sperry Chalets from the Great Northern in the 1950s, continuing, with his wife Kay (1914–2000) and children, the tradition of high mountain hospitality for which the railway had been known. Luding's son, Lanny, along with help from other family members, continues to run Sperry Chalets.

Sweet sound of music

If you visit Glacier, the "Alps of America," it's possible you'll come closer to the *Sound of Music* than if you had traveled to Austria. That's thanks to Kalispell area residents Stefan and Annie von Trapp, whose children are the latest generation of von Trapp family singers. The children have performed frequently in Glacier Park and, on occasion, in Waterton.

Stefan and Annie's kids are the great-grandchildren of Capt. Georg and Maria von Trapp, whose escape from Austria after the 1938 Nazi invasion was dramatized in the 1965 Disney film. Their Opa, or grandfather, is Werner von Trapp of Waitsfield, Vermont, the fourth child of Georg (1880–1947).

Stefan and Annie's children have recorded a CD, which contains a couple of *Sound of Music* songs, but mostly features the sacred music and Austrian folk songs that have been the staple of the von Trapp family singers for decades.

Boxer Tommy Gibbons, left, visited Glacier in 1923 while training in Shelby, Montana. With Gibbons are, left, son Jack, wife Helen holding son Dick, and Tom, Jr. Trainer Eddie Kane and son Billy are on the right.

Vistas with punch

Visiting Glacier is a tradition for the Gibbons family of Minnesota. Starting in the summer of 1923, when boxer Tommy Gibbons (1891–1960) of St. Paul was preparing for a fight against reigning heavyweight champion Jack Dempsey (1895–1983) in a highly publicized match in Shelby, Montana, 72 miles (116 km) east of Glacier, the call of the mountains hit the Gibbons family like a sucker punch.

Tommy Gibbons was invited to preside at the season opening ceremonies for Glacier Park Hotel on June 15, 1923, two weeks before the fight.

The invitation was made by Louis W. Hill, a fellow St. Paul resident whose railway company owned the hotel. It also provided an opportunity for Gibbons to stimulate interest in the upcoming match.

141

The one-day break in training would not be the last visit to the park by Gibbons, his wife and two sons. They would return many times, and after the Gibbons boys went to work in the hotels for the summer, succeeding generations of Gibbons would call Glacier their summer work place, too.

He looked before he chopped

Harvey Reginald MacMillan (1885–1976) played a major role in the formation of Waterton as a national park. His early report on the region is filled with knowledgeable remarks about the natural resources and the importance of protecting them, yet many years later he would become one of the founders of a resource harvester: the lumber giant MacMillan-Blodel.

In 1909, the 24-year-old MacMillan, an assistant inspector of forest reserves, came to Waterton, then known as Kootenay Forest Reserve, to assess the area for the federal government. His subsequent report glowingly documented what he saw in all its pristine glory. He succinctly detailed geologic formations, early human history, wildlife species, value and types of native timber, the importance of forest fire protection and the overall value of the region.

He concluded by saying: "It has been stated that this territory is good for nothing but timber and park purposes, aside from the mineral value. It has been shown that it will make an excellent game reserve. This summer's experience has proven to many that it is a very desirable resort, and there is no doubt that these joined together with its geologic features and its general scientific interest will render it worthy of being made into a National Park or Forest Reserve always available to the people."

MacMillan's information, supported by forest ranger in charge, John George "Kootenai" Brown (1839–1916), and a number of others, was used to designate Waterton as Canada's fourth national park in 1911.

Greasing the wheels of power

Ray Djuff collection

Robert J. Dinning

Construction of the Prince of Wales Hotel in Waterton in 1926–27 put pressure on the Alberta government to allow the sale of alcohol in national parks, despite a swirling controversy over the matter raised by Mormons living in nearby communities. The Great Northern Railway, owner of the hotel, was insistent it would be the first to have a licensed premise in Waterton and, indeed, it was. With Prohibition at an end in Alberta but still in force in the United States, legalized liquor was a draw for American tourists.

Obtaining a liquor license depended on meeting a number of regulations but, most of all, it depended on Robert John

Dinning (1884–1969), first commissioner of the Alberta Liquor Control Board, who ruled with an iron hand from the provincial capital in Edmonton.

The Great Northern Railway made sure Dinning and his family, as well as any in his entourage, were given first-class treatment and special attention whenever they visited Waterton. For his part, Dinning and his family were quite taken with Waterton and, despite the 350 miles (560 km) from Edmonton, spent considerable time in the park over a number of years. It was a symbiotic relationship: Waterton got a much sought after beer parlor and the Dinning family found a great place to relax. Mrs. Dinning, on several occasions, was reported to have rented a cabin in Waterton for a month's stay while her husband dealt with business in Edmonton.

Robert John Dinning's grandson, Jim Dinning, was elected to the Alberta legislature and served as minister of education and provincial treasurer.

And the Academy Award goes to ...

Jerome Hill (1905–1972), one of Louis W. Hill three sons and a frequent visitor to Glacier with his father and, later, on his own, was an artist and filmmaker who won an Academy Award for best Documentary Feature of 1957 for his movie *Albert Schweitzer.*

Jerome Hill's earlier works included scripts for U.S. Army training films during the Second World War. Also during the war, he used his command of the German language to assist the prisoner of war interrogation units.

He later set up the Avon Foundation (now known as the Jerome Foundation) and the Camargo Foundation to support artists, scholars and non-profit arts organizations.

The Hill connection continues

The involvement of the Hill family in Glacier Park did not end with patriarch James J. and his son, Louis W. Hill.

A new generation, in the person of Louis F. Hill, James J. Hill's great-grandson, is carrying on a family tradition of philanthropy when it comes to Glacier.

Louis F. Hill is the chairman of the Glacier Fund.

The Glacier Fund was conceived in 1999 by former park superintendent Dave Mihalic and then Montana governor Marc Racicot, and was set up in conjunction with the National Park Foundation as Glacier's official non-profit partner.

Through private fund-raising efforts headed by Hill and his wife Kathrine, the Glacier Fund provides money to the National Park Service for projects in Glacier that might fall through the cracks because they are not covered by congressional appropriations.

Chris Morrison

Going-to-the-Sun Road, as seen from the Highline Trail, is just a ribbon in the wilderness. From the trail, the sound of vehicles is neither offensive nor apparent, despite the popularity of the road.

7 Oddities

What do you do with hundreds of gallons of human waste at a remote location in a national park? Once upon a time, dumping it over the most convenient cliff was the easy answer. Not so today.

This is just one of many aspects related to Waterton and Glacier that are out of the ordinary, a little strange, unexpected or little known to many visitors to the parks—until now.

Wondering what happened to that overflowing toilet? Read on.

It has to go somewhere

Human waste is a fact of life that takes on expensive considerations when it has to be removed from a national park by helicopter.

In the summer of 2003, Glacier managers proudly announced that only eight helicopter flights would be needed to remove human waste from the public toilets at Granite Park Chalets. Previously they had estimated the removal, which was to include replacing a failing composting toilet from a nearby patrol cabin, would take up to 34 flights.

The composting season at the chalets, shortened by the 6,700 foot (2,010 m) altitude, necessitated the removal of waste from the site. Composting toilets were installed after the chalets were temporarily closed in 1992 by park officials and subsequently turned into a hikers' shelter due, in part, to an inadequate sewage disposal system.

A long-term solution to the composting toilet conundrum has not been worked out.

Blowing away obstacles

The Highline Trail, between Logan Pass, on Going-to-the-Sun Road, and Granite Park Chalets, is one of the most popular and scenic routes in Glacier.

As soon as the road to Logan Pass is open, there are demands from hikers to get access to the trail. The first part of the trail, however, is on a cliff face, protected from the sun and slow to be free of accumulated snow.

To speed up the clearing of trails, park officials may resort to a seemingly unpark-like method: they dynamite the ice off the trail.

The use of explosives to remove obstacles in the park in other tough situations is not unknown. George Ostrom of Kalispell, an avid Glacier hiker, climber and newspaper columnist, reported that the park service once used dynamite to dispose of a dead horse along the Highline Trail.

Blowing away signs

Dynamiting the unwanted isn't limited to Glacier. Waterton had a little dynamite experience of its own in the spring of 2002.

Concrete entry signs which incorporated a stylish logo designed especially for Waterton, and which had welcomed visitors for more than a decade, were suddenly declared to be "non-conforming" with other national parks and historic sites in Canada.

To remove the concrete entry signs, a contractor was hired to blow them to bits, scraping up the remnants with heavy equipment, much to the astonishment of regular Waterton visitors. New green, white and red standard wooden signs were erected at the two park entry points on the highways. The new signs color co-ordinate with new uniforms issued to all park staff, except wardens.

Turning Japanese

The presence of a Japanese couple, wearing authentic costumes and serving tea and cookies in the afternoon at the Glacier Park Hotel and the Many Glacier Hotel was about as odd a sight as one might expect to see in an American mountain resort hotel in 1915.

Japanese paper lanterns hanging in the lobbies were a bit of a tie-in to the couple, but very much out of place amid mounted animal heads, Indian paintings and other western decoration in the hotels.

The Great Northern used the Japanese connection to subtly advertise the fact the company ran two steamships, the *Minnesota* and *Dakota*, to Japan.

Japanese lanterns in Glacier Park Hotel's lobby were not entirely out of character for their time or place.

Fred Kiser postcard, Ray Djuff collection

Whether the company generated much additional business on its ships as a result of these touches is not known.

The Windsor Lounge at the Prince of Wales Hotel, seen here in the 1970s, was carved out of the east lobby. Its location skirted a liquor law that would have otherwise prevented tourists from seeing the mountains.

Sit down and drink up

When changes to the Alberta Liquor Control Act opened the way in 1959 for cocktail lounges, the Prince of Wales Hotel was among the first establishments in the province to apply for a permit.

The Maple Leaf Lounge was created out of a small portion of the north section of the hotel dining room and was governed by strict requirements—rules not exactly conducive to tourism.

The large windows in the lounge that look out on Crandell Mountain had to be kept permanently covered so that drinking patrons could not be seen from the road by passers-by. Patrons could not drink while standing and no stools were allowed at the bar. Singing, dancing and game playing were also forbidden.

Hotel management decided it could bend the rules on entertainment by hiring singing waiters accompanied by a ukulele. The hotel's managers soon learned otherwise and the practice was dropped.

The frustration of having a beautiful mountain view that no lounge patrons could see was overcome, at a cost, in 1960 with the creation of a second lounge, the Windsor Lounge, carved out of the east wing of the hotel lobby. Since no roads pass by the south-facing lounge windows, no curtains were required.

The Maple Leaf Lounge reverted to its original use, as a dining room annex.

Alberta liquor laws have since been revised and the restrictions eased.

History at your feet

When you're visiting Granite Park Chalets, don't spend all your time staring at the incredible scenery. Take a moment to look down at what's beneath your feet.

The stone floors of the chalet feature some of the oldest sedimentary rocks known on earth.

All of the marks impressed at the time of their creation are still visible, including texture, ripple marks, raindrop impressions and mud cracks.

By using local stone, the builders inadvertently created an indoor geology exhibit.

Private enterprise trumps bureaucrats

The first Waterton guide book was not produced by a park naturalist or any other government employee, but by a local newspaperman who saw a need and did something about it.

Donald W. Buchanan (1908–1966), who wrote *A Complete Guide to Waterton Lakes National Park: Its Roads, Trails, Lakes and Mountains*, was the son of Canadian Senator William A. Buchanan, who also owned *The Lethbridge Herald* and had a cabin in Waterton. The first edition of the guide book came out in 1928 and sold for 75 cents. It was regularly advertised in the newspaper.

Over the years, Donald Buchanan personally explored all of Waterton on foot and horseback and wrote many detailed articles on the splendors of the park for his father's newspaper.

Buchanan followed his father into the newspaper business, helping found the weekly *Ottawa Times*.

He played a key role in setting up the National Film Board of Canada and was a founder of the National Film Society (now the Canadian Film Institute).

Looking for dinosaurs

Everyone knows how vast Glacier is: about one million acres (405,000 hectares). But how big is it, really? Seasonal park ranger Doug Follett offers this assessment when asked by visitors: "You could hide a herd of dinosaurs in this place and no one would ever find them."

As proof, he points to the elusive lynx, wolves and mountain lions that inhabit the park, but are seldom seen.

Stamp that name canceled

Glacier's first post office was established in 1905, at the site where Lake McDonald Lodge is now located, and was called Snyder, after hotel owner George Snyder. In 1909, it was renamed Glacier, likely at the request of the hotel's new owners, John and Olive Lewis, who called the building the Glacier Hotel.

The post office name was changed again, to Lake McDonald, in 1913.

Olive Lewis was postmistress from 1909 through to the 1930s, remaining on after she and her husband had sold their hotel to the Great Northern Railway in 1930.

Today, the tiny Lake McDonald post office, a stand-alone facility that was once a gas station building, is the only post office within the park boundaries. It is operated and staffed on a contract basis through the U.S. Postal Service. The post office is open only during the summer months.

The first post office in the Waterton district was in Oil City, a turn of the 20th century boom town that quickly fizzled when repeated drilling failed to produce a commercial volume of petroleum.

Organizing the mail

Waterton has had a number of post offices over the course of 100 years, each in response to changing customer demands.

The first post office was located at Oil City in the Akamina Valley. In June 1905, oil developer John Lineham (1857–1913) was appointed postmaster. When the oil petered out, development plans for the town dried up, too, and the post office was closed in December 1907.

The park area went without postal service for six months, until mid-1908, when Henry Hanson was appointed postmaster at Waterton Mills, located near Maskinonge Lake.

In July 1915, an additional post office was opened about seven miles west in the Hazzard Hotel (now site of the Bayshore Inn) with John Hazzard serving as postmaster. The Waterton Mills' post office closed forever on May 31, 1916.

It was during Hazzard's tenure in 1917 that Ottawa bureaucrats declared "Waterton Park" the official postal name and designated it a year-round operation. Hazzard, known to be somewhat less than thorough, ceased his postal duties on April 30, 1918, but records do not indicate who filled in for him. It was not until mid-November that Carl J. Danielson, a park carpenter, took over. He lasted only three months.

This whirlwind of postmasters ended with the appointment in July 1919 of Arthur H. "Pop" Harwood (1876–1971), who operated out of his home just across the road from Linnet Lake. When Harwood built a new home in the townsite on Fountain Avenue in 1927, the postal operation went with him and he remained postmaster there until January 20, 1950. In the process, he became one of the park's best known and respected citizens.

When Harwood retired and sold his home, the postal operations were moved to a new building across the street, where the post office has been located ever since.

Rockin' and rattlin'

Earthquakes in Waterton are rare, but they do happen and have been noted on at least three occasions.

On June 27, 1925, a very distinct shockwave lasting about 30 seconds was felt in Waterton at 6:20 p.m. Occupants of buildings noted swaying and everyone who felt the effects reported a sensation of fainting and falling. Water standing in pails washed up two or three inches on the side. Those out in rowboats on the lake did not feel it, but some who were driving in cars told of feeling a sort of a dizzy spell. No damage resulted.

On August 17, 1959, earthquakes hit the West, from British Columbia to Wyoming, damaging a southwestern Montana dam and resulting in death and destruction. The rattling was felt in Waterton, as well. At the Prince of Wales Hotel, Indian motif lanterns swayed and creaked and some dishes crashed to the floor. At the then Tourist Café on Waterton Avenue, pots and pans rattled, and in the dormitory portion of Frank's Café, now New Frank's, bunks were shaken, nearly throwing their occupants out of bed.

The most recent earthquake to hit Waterton was on March 5, 2000, at about 8 p.m. Some 90 residents and visitors were in the townsite at the time. Aside from creating a topic of conversation, the quake caused no injuries or damage.

Energy, Mines and Resources Canada now has a remote earthquake monitor on Crandell Mountain not far from the Waterton townsite.

German "cowboys"

It is a curious fact that many of the early artists associated with Glacier were Germanic—John Fery, Winold Reiss, Joseph Scheuerle and Julius Seyler—and all but Fery painted portraits of the Blackfeet.

Reiss and Scheuerle's art of the Blackfeet was widely used by the Great Northern Railway to promote Waterton and Glacier.

The common denominator in this interest in the Rockies of Montana was German writer Karl May's (1842–1912) books about life in the Wild West with cowboys and Indians. May single-handedly started a wave of German immigration to the United States and Canada by young men wanting to both experience the tales of Old Shatterhand and Mescalero that he'd written about, and to meet Native Americans, such as May's fictional Winnetou.

Winold Reiss

May, however, did not write about the American West from first-hand experience. His first visit to the United States was in 1908, four years before his death and almost 40 years after he began writing westerns. He was a teacher by training, but his career was interrupted when he was sent to prison for eight years for impersonating a police officer.

He then took up writing fiction.

First African-American visitors

The first recorded visit by African-Americans to Glacier was by members of Lt. George Ahern's expedition in August 1890. Ahern (1859–1940) led the expedition from Fort Shaw, in Montana Territory, where four companies of the 25th Infantry, a regiment of "colored men" dubbed "buffalo soldiers" by the media, were stationed.

Ahern's orders were to explore and map Glacier territory, which involved trekking near Chief Mountain, then into what is now the park via the Belly River Valley, crossing Ahern Pass with horses (after two days of labor to create a trail in pouring rain).

Except for the valets of wealthy visitors, such as William Whitener, who worked for many years for Louis W. Hill (1872–1948) of the Great Northern Railway, and the railway's porters, African-Americans would not become regular visitors to Glacier until well after the Second World War.

Unspoken color bar

For 40 years, the officials who ran the Great Northern Railway's resort hotels in Glacier worked diligently to ensure no African-Americans were hired as staff.

This was done by requesting information on "nationality, white or colored," on application forms. Until the National Park Service called the hotel company on its practice in 1949, railway officials were able to privately claim only one "colored" student had slipped through the review process, and that was because the hiring was done "through correspondence" rather than a personal interview, as was the norm.

When confronted about its application form asking for race and religion, Great Northern's lawyer responded that the policy "is and always has been ... not to discriminate." Religion was requested so the hotel company could "make employees' living conditions as good as possible. We don't want to put kids in a camp where they are unable to attend church, become dissatisfied and will leave."

The old application forms were destroyed only to be replaced by new forms, which asked for the color of the applicant's eyes, hair and complexion. Forms continued to ask about hair and eye color and complexion into the 1970s, well after the railway had sold the company, although visible minorities had started obtaining positions at the hotels by then.

Second-class on their own land

The Great Northern Railway liked to call the Blackfeet "Glacier's Indians" and used them extensively in its advertising to lure tourists to Glacier, but the relationship was very limited.

Natives could enter the hotels in costume for entertainment purposes, but were not welcome otherwise. Payment was sometimes in food issued from the hotel kitchen.

They were paid to perform, but few found work as staff at the railway resort hotels, even though Glacier Park Lodge is surrounded by their reservation. It was not until the 1980s, when a deal was struck between the Blackfeet and Glacier Park, Inc., that the hiring of natives by the hotel company was encouraged to promote training in tourism-related fields.

The second-class status of natives, as for African-Americans, was as much an institutional problem as a racial one. For years the Blackfeet could not vote in the United States, as they were not considered American citizens. That changed in 1924 with the passing of the General Citizenship Act (Snyder Act).

Scrapping tradition

The Great Northern Railway's publicity department liked to boast that the Blackfeet who entertained at its hotels in Glacier were authentic in manner and dress, with some of the native elders recalling life during the "buffalo days."

That authenticity, however, only went so far.

Great Northern officials issued a memo stating the need for the Blackfeet to don, "Plains style headdress for those wishing for employment ... 1917."

As a result, the Blackfeet modified their headdresses from the traditional stovepipe style, with eagle feathers encircling the head and pointing straight up, to the familiar (read Hollywood) Sioux-

Postcards, Ray Djuff collection

Three Bears, right, wears a traditional stovepipe-style Blackfeet headdress. Later, tribe members such as Bird Rattler adopted the Sioux style headdress, with shoulder-hangs.

style that points up and back, with shoulder-hangs. The Blackfeet headdress has been that style ever since.

Who's in charge?

Members of the Blood Tribe, northeast of Waterton, have over the years put on dancing and drumming presentations at the Prince of Wales Hotel and in the townsite.

During these sessions, tourists usually learn that while European explorers called them Bloods or members of the Blood Tribe (for the red ochre they used on their face for ceremonial purposes), the Native Americans referred to themselves by another name.

Members of this Blackfoot Confederacy call their tribe Kainai or Kainaiwa, meaning "many chiefs." The origin of that name comes from an incident possibly 200 or 300 years ago, when a visitor arrived at a Kainai camp and asked: "Who is the chief here?"

"I am," said the first man he met.

"I am a chief," said a second man. A third added: "I am the chief."

The name, Kainai, stuck.

Blackfoot or Blackfeet?

While the natives whose reservation borders Glacier are called Blackfeet, they are members of the Blackfoot Confederacy. The other tribes in the confederacy, all in Canada, are the Piikani (Peigan), Kainai (Blood) and Siksika (meaning Blackfoot).

153

The names Blackfoot or Blackfeet can be used interchangeably and are recognized as such legally on both sides of the border, although Canadian ethnographers tend to call the tribes in Canada the Blackfoot and the American tribe Blackfeet.

The term Blackfeet was given to the tribe by others, who noticed their blackened moccasins from walking through prairie grassland charred by fire.

The Blackfeet, in their own language, refer to themselves as Soyi-tapi, or Prairie People. Ethnographer and Blackfeet expert Hugh Dempsey says an older term is Nitsi-tapi, or Real People.

Tom Dawson, Mountain Man

Postcard, Ray Djuff collection

Tom Dawson was a "mountain man," as artist Winold Reiss portrayed him, but those aren't his clothes.

Thomas "Tom" Dawson (1859–1953) was a popular guide with visitors to the eastern portions of Glacier prior to it becoming a national park. His clients included Louis W. Hill, Dr. Lyman B. Sperry (1838–1923) and Henry L. Stimson (1867–1950).

Dawson was immortalized as the penultimate old-timer and trapper in a painting by Winold Reiss (1886–1953), as part of a series of portraits of Blackfeet and Glacier pioneers done for the Great Northern Railway to use for its calendars.

The portrait shows Dawson in buckskins, wearing a fur hat with a raccoon tail and holding a Winchester rifle. Mary Murphy of Spokane, Washington, Dawson's granddaughter, said only the gun and mountain setting are reflective of the man. The hat and coat were borrowed and put on him by Reiss, not an unusual custom for the artist, who often dressed his subjects with borrowed items.

Murphy said Dawson never owned such a hat and would never have worn one, adding that raccoons are not common in Glacier. She also pointed out that the coat Dawson is wearing is obviously too short in the sleeves.

Presumptuous assumption nixed

In 1927, when Great Northern officials were deciding what to call their new hotel in Waterton, railway president Ralph Budd (1879–1962) made a bizarre suggestion.

He told railway chairman Louis W. Hill that the company had enough political clout in Canada to persuade the government to change the name Upper Waterton Lake to Boundary Lake, to match Budd's proposed name for the facility, Boundary Hotel.

Hill rejected the suggestions and named the hotel Prince of Wales after the popular Edward, Prince of Wales, who would later, as Edward VIII, abdicate the throne to marry Wallis Simpson (1896–1986).

Hotel renamed three times

What we now call Lake McDonald Lodge, seen here in the 1920s, has had two other names: Lake McDonald Hotel until 1957 and, earlier yet, the Lewis (Glacier) Hotel.

In 1930, Olive and John Lewis, owners of the Glacier Hotel at Lake McDonald, sold out to the Great Northern Railway. Two years later, the railway sold the hotel and land to the National Park Service in exchange for an operating concession for the facilities. During the course of changes, the name became "the thing."

Wanting to make a clean break from the old name, Great Northern had renamed the facility Lake McDonald Hotel. When the National Park Service became the owner, it suggested three new names: the Charles M. Russell Hotel, the George Bird Grinnell Hotel or Heaven's Peak Hotel.

All of the names were rejected for fear that in time they would be abbreviated and the significance to either Russell or Grinnell would be lost.

The name remained Lake McDonald Hotel until 1957, when it was changed to Lake McDonald Lodge.

Before there were infomercials ...

The Great Northern Railway teamed up with NBC in January 1929 to launch radio broadcasts of The Empire Builders, a weekly series about events of the Northwest, including Glacier, and related matters.

The February 18 program was about the Louisiana Purchase and the Lewis and Clark expedition, while February 25 was about the discovery of Marias Pass. An April program had author Mary Roberts Rinehart's character Tish regale the audience with her adventures in Glacier.

The radio program was little more than a promotion for the Great Northern's new train, the Empire Builder, and was meant to encourage travel to Glacier and the Northwest.

A recurring character, the Old Timer, played by Harvey Hays, did most of the promotional plugs through his "reminiscences."

The Empire Builders, which was broadcast Monday nights, lasted until 1931.

Bernadine Flynn and the Old Timer, Harvey Hays, rehearse an episode of the *Empire Builders* radio show, named for the Great Northern train.

Antelope just want to play

Pronghorns, often incorrectly called antelope in Alberta, are a big-game animal whose usual domain is the open prairies that stretch eastward from Waterton for hundreds of miles. Yet in the winter of 2003–04, a herd of between 40 to 60 pronghorns wandered into Waterton, a migration that researchers said was a first for herd activity.

It is not known why the pronghorns moved into the mountains. Some experts speculated it was an early winter weather system that forced them from their usual home range; some amateurs said it was a late fall forest fire east and south of the park that frightened and disoriented them. By summer the animals had moved back to their normal habitat.

Where there's no fire, there are beetles

In the late 1970s, a large number of lodgepole pines in Waterton and Glacier started dying. As they turned red and subsequently lost needles, visitors wondered about the cause.

The mountain pine beetle (*Dendroctonus ponderosae*), which has been present in lodgepole pine forests virtually forever, was making its growing presence apparent in the forest life cycle. This is a natural ecosystem response to the lack of forest fires.

The beetles bore into the tree and deposit eggs that hatch into a worm-like larvae. These larvae girdle the tree and eat through the phloem, eventually killing it. After being infested, the trees take from three to four years to die as the sap flow dwindles.

A natural regeneration of the forest usually comes after a fire, but in areas not burned, the oldest lodgepole pines, for reasons not entirely clear, are the ones most susceptible to the beetles. So if fire or disease doesn't take the pine trees, the beetles will.

Ironically, once the trees die from the pine beetles, they become an even greater fire hazard, especially during seasonal dry periods. A dead, standing tree can literally explode if struck by lightening.

No action has been taken in the parks to slow down the insects' attack since it is considered a normal component in the forest life cycle.

High-flying adventurer

The first trip by hot air balloon over Glacier Park was made in October 1999 by pilot Darren Kling of Whitefish, Montana. The trip took two hours, starting at Kruger Helicopter in West Glacier and ending near St. Mary. Along for the ride was Kling's friend, Rick Bretz, also of Whitefish.

Whitewater adventure

While whitewater rafting trips on rivers just outside Waterton and Glacier are popular tourist activities today, in earlier years they were a dreaded part of exploration of the frontier.

The earliest recording of a whitewater rafting trip in Glacier for pleasure was by author Mary Roberts Rinehart (1876–1958) in her book *Tenting To-Night*. In it, she tells of a 1916 guided horseback trek up the North Fork Valley to Kintla Lake with her husband and three sons, taking with them boats on horse-drawn wagons, following the trail to the abandoned oil well drilling site.

They then floated south on the North Fork of the Flathead River to Columbia Falls, Montana. Rinehart described the North Fork as a "riotous, debauched, and highly erratic stream."

Sixty years later whitewater rafting on local rivers would become a commercial activity. The availability of high quality, affordable rubber rafts opened the door for the founding of Glacier Raft Company in 1976. As the oldest such outfitter in Montana, Glacier Raft Company's expertise was called on for the making of the 1994 movie *The River Wild*, starring Meryl Streep and Kevin Bacon. It was mostly filmed on the Middle Fork of the Flathead River, which runs along Glacier's southern border.

Buttering up a story

An investigation into a hiking accident on the Blakiston Falls nature trail in July 1982 turned up some strange details. According to reports, a three-year-old Calgary boy slipped off the trail, fell under a newly constructed fence and into the swift-moving Blakiston Creek and over the falls.

According to the child's father, someone had been picnicking along the trail and left a pat of butter behind. The child slipped on the butter starting the chain of events.

Max Winkler, then chief park warden, expressed some skepticism over the incident, for which the boy was checked at a hospital and released, but said he would investigate further.

The final report was not made public.

When size really matters

The trend to megastores in marketing at the end of the 20th century, where bigger is better, need not always hold true. Glacier Park, Inc. discovered this at Lake McDonald Lodge when the gift shop was remodeled in the 1990s.

While the size was reduced by 50 per cent, gross revenue increased because the layout was more attractive and efficient.

Stork too quick

Lindsay holds a special honor. The daughter of Glacier naturalist Lynn Murdock is one of the few people in modern times who can claim to have been born in Glacier.

Murdock was being driven across Going-to-the-Sun Road to a Kalispell hospital in June 1992 when the vehicle was forced to pull over at Logan Creek so Murdock could give birth to Lindsay. Mother and daughter were taken the rest of the way to the hospital by air ambulance.

With medical services in easy reach of Glacier, it had been a generation or more since a baby was born in the park to a staff member or in-holder resident.

Waylaying the stork

With the arrival of her child imminent, Waterton resident Carolyn Lunn got in the park ambulance on March 28, 1984, expecting a speedy, safe arrival at the Cardston hospital, 30 miles (48 km) east of the park.

Aboard to provide moral support was husband Simon, assistant chief park interpreter. The pair had every confidence in the ambulance driver, Derek Tilson, a park warden.

As he sped toward the hospital, what Tilson could not anticipate was the sudden appearance of a cow elk on the road at a location known as Knight's Hill.

Tilson hit the animal and rolled the ambulance, effectively totaling it. But he was able to radio for help and the Lunns made it to the hospital just in time for the birth of the baby.

New passport regulations inconvenienced *Motor Vessel International* passengers during the first part of the Second World War. Fuel rationing later shut down the cruises.

Guarding the border

The terrorist attacks of September 11, 2001, created fallout that even extended to Waterton–Glacier, the birthplace of international peace parks.

Due to border security concerns, for the next two summers the U.S. government imposed various restrictions on excursion boats which normally landed at Goat Haunt on the Montana end of Upper Waterton Lake, at first prohibiting the unloading of passengers who were not U.S. citizens. Amid protests from the boat concessioner, the rules were modified to allow all passengers to disembark, but limited their strolls to no farther than the ranger station, about a quarter mile from the dock.

Those who hiked the lakeshore trail from Waterton to Goat Haunt were required to carry proof of citizenship and report directly to the rangers, who were also assigned immigration detail.

Until then, the procedure for passengers visiting Goat Haunt was very informal. But it was not the first time regulations had been imposed at the U.S. head of the lake. In the summer of 1942 and for the duration of the Second World War, no excursion boats were allowed to land at Goat Haunt due to wartime regulations imposed by the U. S. government.

An international body of water

Upper Waterton Lake, which is intersected by the Canada–U.S. border, is, technically, subject to two sets of rules: one to the Canadian portion, the other to the U.S. portion. But where possible, park managers have tried to make the rules as uniform as they can, though it is not always an easy task.

Until the spring of 1994, personal watercraft, or jet skis, were allowed only on the northern end of the lake, until the Canadian government banned them.

Fishing on the lake, however, continues to be problematic. While the fishing season and catch limits on that lake are compatible on both sides of the border, people fishing on the Glacier side do not need a license, while those fishing on the Waterton side do. Since the only practical boat access is from Waterton, proving where the fish were caught is impossible. Wardens enforcing fishing regulations must take fishermen at their word, unless they can prove otherwise.

But when a forest fire strikes along the Upper Waterton Lake Valley, the border makes no difference. Whatever is required is called into action: crews, aircraft or boats. A reciprocal fire fighting agreement allows park managers to act as if the entire valley is one big park, without regard to the 20-foot (6 m) swath that marks the border.

The millennium panic

In anticipation of the new millennium, late in 1999 various experts insisted that problems in computer-operated systems, called the Y2K bug, might occur on December 31, 1999, or January 1, 2000.

Chris Morrison

Like sentinels, these propane tanks, remnants of the Y2K panic, are stored out of public view in Waterton awaiting disposal.

The managers in Waterton leapt into action to make preparations for the threat of malfunctions or total failures, at the same time upgrading long-term emergency and backup systems.

Fearing that the most critical failures might be to natural gas or electrical power in the townsite, Parks Canada's offices and staff housing were equipped with backup heating systems and fuel sources. The water and sewer systems were fitted with generators in the event of an extended electrical failure. Leaseholders, both commercial and residential, were advised to prepare their properties as well.

In the end, nothing untoward came of the Y2K bug. The propane tanks installed at each park staff member's house were removed to be stored out of public view in a government enclosure.

A two-for-one deal

In November 1992, Historic Sites and Monuments of Canada added Waterton's Prince of Wales Hotel to its list, but it would be another two-and-a-half years before the public would be invited to a ceremony to mark the event.

The hotel's one-of-a-kind architecture in its unique location, high on a windy hill, was commemorated with the unveiling of a plaque on July 23, 1995, before a crowd of more than 150 people.

The ceremony had been delayed to coincide with the park's 100th anniversary.

Watching the listener

In the summer of 1935, a portable radio station set up in the Waterton Park Transport garage in Waterton drew a crowd.

Visitors watched radio operator Jack Frost, seated at a table, earphones in place, a loudspeaker to his left, a map of Waterton and a pad of paper in front of him, writing down messages.

From early morning to late at night, Frost used the shortwave set to keep in touch with similar stations all over the district as details were exchanged between wardens and rangers about forest fires: station KNIQ at the head of the lake; KNIR at Boundary Bay; KNIA at Glacier's headquarters near Belton (now West Glacier); KNIF on the north fork of Kennedy Creek; KNIW on Kennedy Ridge, four miles further down the canyon; KNIJ at St. Mary; and KNIO on the Belly River. The Waterton station was KNIY.

Watching someone listening to a radio had never been so interesting.

No time like the present

Alberta was the most recent province in Canada to mandate daylight saving time, doing so in 1972. For a period after Montana adopted daylight saving time, the Prince of Wales Hotel followed suit, so its clocks were an hour ahead of those of the rest of the businesses in Waterton Park townsite.

For a period after Montana adopted daylight saving time, having the Prince of Wales Hotel on daylight saving time worked well for American visitors on tours organized by Glacier Park Inc., which ran the hotels.

However, it caused no end of grief for staff at the Prince of Wales Hotel who had to placate disgruntled Canadian visitors who missed meals when the hotel dining room closed an hour earlier than the visitors anticipated. In letters to the editor in Canadian newspapers, the hotel was accused of favoring Americans over Canadians.

Jim Morrison, left, and Randy Slen at the international boundary on Upper Waterton Lake in 2004 after the 20-foot (6 m) swath was re-cleared and the monument coated with silver paint.

Chris Morrison

8 What Were They Thinking?

Almost everyone who visits a national park can become a critic. Bad ideas that have been implemented, projects that have failed or been too costly, plans that fell apart in the application, or a slip of the lip to the media are all fodder for those who love to find fault. But the faults are sometimes too difficult or humorous to ignore.

Between the two of us

Every two decades or so, a 20-foot (6 m) swath is renewed along the 49th parallel to mark the international boundary, a practice mandated by treaty. The cutting of that swath between Waterton and Glacier, the world's first international peace park, has raised the ire of many over the years but never more so than when the International Boundary Commission decided to do the job chemically.

In 1968, much to both the surprise and horror of the two park superintendents who had not been consulted, a chemical defoliant, Tordon 101, was sprayed on the boundary line from a helicopter. Unable to prevent the chemical from drifting in this windy area of the continent, crews could do nothing to prevent trees and other plants outside the boundary from being dosed. Algae in streams and lakes, a major food source for aquatic life, was destroyed. Grazing wildlife and small mammals such as squirrels, chipmunks and other small rodents, as well as their predators, were also subjected to the toxic chemical. Long-range side-effects were not known at the time.

Enough pressure was brought to bear on both sides of the border—by parks officials, politicians and the public—that chemicals were not used again. The border between the two parks is cleared by crews who use chainsaws and hand tools.

The first clearing in this century was done in 2004.

Too many bears

After Glacier backcountry ranger Jerry DeSanto was mauled by a bear in June 1983, he told a local newspaper there might be too many bears in the park. This statement bothered some park officials, who felt the opposite was true. The controversy over how many bears are enough raged for decades, heating up with every new human encounter or attack.

Surprisingly, DeSanto's comments resulted in no official reprimand.

If we only had more money

Improvements at Waterton and enough money to carry them out was the cry of the Associated Trade Boards of Southern Alberta in early December 1929.

The group sent the federal government a resolution detailing what it wanted done. Among the more "radical" ideas was the provision for a landing field for "aeroplanes in the park;" additional residential lots; construction of a foot bridge across the narrows below the Prince of Wales Hotel to connect with trails to be built on the east side of the lake; construction of a road connecting the Pass Creek area with the Akamina Parkway over the Lineham lakes summit; extension of Akamina Parkway to the British Columbia border; and establishment of five or six "paddocks for wild animals in the park" where tourists would be guaranteed to see deer, sheep, goats, moose, elk and bison.

With the exception of the bison paddock, none of the suggestions was acted on. One reason the government declined was timing. Just six weeks before the group submitted its resolution, the world stock markets crashed, and while the full effects would not be felt in Alberta for some months, the federal government had more pressing matters to attend to.

Other suggestions would be implemented, but would take years to see the light of day, including year-round electricity and water supply for the townsite, expansion of the golf course from nine to 18 holes, re-grading and widening of the road to Red Rock Canyon and establishment of a campground at Cameron Lake (since removed).

The potential wonders of engineering

When history has a way of repeating itself, often it's not verbatim but, rather, an old idea with a new twist. Such was the proposal for a dam on Upper Waterton Lake.

The first time, it was suggested by irrigation advocates in Canada that a dam be built at the narrows below where the Prince of Wales Hotel now sits. That idea dried up by 1923 because the lake is an international waterway and U.S. officials refused to allow water to be backed into Glacier.

Another dam was suggested in the mid-1950s by U.S. officials, who proposed a 6,100-foot (1,859 m) long, 700-foot (213 m) high structure across the American end of the lake. A 20-plus mile (32 km) tunnel through the mountains would drain off the water for irrigation in Montana.

The proposal was met with disbelief in Waterton. One resident was quoted, tongue in cheek, saying: "Waterton will become even more famous as a tourist resort because people will come from all over to see this eighth wonder of the world."

Another Watertonian thought it would be easier for the U.S. to build a railway to the lake head and carry the water out during the winter when it is frozen.

By year-end, the dam-tunnel idea was dropped as unfeasible.

If you don't build it, they will come

In the late 1940s, the U.S. Army Corps of Engineers proposed the building of a dam in the North Fork Valley, on Glacier's western boundary, flooding some 20,000 acres (8,100 hectares) of parkland. The proposal was made because, it was suggested, hardly anyone used that section of the park.

The Army Corps of Engineers must have been surprised that its so-called Glacier View Dam was almost universally opposed.

To prevent a dam from being built, and enhance the tourism prospects of the area, park superintendent John W. Emmert proposed an automobile road be built into the North Fork, along with campgrounds and picnic sites.

The 10-mile (16 km) "inside" road was built and the dam proposal was dropped.

A four-storey dam at the Narrows, below the Prince of Wales Hotel, was proposed in the 1920s to irrigate drought-stricken farmland to the east.

Eat what swims in it but don't swim there

Waterton's Crandell Lake was purposely poisoned by the Canadian Wildlife Service in the summer of 1950 to rid the lake of an estimated 3,000 suckers which had been destroying the rainbow trout population. The suckers had been introduced to the lake by fishermen as live bait that either got away or were jettisoned at the close of a fishing day.

Following the poisoning, park employees were invited to take all of the trout and suckers that were killed off, with the assurance that the poison would not affect the eating quality of the fish. But swimming in the lake was prohibited for the balance of the summer.

165

The lake was later restocked using trout raised at the Waterton fish hatchery and fishing was not permitted again until the 1952 season.

Use 'em or lose 'em

Sometimes an administrator's enthusiasm for one project gets in the way of everyday management.

When Jim Atkinson, Waterton's superintendent, wrote to Ottawa in 1954 requesting permission to start a small display museum of mounted specimens he had recently received from the National Museum, he told his boss, J.B. Coleman, there would be no additional labor cost for the new facility because "I can utilize local labor for such a project in that quite often, I have men who have very little to do and it is of advantage to have small projects of this nature to deal with."

Coleman told Atkinson in no uncertain terms that if the superintendent had no work for his staff, he should not be paying them for idle time.

The museum idea was immediately quashed.

Their plans were too big

Plans to build two museums featuring the culture of the Blackfeet Indians, with one in Glacier and the other in Browning, just 13 miles (21 km) east of the park, were announced in the late 1930s.

The redundancy of two museums featuring the same theme was justified by several arguments: Preservation and display of existing relics and artifacts because tourists were eagerly buying them for their own collections; the Blackfeet craftsmen would have places to sell contemporary crafts; the disparity between Yellowstone National Park, which had six museums, and Glacier, which had none; and probably most important, the building of two museums could be authorized as a Public Works Administration relief project.

Strangely, the announcement was not made by the Indian agent for the Blackfeet reservation, nor by the park superintendent. Instead, Glacier concessioner Howard Hays (1883–1969), president of Glacier Park Transport Company, broke the news to the Great Falls Rotary Club at its August 1937 meeting. According to the *Great Falls Tribune*, the two museums would "tell the whole known history of the Blackfeet tribe."

It was ironic that the facility in Browning was originally to be a memorial to the late general Hugh L. Scott (1853–1934), a pioneer Indian fighter. Presumably it was to have been his later friendship with the Indians that would have been highlighted and not his war record. When Browning's Museum of the Plains Indians opened on June 29, 1941, the focus was on the natives, not Scott.

Perhaps no other proposal has been more discussed and subsequently shelved over the last six decades than a museum for Glacier.

Would that be a federal "yin yang"?

There's nothing like being quoted by a newspaper reporter who is intent on reporting words exactly as spoken in the heat of the moment. Once in print, sometimes frankness doesn't come off as politically correct. Long-time business woman Wendy West, known for her outspoken opinions of Waterton officials, told Garry Allison of *The Lethbridge Herald* that the 1986 increase in the park entrance fee from $10 to $20 was hurting business.

"What they should do with that park gate is shove it up the minister's yin yang," West said, referring to the federal minister responsible for national parks.

Park officials declined to comment.

Grazed but not wounded

In a tussle between patriotism and common sense during the First World War, land was opened in the U.S. national parks to allow grazing by sheep and cattle to supposedly aid the war effort by feeding "our boys" overseas.

Horace Albright (1890–1987), at the time temporarily in charge of the National Park Service, opposed it and threatened to resign if grazing was implemented. He was ordered not to quit and told to keep quiet and get on with the job, making whatever compromises

Chris Morrison

Some cattle call the area adjacent to Waterton home, but at one time cattle and horses were allowed to graze, by permit, within the park.

Courtesy, National Parks Service

Horace Albright

were necessary to ensure there would be little or no public backlash.

Albright's conundrum in Glacier was Montana Senator Thomas Walsh (1859–1933). Albright said Walsh had a connection to "a rather sleazy outfit" called the Penwell Sheep Company that was after the grazing lease. Albright feared Penwell wouldn't follow the tough guidelines controlling grazing in the park and would damage its meadows.

By coincidence, Albright ran across rancher and meatpacker Walter Hansen while in Glacier. Hansen offered Albright a sympathetic out.

"Hansen suggested that I grant him a permit for a small herd to graze on some isolated chunk of land of my choice, and thus all other applications for grazing could be denied," Albright wrote later in an autobiography.

The lease was arranged and at the end of the war, Hansen removed the few cattle, "leaving Glacier unharmed."

Four-footed safety hazards

In retrospect it seems a little strange for a national park, but until 1948 Waterton granted grazing permits to area ranchers during the summer months, the only national park in Canada to do so.

Free-roaming horses and cows continually created safety hazards for motorists, especially at night. As visitor numbers increased following the Second World War and several animals were struck and killed on the road, the hue and cry to discontinue the practice grew.

A newspaper noted delays caused by the free-roaming domestic animals, such as an incident in 1947 when an incoming Greyhound bus filled with visitors was forced to stop seven times between the park gate and the village.

What eventually brought the matter to a head, however, was not only safety, but hungry elk. In the fall and winter, herds numbering as many as 600 animals began invading neighboring ranches in search of food because the domestic animals had consumed much of the park grass in the summer.

Is the grass greener in the park?

A drought in southern Alberta in the summer of 1977 prompted the federal government to consider once again opening some parts of Waterton to grazing cattle.

Parks Canada, the Canadian Wildlife Service and Agriculture Canada all rushed into action, preparing a grazing land inventory, determining how much grass the wildlife needed, calculating the maximum number of cattle to be allowed on how much land and for what time period, and specifying health regulations. Meanwhile, stockmen awaiting permission to move their animals onto park land had to assess whether starvation or predation by the park's bears, wolves and coyotes was the lesser of two evils.

The idea to use the park for grazing in 1977 was short-sighted. By the time each government department got organized, the summer grazing season was nearly over. The number of cattle (no sheep were allowed) was limited to 400 head, all of which had to be vaccinated for tuberculosis, brucellosis, red water, black leg and anthrax, as well as being branded. Also required were round-the-clock range riders.

With just four weeks left in the allotted park grazing scheme, federal officials abandoned the plan, noting that the strict regulations would create more problems than the grazing was worth.

Providing winter feed to Glacier's deer in 1930, as shown in this publicity photo, led to overpopulation and overgrazing.

Policy hit the target, but missed the mark

In the early years of the 20th century, predators such as wolves and cougars were wiped out, shot on sight by Glacier's rangers, with an aim to protect the more tourist-friendly species, such as elk and deer. Had anyone stopped to work through the consequences, officials in the parks might have reconsidered the policy long before they did.

The deer and elk flourished, and it wasn't until 1945 that Glacier stopped its deer feeding and predator extermination programs.

Park officials waited, hoping for a return of predators to resolve the deer and elk overpopulation problem. When it didn't happen quickly, Blackfeet natives were encouraged to hunt near the park to get ungulates that wandered from the protected area. And in 1955 and 1956, rangers had to kill many elk and deer or drive them onto the Blackfeet reservation to try to reduce the park populations. It took much longer than anyone anticipated for predators to again prowl the park valleys, with wolves not returning until the 1980s.

Today, there's more predator-prey balance, with cougars and wolves again roaming Glacier. This means hikers and backpackers must be more vigilant on their outings.

Truth in advertising

When 300 tourism industry representatives gathered in Calgary in February 1972, the message they heard from one speaker at their convention was not the most optimistic.

Ron Malis, regional director of Canada's national and historic parks branch, said the time would come when the number of day visitors to national parks would have to be limited and the only way to relieve crowding in Waterton was to enlarge the park.

Perhaps forgetting just who he was addressing, he told resort operators to stop promoting parks "in scenes of glowing color and instead inform visitors of the lineups, delays and shortages of accommodations they will face during peak periods."

Malis was a trifle pessimistic: no limits were placed on the number of day visitors, nor was the park enlarged.

Playing loose with the facts

In its efforts to promote Glacier, the Great Northern's publicity department commissioned postcards and a seemingly endless number of advertisements touting the beauty and marvels of the park. Unfortunately, sometimes reality was missed in the effort.

In one of a series of animal cartoon postcards issued about the time of the First World War, the artist drew a pair of raccoons inviting people to visit the scenic wonders of Glacier.

A Great Northern promotional stamp.

Too bad railway officials hadn't checked with park rangers before approving this postcard, as they would have learned raccoons don't frequent Glacier.

Likewise, in the 1910s, Great Northern published a series of stamps featuring the animals of Glacier, including a bison, a wolf and a cougar.

The idea was to lure potential tourists to the park to see the animals, except bison had been killed off in the park by the 1880s and there was no captive herd, and wolves and cougars were being hunted as undesirable predator species.

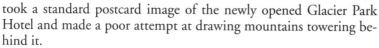

Luxurious New Glacier Park Hotel, Eastern Gateway to Glacier National Park, Montana. Accommodations for 200 guests. Built of massive logs, 4 feet in diameter, 50 feet long. Huge fireplaces, open camp-fire in lobby, swimming pool in basement. Season June 15 to October 15. Rates per day $3.00 to $5.00 American plan. See America First. Great Northern Railway.

Postcards, Ray Djuff collection

An unidentified artist took the 1913 post-card view of Glacier Park Hotel, above, and, probably for dramatic effect, added very non-Glacier type mountains to the background where there are none.

New $350,000 Glacier Park Hotel erected by Great Northern Railway. Glacier National Park, Montana.

Playing loose with the facts 2

When the railway deemed it necessary, the mountains were at Great Northern's beck and call. About 1913, someone took a standard postcard image of the newly opened Glacier Park Hotel and made a poor attempt at drawing mountains towering behind it.

It's bad enough the artwork was amateurish, which harmed the quality of the image, but the mountains shown on the postcard were located to the east of the hotel, where in reality the mountains are to the west and the land to the east is rolling prairie.

Another scene, advertising the Belton Chalets, took interesting liberties as well: the artist moved existing mountains closer to the chalet, but erased railway tracks in front of the buildings. The artist then put a rider on a horse where the tracks should have been, and had horse rentals at a chalet site where there were none.

Playing loose with the facts 3

Great Northern's publicity department sent photos of Waterton and Glacier to newspapers and magazines across the United States (but seldom if ever to Canadian periodicals), hoping they'd be run and thus promote tourism.

While the images were always striking, if not exotic on their own, sometimes captions were included that, in hindsight, read like

171

a copywriter's imagination gone wild. A Roland Reed (1864–1934) photo from about 1911 of two Blackfeet standing on the shore of St. Mary Lake carried this fanciful claim:

"Released for immediate publication. Earliest stage in evolution of eugenics evidently dates back to American Indian: Down to the water's edge the Blackfeet newlyweds go to pray to the Great Spirit for their papooses that are to come. The bride with an empty papoose cradle slung over her back stands in solemn supplication behind her kneeling brave who is visualizing what he wants his offspring to be like—generally 'strong, brave and true.' "

Walt Dyke postcard, Ray Djuff collection

That splash the fisherman is reaching to net is not a prize catch, but a rock thrown by John Mauff, just out of camera range.

Playing loose with the facts 4

Fishing has long been promoted as a reason to visit the national parks and is frequently featured on postcards of Waterton and Glacier.

Photographer Walt Dyke overcame that challenge in a series of shots commissioned by Great Northern in the 1950s.

When no fish were biting after a series of casts at Two Medicine Lake, Dyke enlisted the help of bystander John Mauff (1912–2004), a tourist from Chicago who had been watching the photo shoot.

On Dyke's command, Mauff threw a large rock from shore to splash in front of the angler just as the fisherman was apparently reaching to net his "catch."

First it did, then it didn't

One of the more bizarre ideas tested in Glacier to reduce the threat of avalanches for crews clearing Going-to-the-Sun Road occurred in the 1960s.

In March 1960, two U.S. Air Force jets from Geiger Field, Spokane, Washington, used sonic booms in the park to bring down avalanches before plows started working under steep slopes on the Going-to-the-Sun Road.

A newspaper account of the trial said, "it was a warm day and good results were reported."

However, two years later when two Delta Darts from Geiger "sonic boomed' the Garden Wall section of road, the test failed.

Treading lightly on the landscape

For a time in the early 1970s, there was a boardwalk constructed at Logan Pass much of the way to an overlook for Hidden Lake. Its purpose was to keep tourists off the alpine meadow, and thus preserve the delicate plants growing there.

The 3,720-foot (1,134 m) long boardwalk turned into a fiasco when it was alleged the lumber was treated with toxic creosote, negating any environmental benefit of having it.

It has since been replaced by a hard-packed pathway.

In another experiment to keep tourists off the delicate alpine landscape at Logan Pass, the park service has installed a metal grate walkway for pedestrians and the handicapped to a lookout with a view of the Garden Wall.

Reputation for purity flushed

Washroom facilities have been a continued source of grief for Glacier officials.

The National Park Service was embarrassed in 1969 when it was revealed that sewage from the Logan Pass visitor center escaped treatment and flowed directly into Reynolds Creek and then into the scenic and much photographed St. Mary Lake.

The Logan Pass visitor center had opened a few years before, built as part of the Mission 66 project to mark the 50th anniversary of the creation of the National Park Service in 1916. Mission 66 was supposed to represent a modernizing of the parks, correcting long-standing maintenance issues and completing needed capital projects.

The situation has since been corrected.

Dubious accessibility

The Web site *www.jldr.com* featured an "Outhouse Tour," which singled out the restroom above Granite Park at Swiftcurrent Lookout, at 8,300 feet (2,530 m), as noteworthy.

"This is a picture of an outhouse that will knock your socks off. It has a million dollar view, it's bear proof, lighting [sic] proof, able to withstand gale force winds and to top it off, it is handicap accessible.... To get to the door you have to climb down a rock ledge. Since this hike is 8 miles one way and 3500 feet up, I think wheel chairs are out."

American spoken here, eh!

American visitors sometimes fail to grasp some basic concepts about their neighbor to the north. For example, as a country in its own right, Canada has its own currency. In tourist areas such as national parks, most merchants will accept U.S. currency at the exchange rate, giving any change in Canadian funds.

Looks of total bewilderment are commonplace when customers receive money in coins or bills they have never seen before. When the rate favors the U.S. dollar, the amount of change received can overwhelm the customer.

Likewise, Canada has its own postal service, its own stamps and its own prices for postage. Post office folk in Waterton say Americans frequently expect to purchase U.S. stamps there.

It's the verbal interaction between American visitors and Canadian postal workers in Waterton that is often amusing.

In July 2003, a visitor from Utah came into the post office and announced he had to send a postcard to his brother. "I'm writing to tell him you people speak American up here," the visitor said to the clerk.

Without missing a beat, the clerk replied, "Well sir, we try to be as accommodating as possible."

Finding different ways to say "no"

Tourist attractions—as ideas—come a dime a dozen in Waterton. Bringing the ideas to fruition, however, takes a combination of many approvals by parks officials, both locally and nationally, and investor willingness.

One of the hottest ideas of the 1960s was a gondola lift in the park for winter skiing and summer sightseeing. The first application to build came in the spring of 1961. Ottawa officials reacted by immediately ordering staff to survey the park for suitable locations and made it clear to the applicant that, were one to be found, a public call for tenders would be made.

The survey drew a blank for a dual purpose facility, but suggested the possibility of a summer-only gondola on the north side of Mount Crandell off the Red Rock Parkway. The survey also noted that the idea would probably be economically unfeasible.

By the end of the year, a consortium of Banff businessmen, unaware of the survey results, made a submission for a summer-only sightseeing gondola on the Bear's Hump. Early in 1962, that idea was turned down as being "unwise," but the concept didn't die.

Late in 1963, a Lethbridge man inquired about building a dual purpose lift on Mount Rowe, near Cameron Lake. Although the lift was considered by park personnel as generally economical at this location, they feared increased traffic, the need for parking and ground clearing would be "obtrusive and not at all in keeping with the natural beauty the area now affords."

The final bell was sounded in 1968 when once again the gondola idea surfaced, this time by a well-known Banff businessman who came to the park to discuss two possible sites: one above the visitor information bureau and one on Mount Bertha, adjacent to the west side of the townsite.

In the 1960s, there was a proposal to build a gondola to the top of Mount Crandell, behind the Prince of Wales Hotel. The plan was nixed.

Park superintendent Jim Lunney delivered the decision in a letter: "It has been agreed that we cannot permit infringement upon the two main features of this park, the sudden junction of the prairies and mountains and the view down the mountain-rimmed main lakes. Therefore, no lift of any type will be permitted if it is obtrusively visible from the main valley.... In short the impact upon intrinsic values of this small park will be a determining element in assessing any proposal."

It had taken Parks Canada eight summers to come up with the definitive answer: "No." Further talk of a gondola in Waterton ceased completely.

It pays to co-operate

It never hurts for various bureaucratic agencies to check with each other from time to time and, failing that, for employees to question orders.

In the late summer of 1951, the task of making a new directional sign and placing it at the junction of Highways 6 and 3 at Pincher Station, Alberta, was up to the Alberta Department of Highways. The installed sign read: "Waterton–Glazier."

A newspaper photo drew attention to the spelling error and the sign was removed, improved and replaced.

Not a tree-mendous idea

In the Great Northern's efforts to get the U.S. Department of the Interior to spend more money on Glacier infrastructure, railway chairman Louis W. Hill (1872–1948) tried buttering up Mark

Daniels, the general superintendent of parks. This included shepherding Daniels in Hill's private railway car from the railway's headquarters in St. Paul, Minnesota, to the park, with plenty of food and "wet goods" to smooth the long trip.

During a leisurely horseback ride, Hill commented to Daniels on the fact that Mount Henry was bald, with trees growing only part way up the sides, and wondered why that was so.

Daniels apparently consulted his information notebook on how much money was in that year's congressional appropriation for Glacier. It was $3,000 for everything: administration, protection of the forests and wildlife, construction and manpower.

Daniels, nonetheless, made a grand gesture and said: "Mr. Hill, I have $3,000 with which I will reforest Mount Henry. There will be trees all the way to the top."

Hill was outraged at the idea, canceled the trip and returned to St. Paul, where he ordered his lawyers to file charges against Daniels. Fortunately for Daniels, nothing ever came of it.

Scrambled thinking

For a time in the 1950s after the Luding family took over operation of Granite Park Chalets from Great Northern Railway, they found it was cheaper to use an airplane to fly in supplies than mule trains.

The plane would drop the food load by parachute, aiming for a white circle marked by sheets on the ground laid out by chalet staff.

A photograph of such a drop, taken by none other than Conrad Wirth (1899–1993), the director of the National Park Service, was run in National Geographic in May 1956.

The practice came with risk, however, and once when the chute opened, milk, eggs and other food stuffs were scrambled all over the countryside—an unwanted attraction for bears.

Not in my backyard, please

Development adjacent to the boundaries of Waterton has long been a sore point, one that has pitted park officials against developers. A proposed waterslide on the northeastern edge of the park set off a major dispute in 1985. Claiming the waterslide would have a "negative visual impact on the park" and encourage other entrepreneurs to come forth, park superintendent Bernie Lieff urged municipal officials responsible for permits to turn down the proposal.

Parks Canada's insistence on having a say in developments outside the park and outside its jurisdiction angered many citizens on a point of principle. Although the project was eventually given the nod, as it turned out, it was the climate that settled the matter. A lack of consistently warm days over a long period of the summer made outdoor waterslides in southern Alberta not economically viable.

The old argument flared to life again in 2001, when Jim Garner, a rancher east of the park boundary, sought permission from Cardston County to subdivide his property for a housing development. Park officials, arguing against the subdivision, said the land was a major wildlife corridor and the residential development would be subject to major wildfires.

While Cardston County did approve the subdivision, the asking price for the land and the cost of the requisite utility connections seemed to significantly quell a rush to purchase and build.

We won't tell—wait for the smell

In the fall of 1986, Shell Canada was given permission by British Columbia authorities to drill for potentially lethal sour gas just west of Waterton and north of Glacier, but nobody bothered to inform park officials about the decision.

Concerns that a well blowout could spew poisonous gas into the parks were calmed when Shell's seismic exploration failed to result in a promising drilling location.

Emerald Bay, sheltered from the wind and waves, was the first choice of boaters in the early part of the 20th century, and today remains the most sensible location for a marina in Waterton.

Smack into the wind

Occasionally, ideas are proposed for Waterton's boating facilities by those who are not in touch with actual conditions.

The Great Northern Railway, which commissioned the building of the excursion boat *International* in 1927, began building a dock for it below the Prince of Wales Hotel at the north end of Upper Waterton Lake.

To those at railway headquarters in St. Paul, Minnesota, the dock's proximity to the hotel seemed like a good idea. What officials failed to take into consideration were the prevailing winds and lack of shelter. They quickly changed plans and built the dock across the bay, next to the other boats in the area.

Thirty-five years later, in August 1962, officials in Waterton, wanting to add facilities, suggested a new boat dock and launching ramp. A day-use area for boat owners, a fueling station and possibly a repair center were all to be located on the north shore of Middle Waterton Lake. While a small day-use dock and ramp were built, the balance of the project was never developed. The wind was a major deterrent.

In 1967, park planners suggested the marina be expanded, but this time noted the chief factor for a new location would be the wind. They suggested the expansion take place in Emerald Bay to the northwest of the existing marina. What they failed to consider was the shallowness of the water as the summer progresses. The expansion was abandoned.

Reduce, reuse and recycle

Little did brothers John and Henry Hanson realize a relic of their failed business venture would, several generations later, prove interesting to others.

The Hansons were among the area's first international business men, capitalizing on access to timber on the U.S. side of Upper Waterton Lake (Glacier had not yet been established) and milling it on the Canadian side near what is now Maskinonge Lake (outside what was then Waterton's border).

They hired 45 men at their 1906 operation, which they named Waterton Mills. To transport the timber from source to mill, they had built a model of environmental ingenuity: a 100-foot (32 m), wood-fired steamboat christened the *Gertrude* that had a draft of only eight inches (20 cm), suitable for the shallow sections between the lakes.

After a flood wiped out the mill two years later, forcing its closure, *Gertrude* continued to run on the lake as an excursion craft. In 1916, she was leased to W.O. Lee and Sons, a camp operator, who moored the boat and used it as a tea room and restaurant for two seasons.

In 1918, park officials ordered the deteriorating steamboat removed and consented to her being sunk in Emerald Bay in 40 feet (13 m) of water. But *Gertrude* does not simply lie at the bottom of the bay unseen and forgotten.

Local scuba diving schools now use the old boat as a destination, making *Gertrude* the oldest recycled tourist attraction in the park.

Great Northern Railway promoted fishing in St. Mary Lake, but failed to tell tourists that it operated a commercial fishery on the same lake.

Unfair competition

In the early days of Glacier, brochures and postcards were produced touting the fishing in the park, particularly focusing on St. Mary and McDonald lakes, where exceptionally large trout were caught and photographed.

What few of the anglers lured to the park knew, however, was that until 1939 they were competing with what amounted to a commercial fishery operated on the lakes by the Glacier Park Hotel Company under the terms of its agreement with the Department of the Interior. The hotel company, which had permission from the Department of the Interior, caught the fish with gill nets set up to provide fresh catches daily to diners at its hotel restaurants.

The practice, which should have been anathema in the park, was finally stopped prior to the Second World War on ecological grounds.

Julius Seyler, right, a relative by marriage to Great Northern's Louis W. Hill, displays some of his 1914 paintings, much to the interest of Two Guns White Calf, pointing, and other Blackfeet.

9

Creatively Speaking

The beauty of Waterton–Glacier, with its ever-changing light and dramatic seasonal presentations, its animals, mountains, lakes and streams, has called to artists of all types for generations. Their creative endeavors, in turn, have inspired many people to visit the park and experience the sights, sounds and smells of the mountains for themselves. Here are some who made a contribution to getting these parks widely recognized.

... With photographs

Bringing photos to the masses

Before the View-Master, that popular stereoscopic viewer introduced in the 1950s, there were the stereoscopes of the Gilded Age.

The stereoscope photographer who put images of Glacier into the parlors of wealthy eastern travelers in the 1910s was Norman Forsyth of Butte, Montana.

Forsyth (1869–1949) visited Glacier between 1902 and 1912, amassing a series of stereoscopic pictures that were reproduced as Keystone View images by Underwood & Underwood of New York. The stereoscopic cards of Glacier were sold in sets of 30 and proved to be a useful adjunct to the Great Northern Railway's early advertising efforts, creating additional interest in travel on the company's line to the newly created park.

Forsyth changed his shooting format after the stereoscope fad had passed in the 1920s, and his last collection of 10 images of Glacier was published in 1947, two years before his death.

Word man remembered for photos

Walter McClintock (1870–1949) of Pittsburgh, Pennsylvania, an accomplished lecturer and photographer, first came to northwestern Montana and the Glacier region in the spring of 1896. He was the photographer for a government expedition commissioned to make recommendations for a national policy on forest reserves.

Ray Djuff collection

Walter McClintock

When the party's work was done, McClintock stayed behind with the group's Blackfeet guide, William Jackson (Siksikakoan), camping in the Rocky Mountains before working their way eastward to the Blackfeet reservation. It was a journey that marked the beginning of McClintock's life-long association with the Indians.

In 1910, McClintock published *The Old North Trail: Life, Legends and Religion of the Blackfeet Indians* in which he described his trip and his view of life with the Blackfeet, amply illustrated with his photos.

The enduring quality of the book for the Glacier aficionado, then and now, is McClintock's explanation of the cultural interrelationship between the Blackfeet and the mountains, which they call the "Backbone of the World." His photographs of daily life on the reservation are a remarkable addition to the text.

His photo collection and papers are held by his alma mater, Yale University in New Haven, Connecticut, and by the Southwest Museum in Los Angeles, California.

Dream unfulfilled

Photographer Roland Reed (1864–1934) dreamed of being the next Edward S. Curtis (1868–1952), producing volumes of pictures documenting the Native Americans of the West.

After a stint as the Associated Press photographer in Alaska's gold fields, Reed returned to the Lower 48, set up a studio in Ortonville,

Roland Reed postcard, Ray Djuff collection

A group of Blackfeet, outfitted as they would have been in "buffalo days," pose for photographer Roland Reed circa 1910 for an image he called "Pass Finders."

Minnesota, and began regular trips to the West to photograph Indians.

Reed's photographs of the Blackfeet were elaborately staged to show the natives in authentic costumes and poses, as they would have lived in the days before the arrival of white settlers. The pictures, which were taken both on the reservation and in Glacier, immediately attracted the attention of the Great Northern Railway's publicity department. The railway soon had a deal with Reed to use the photos in its promotional brochures, to reinforce its claim the Blackfeet were "Glacier's Indians."

Author James Willard Schultz invited Reed to join him and elders of the Blackfeet tribe on a tour of the park in 1915. The resulting photos were used in Schultz's book *Blackfeet Tales of Glacier National Park*.

That would be Reed's fate: illustrator of books, such as Schultz's and Agnes Laut's *Enchanted Tails of Glacier Park*, but never producing the Curtis-like tome he'd started out to make.

This Fred Kiser photograph of Two Medicine Chalets, taken about 1912, was made either using a ladder or with the camera on a pole to show the chalet buildings from elevation.

First and good

Fred Kiser (1878–1955) was one of the first commercial photographers to work in Glacier. The Portland, Oregon-based Kiser was said to be one of the best-known landscape photographers in the Pacific–Northwest prior to the First World War.

Named official photographer of the 1905 Lewis and Clark Centennial Exposition, Kiser went on to distinguish himself in 1907 with a major exhibition of 1,000 photographs of Oregon scenery which took eight years to amass.

The display traveled to 20 major cities in the East.

In 1909, Kiser was hired by both the Spokane, Portland & Seattle Railway and its Great Northern Railway parent to illustrate travel brochures, work that lasted six years. During his tenure with the Great Northern, he sold hand-colored photos and postcards of Glacier in its hotel and chalet gift shops, some of the earliest commercial pictures of the park.

In 1915, Kiser sold his business and moved on to other projects until, in 1921, he concentrated his considerable photographic talents on Oregon's Crater Lake National Park. In Oregon, he built a studio and worked for 10 years, until bankruptcy forced him to sell his studio to the National Park Service.

An uncredited photographer

Roy "Ted" Marble (1883–1938) may be Glacier's most under-appreciated landscape photographer.

Marble was hired by the Great Northern starting in 1913 to take publicity shots in Glacier, but his work was seldom if ever credited in the railway's brochures. The most obvious example is Mary Roberts Rinehart's book *Through Glacier Park in 1915*, which is illustrated with Marble photos. Marble failed to make the list of the book's contributors, while the author took great pains to comment on the presence of painter Charlie Russell and others.

Photographer Ted Marble climbed over the retaining wall of Going-to-the-Sun Road and down the mountainside to obtain this shot of Mount Clements, a stunt not recommended for anyone.

(caption side text) Ted Marble postcard, Ray Djuff collection

Marble's work for Great Northern lasted until about the First World War, when he joined the Army Air Services as a photographer.

After the war, Marble found himself replaced on the Great Northern's payroll by another local photographer, Tomer J. Hileman, who had an exclusive contract to provide photographic services at the railway's hotels in Glacier, thus shutting out Marble.

Marble set up his own studio in Whitefish and didn't return to doing scenic studies of Glacier until 1932, when he built a darkroom and studio in Belton (now West Glacier) to capitalize on tourism created by the newly opened Going-to-the-Sun Road. He spent his summers at a cabin/studio near Lake McDonald Lodge.

Marble's return to Glacier would be short-lived; he died in 1938 of a heart attack at age 55.

The two-park photographer

Tomer J. Hileman (1882–1945) was Glacier and Waterton's most prolific and widely recognized photographer.

A graduate of the Effingham School of Photography in Chicago, he came to Montana in 1911 and opened a studio in Kalispell, 30 miles (48 km) west of the Glacier.

He quickly came to the notice of Great Northern officials for his scenic photographs of the park, and after the First World War was hired as a contract employee and paid a stipend of $125 a month to produce publicity shots of Glacier's mountains, lakes, hotels and chalets. Hileman also photographed all the visiting groups and dignitaries, pictures that the Great Northern distributed to newspapers.

He also made a point of keeping up with developments. When the Great Northern opened the Prince of Wales Hotel in Waterton in 1927, Hileman came north to ensure the railway had all the pictures it needed of this new tourist destination. Each time the Glacier Park Transportation Company updated its bus fleet, he'd retake familiar scenes with the new equipment.

As a result, Hileman's photographs were used extensively by the Great Northern's publicity department, appearing in just about every brochure and flyer produced between 1925 and 1960, when the railway sold its resort hotels.

Under his agreement, Hileman kept the copyright on all his work while the Great Northern could purchase copies for 35 cents per print. He sold thousands of prints and print postcards to the public during his career, and almost all his work was credited, ensuring broad recognition.

Ray Djuff collection

For once photographer Tomer Hileman is in front of the camera instead of taking the picture. He earned his nickname "mountain Goat" Hileman for hauling his large-format camera everywhere.

During the Depression, Hileman's wage was cut to $25 a month. However, with the film processing and print studios he operated at Many Glacier Hotel and Glacier Park Hotel, as well as his main studio in the Alton Pearce Building in Kalispell, Montana, Hileman was

Long before one-hour photo labs, Tomer Hileman had outlets in park hotels to process and print visitors' film.

able to make a good living. In 1931, he built a new home on Flathead Lake.

Curiously, in the 1930s when the Great Northern started using color photographs in its brochures, it contracted the work to other photographers.

Within a decade, Hileman had sold his Kalispell and park studios but continued to do work for the railway. In 1943, he suffered a stroke, and in 1945 he died suddenly at his home.

Many of his photos and negatives were acquired by the Glacier Natural History Association and Glacier National Park archive.

Government photography

The photographic history of Waterton, unlike that of Glacier, was primarily the result of work doled out by the Canadian government.

One of the outstanding photographers commissioned by Ottawa was William J. Oliver (1887–1954) of Calgary, who worked for newspapers and was much in demand as an outdoor photographer. In 1910, he took up cinematography and in the 1920s and 1930s produced an impressive series of films for the federal parks branch.

In 1934, he spent two weeks in Waterton shooting both movie film and stills for publicity. His assignment was to show visitors what activities were available, including golf, tennis, swimming, fishing, hiking and horseback riding, as well as motor boating. Oliver shot film in the townsite, from excursion boats on Upper Waterton Lake and from various locations on the Chief Mountain International Highway, then under construction.

Right time to cash in

Alfred E. Cross (1890–1951) couldn't have picked a better time to get into the photography business in southern Alberta. A native of England, he set up his shop, A.E. Cross Studio, in Lethbridge just as tourism development in Waterton was taking off.

Not only did Cross take commercial photographs to promote newly opened businesses in the park, such as the Ballinacor Hotel, he also produced a series of postcards of Waterton. His studio also provided photofinishing services for Lethbridge and area residents who had visited the park and taken their own snaps.

Cross, however, was not able to land the job of photographing the biggest commercial development in the park at the time, the opening of the Prince of Wales Hotel in 1927. That went to Tomer J. Hileman, contract photographer in Glacier for the Great Northern Railway, which had commissioned the building.

G. Adelle Rackette's photograph of smoke from the 1935 forest fire nearing Waterton townsite from the south spoke volumes about the situation in the valley.

G. Adelle Rackette photo, Chris Morrison collection

From snapshots to history

G. Adelle Rackette (1903–1954), was a gifted photographer who opened the Lakes Photo Shop in a building on Waterton Avenue in 1933, which was later replaced by the Ballinacor Hotel (now part of the Bayshore Inn).

She and her husband, James, provided a developing and printing service for tourists, and also sold photos and postcards of Adelle's creation. One of her most widely published photos was that of the smoke-filled main street during the August 1935 Boundary Creek fire that threatened the townsite.

In 1937, Frank Goble (1916–2004), who had recently completed a photography course in Calgary, purchased the shop from the Rackettes and made hand-colored photos his specialty.

Goble's photo business was interrupted after its first season when a fire destroyed his equipment, which was being stored for the winter in the Waterton Dance Pavillion.

By 1940, Goble was back in the photo-finishing business. In 1941, he purchased Nixon's Café, operating the photo shop in connection with the restaurant.

Goble's photos, now in the hands of family members, have become an important record of life in Waterton, and many are on display in Waterton businesses.

Some of Rackette's photos have been donated to the Waterton Natural History Association.

He left his stamp on Glacier

George Grant (1891–1964), the National Park Service's first official photographer, spent three summers in the early 1930s in Glacier building a bank of photos for use in reports, interpretive projects, education and public information.

George Grant photo

George Grant submitted several versions of this scene of Two Medicine Lake and Mount Sinopah, with and without people, for the stamp.

Ray Djuff collection

On occasion, Grant worked in conjunction with the Great Northern Railway's photographer in Glacier, Tomer Hileman, producing near-identical pictures.

To mark the Year of the National Park in 1934, the Post Office Department issued a series of 10 stamps featuring national parks across the United States. They turned to Grant for images. Grant's photos were the basis for five stamps, those of Glacier, Crater Lake, Zion, Grand Canyon and Mesa Verde.

A Grant photo of Two Medicine Lake and Mount Sinopah (8,271 ft, 2,521 m) was selected for the nine-cent Glacier stamp.

It was issued on August 27, 1934, with 66,018 being sold in Glacier and 53,632 in Washington, D.C., on the first day of issue.

Taking in the big picture

For two decades artists had been commissioned to paint murals on the walls of the Department of the Interior building in Washington to illustrate the beauty of the national parks.

Until Secretary of the Interior Harold Ickes (1874–1952) spotted the work of Ansel Adams, photographs had never been considered for use as a mural.

Adams (1902–1984) was commissioned in 1941 to undertake the Department of the Interior's Mural Project, visiting national parks across the U.S. to take images for possible use in the department's Washington headquarters.

He toured Glacier in the early summer of 1942, turning out 11 prints for consideration, particularly scenes of Lake McDonald that would have been well suited for a mural.

Budgetary restraints brought on by the Second World War, however, caused the project to be cancelled.

Newspaperman extraordinaire

No professional has photographed Glacier for longer or as extensively as Mel Ruder (1915–2000). During 32 years as owner/publisher/photographer and reporter for the weekly *Hungry Horse News* in Columbia Falls, Montana, Ruder was constantly in and around Glacier, covering events from the outstanding to mundane.

Ruder at first ran four pictures per issue of the paper, which was started in 1946. By the time he sold the paper in 1978, there were at least 25 pictures per issue, almost all taken himself, and seldom was there an issue without at least one image of Glacier.

His favored camera was a Speed Graphic, which gave him large negatives for blowing up into prints that reproduced well.

Ruder's coverage of Glacier was considered so thorough and well-illustrated that the *Hungry Horse News* soon had subscribers, and Glacier fans, around the world.

It was Ruder's reporting of flooding in Glacier and environs in June 1964 that brought him national attention. Although a weekly newspaper, he published four editions of the *Hungry Horse News* in four days to ensure local residents were up-to-date on the most severe flooding the state had seen in a century. Ruder was awarded a Pulitzer Prize for distinguished general local reporting, the first Pulitzer win for a Montanan.

Ruder sold the *Hungry Horse News* to Bruce Kennedy in 1978. The paper continues to be published today.

Close up and crisp

Danny On's photographs and prints of wildlife were hot commodities in Glacier in the 1960s and 1970s. His close-ups of park animals were so stunning and crisp, they were sought to illustrate a variety of books about Glacier, and were the subject of his own books (*Along the Trail* and *Plants of Waterton–Glacier National Parks and the Northern Rockies*).

A native of Red Bluff, California, On was trained as a forester, earning bachelor's and master's degrees at Chicago State College and the University of Montana. For a while, the Second World War veteran was a silviculturist with the Flathead National Forest. Photography was a hobby that grew into a passion and eventually a profession.

What many people didn't realize was that not all of On's wildlife photos were taken in Glacier or portrayed animals in the wild. As models he sometimes used animals on the Triple D game farm near Kalispell. By carefully selecting his scenes and poses, and being able to work very close to the animals without the need for very long lenses, On was able to produce outstanding, natural-looking images that are no less impressive than if they'd been taken in the wild.

Engineer turned calendar photographer

Larry Burton, who died in Missoula, Montana, in 2004 at the age of 65, had degrees in electrical engineering, physics and pure mathematics, but abandoned his education to pursue his passion for the outdoors and his hobby of photography.

Following the tradition of earlier landscape photographers of the parks, Burton used a 4 x 5-inch view camera to capture some 125,000 images of Montana's landscape. While the camera was bulky and difficult (65 lbs, 29.5 kg) to carry up mountain trails, and required him to use a cloth to cover his head so he could see the viewfinder, the resulting negatives were incredibly detailed.

For 35 years the former Glacier ranger's images were used as art for popular and widely sold calendars produced by his firm, Creative Arts Publishing Co. The company continues to sell note cards with his photos.

... In words

Creating classics

They came, they saw and they wrote—and it all happened in 1915 in Glacier.

Frank B. Linderman's *Indian Why Stories*, released in the fall of 1915, was initially considered a book of children's stories about the Blackfeet, Chippewa and Cree. It was illustrated by cowboy artist Charlie Russell, a summer resident of Glacier and friend of Linderman (1869–1938).

Ray Djuff collection

Writer James Willard Schultz interviews Blood Tribe members Many Mules, center, and Weasel Tail in Waterton in the summer of 1927. Schultz, who had lived among the Blackfeet for 20 years, wrote dozens of books about native legends.

Adults quickly discovered the pleasure of Linderman's well crafted and detailed retelling of Indian legends, and Great Northern Railway officials ensured it was stocked in the gift shops at its hotels in Glacier for both old and young.

James Willard Schultz's *Blackfeet Tales of Glacier National Park* was the outcome of a camping expedition he led for 33 of his Blackfeet tribe members, with the stories a composite of their recollections of the region before it had become a national park. For Schultz (1859–1947), who had moved away from Montana in 1904, it was a nostalgic trip to his old stomping grounds in Glacier with missed friends.

Mary Roberts Rinehart (1876–1958) had just broken into the big time of popular fiction writing when she went on the 1915 tour of Glacier led by Wyoming dude ranch operator Howard Eaton. Her first major literary success was *The Circular Staircase* (1907), and by the time she arrived in the park, she had about a dozen more books and short stories in print.

Rinehart's *Through Glacier Park in 1915*, like Linderman's *Why Stories* and Schultz's *Blackfeet Tales*, impressed Great Northern's publicity department and was added to the suggested reading list for park visitors and would-be tourists.

Rinehart, Schultz and Linderman's books have all recently been reprinted, a testament to their universal appeal despite the lapse of almost a century since they were written.

The Brit and the Yank

While Mary Roberts Rinehart is probably the best-known author to write about the early days of hitting the trails in Glacier (*Through Glacier Park in 1915* and *Tenting To-night*), she's not the only author to have written about those halcyon days.

British writer Stephen Graham (1884–1975) tramped through Glacier in 1921 at the invitation of, and with, American poet and troubadour Vachel Lindsay (1879–1931).

Graham then set pen to paper to compose *Tramping with a Poet in the Rockies* (D. Appleton, 1922).

Lindsay took a year to consult his muse following the Glacier trip before

Ray Djuff collection

Writer Mary Roberts Rinehart returned to Glacier after her initial 1915 visit for a rafting-fishing trip on the North Fork.

writing a book of poetry, *Going-to-the-Sun* (1923), inspired by the peaks in the park. Lindsay referred to his book as "a sequel and reply" to Graham's account. They enjoyed brief celebrity after the release of their works, but the books never caught on with the public like Rinehart's, and have since faded from public memory, except for collectors.

Rinehart's *Through Glacier Park in 1915*, meanwhile, has since been reprinted, starting in 1983, and is again a popular seller in the park.

Penning books about the West

Long-time Waterton cabin owner Harlan Thompson (ca. 1886–1988) found a silver lining in a dark cloud when a farm accident provided an opportunity to start a new career.

While working as a manager of four farms near Spring Coulee, Alberta, 53 miles (85 km) east of the park, Thompson was injured and went to California for treatments. It was there he began writing books for boys under the pen name Stephen Holt.

Drawing on his experiences in southern Alberta, Thompson crafted *Prairie Colt* in 1947, which earned the Boys' Club of America Book Award the following year.

It is a story set in the ranch country of Magrath and Lethbridge that tells of a boy's courage and determination to help his father save his farm implement business.

With considerable literary license, the drama takes the protagonist to Waterton Lake where he gets help from Glacier Park ranger Joe Cosley.

Thompson, who served as president of Pen International, a writers' organization, went on to write a dozen adventure books for juveniles, many set in the Canadian West. Although he made California his permanent home, he regularly visited Waterton, where the original cabin is still in the family.

Thoroughly modern woman

Clare Sheridan (1885–1970), the English sculptor and author, was fascinated with Glacier and the Blackfeet Indians. In 1937, Sheridan, a decidedly independent and adventurous woman, had her car shipped from Southampton, England, to New York so she could learn more about the United States while driving to Glacier to attend Winold Reiss' art school at St. Mary Lake.

The art school, which specialized in the use of Indian models, attracted a variety of attendees, both established and learning, during the 1930s.

Sheridan was, without doubt, one of the school's most unusual students. In addition to sculpting local Indians and making a point of befriending many, she made copious notes about her meetings. She had already published one book, *Naked Truth*, after having lived for 10 years among Arabs in the Sahara desert.

Earlier, she created a sensation by disappearing to Moscow during the Russian Revolution and appearing some months later with the sculpted likenesses of Lenin and Trotsky. Her other models were Mahatma Gandhi, Marconi, Lord Oxford and Asquith, Charlie Chaplin and Sheridan's own cousin, Winston Churchill.

She turned her trip to Glacier, Waterton and southern Alberta into a book entitled *Redskin Interlude* (1938).

Fiction takes strange turns

Usually authors writing about the parks have painted in glowing words great images of natural beauty. Rick Mofina and Nevada Barr are exceptions to that rule.

Author Nevada Barr came to prominence in Glacier when she set her novel, *Blood Lure*, in the park.

There are numerous parallels between Barr and her alter-ego, Anna Pigeon, the sleuth in *Blood Lure*. Anna is a National Park Service employee while Barr worked for the park service from 1989 to 1995. Both have sisters named Molly and both have first-hand knowledge of the theatre. Barr was a struggling New York actress and Anna is an actor's widow. Unlike Anna, who solves a killing in Glacier in *Blood Lure*, Barr never worked in Glacier. Barr did, however, spend part of a season in Glacier to do research for the book, published in 2001.

When author Rick Mofina wrote *Cold Fear*, he initially set the murder-mystery in the Canadian Rockies, not far from his home at the time in Calgary, Alberta. His American editors, however, convinced him to move the action south, to Glacier, to increase the appeal of the book to U.S. readers, an audience 10 times that of Canada.

This entailed Mofina, a newspaper reporter who now lives in Ottawa, having to do additional research about the FBI to ensure the authenticity of his tale.

Historian for hire

Agnes C. Laut (1871–1936) was a frequent contributor to the Great Northern Railway's publicity efforts in the 1920s and 1930s, writing articles and introductions for the railway's illustrated brochures promoting trips to Glacier and Waterton.

The railway chose her because the Ontario-born Laut was, by the 1920s, a well-recognized journalist and author in the United States. Her history books and novels include the *Romance of the Rails, Heralds of Empire: Being the Story of One Ramsay Stanhope, Vikings of the Pacific* and *Fur Trade of America*.

In 1925, Laut was among a group of dignitaries invited to the Upper Missouri Historical Expedition, which traced Great Northern's expansion and influence from its headquarters in St. Paul, Minnesota, across the plains to the Rockies.

Laut produced two books from the trip: *Blazed Trail of the Old Frontier* and *Enchanted Trails of Glacier Park*, both popular sellers and, not coincidentally, promotion to travel on Great Northern.

Popular journalist and historian Agnes Laut composed introductions to Great Northern Railway publicity brochures about the parks and wrote *Enchanted Trails of Glacier Park.*

Ray Djuff collection

Best basic Glacier book

Warren Hanna (1898–1987) was a law student at the University of Minnesota when he came to Glacier in 1918 to work as a transportation agent at Many Glacier Hotel. Three summers of work there helped finance his college education, but the park itself stirred some-

thing deep inside Hanna, something outside his profession as a lawyer.

Hanna would write several books, but his most enduring was published in 1976. *Montana's Many-Splendored Glacierland* was years in the making, having been laid aside for a time and then revitalized as a final manuscript.

The work brought Hanna back to Glacier after a long absence. Despite nearly threes decade since its first printing, it is still considered one of the best all-round works ever published on the park.

Once he'd started, Hanna seemed unable to contain his interest in Glacier and continued writing about the park and its people, such as *Stars Over Montana* and *The Grizzlies of Glacier*.

Warren Hanna

He became particularly fascinated with author James Willard Schultz's life among the Blackfeet in and around Glacier, eventually writing a biography, *The Life and Times of James Willard Schultz*. His research also turned up early lost writings by Schultz that were republished as *Recently Discovered Tales of Life Among the Indians*.

From nightmare to non-fiction

Jack Olsen (1925–2002), a former sheriff's deputy from Colorado turned journalist and author, took the biggest news story to ever come out of Glacier and turned it into a riveting non-fiction book.

The event was the mauling deaths of two women, at separate locations in the park, on the same night, August 13, 1967, by different bears. They were the first fatal grizzly attacks in Glacier history.

For *Night of the Grizzlies*, Olsen stuck to his formula of letting the facts, presented in the same dramatic fashion of fictional crime writers, draw readers into the story. The book, one of Olsen's 31 works, was a bestseller and later very loosely adapted into William Girdler's 1976 horror movie, *Grizzly*, about a giant killer bear.

Olsen's *Night of the Grizzlies* was critical of a history of bear-baiting—luring bears with spotlights and food scraps—a practice that had been tolerated for decades at Granite Park Chalets.

Olsen was also critical of the building of a campground in the area and brought to light poor bear-human management policies of the National Park Service.

Publication of Olsen's book helped reinforce the need for reforms to bear management policies in the national parks.

A few pertinent facts skipped

Margaret Thompson's book *High Trails of Glacier National Park* provides a gushing description of the beauty of Glacier, evidence of her love of the region.

It also contains a strong endorsement to see the countryside from horseback, the traditional manner of touring the park promoted by the Great Northern Railway.

The book, which was serialized in newspapers, was published in 1936, three years after the opening of Going-to-the-Sun Road, which made the interior of the park accessible to auto travel. As a consequence, interest in trail riding plummeted.

Thompson (1892–1969) makes no mention in the book of her longtime association with Glacier, instead writing as though she were simply a park advocate.

She had lived in Glacier for a number of years with her husband, Otto, the chief engineer (head of maintenance) for the Glacier Park Hotel Company, which ran the hotel chain for the Great Northern.

Otto left the company after 15 years and met a tragic end in Seattle in 1929. He was 38 years old.

Wonderful Waterton

Newspaper articles written by local correspondents have made a substantial contribution to Waterton's recorded history, thanks in large measure to the interest in the park by *The Lethbridge Herald* and its publisher.

William A. Buchanan (1876–1954), the newspaper's first owner and publisher, owned a cabin in Waterton and had a long-standing love of the park. Once the townsite began to grow substantially in the 1920s, news coverage of the park was established and has not stopped since.

One of the early Waterton correspondents for *The Lethbridge Herald* was Ernest Haug (1892–1952), whose father, son and grandson all shared the name Ernest. As the owner of several businesses in the park and a man who was at the social center of activities, Haug was a well-placed park advocate and the first to write under the column heading "Wonderful Waterton."

G. Adelle Rackette (1903–1954), stepdaughter of Waterton postmaster Arthur "Pop" Harwood (1876–1971) and wife of park employee James, followed Haug, writing solid news stories and taking photos, as well as submitting humorous fiction for the paper until the death of her husband in 1949. She later published small volumes of poetry.

The most prolific year-round correspondent was Bessie (Vroom) Annand, whose articles appeared for 15 years under the banner "Wonderful Waterton" and covered all aspects of life in the park.

Courtesy, Edith Smithies

Bessie Ellis

Annand quit in 1965 when she resumed her career as a school teacher. In 2003, Annand (now Ellis) published a book about growing up in the area. She is working on a sequel.

There was a 20-year gap in correspondents until professional journalist Chris Morrison began spending summers in Waterton in 1987. Morrison provided articles for the next 15 years, until newsroom budgets were cut and coverage was handed over to the occasional visiting journalist. Morrison is co-author of three books on Waterton–Glacier, including this one.

Poet of the Rockies

Dude wrangler James Whilt (1878–1967) of Kalispell quickly distinguished himself among his fellow saddle horse tour guides through his western poetry and storytelling.

By the mid-1920s, he had been asked by the Great Northern Railway to take his "spiel" on the road, talking about Glacier Park, trail rides and reciting his poetry at Rotary Club meetings. He later was heard regularly on NBC radio.

Ray Djuff collection

James Whilt

The "poet of the Rockies" soon found himself working as many months away from Glacier on speaking tours as in the park guiding tours. He eventually wrote five books of poetry.

Whilt ended his touring after his marriage in 1928 to Edith Smejkal of Chicago, whom he met while working as a guide. She was a dude. He tried settled life in Iowa for a few years, but was back in Glacier by 1932.

By 1938, Whilt had sold more than 50,000 copies of his books, which included *Mountain Memories, Rhymes of the Rockies, Giggles from Glacier Guides* and *Our Animal Friends of the Wild*. This latter book, liberally illustrated by Jack Todd, was considered by the U.S. federal government for inclusion as a school text book because of its extensive descriptions of wild animal behavior.

A major part of his life was spent in the outdoors working as a timber cruiser, packer, guide and trapper. Once an avid hunter, he turned his expertise to conservation and in two years captured alive more than 100 mountain lions in Glacier.

After the Park Saddle Horse Company folded during the Second World War, Whilt worked for 11 years in Glacier as the "camp-tender" at Rising Sun, where he continued to recite his poems and tell stories as an added feature of the naturalist programs. His last summer was 1964.

In his retirement, he worked as a bailiff and dog catcher in Kalispell, Montana.

Ministering to many flocks

Archdeacon Samuel H. Middleton (1882–1964) was quite literally a man with a mission. As an Anglican minister, Middleton was a devoted church leader, the principal of St. Paul's Indian residential school for the Blood Tribe, the longest serving clergyman of Waterton's All Saints Anglican church and well respected inside his flock and out.

Rev. Samuel H. Middleton

Many in southern Alberta came to know him through his writing. Under the simple byline "Canon," a church title by which he was long known, Middleton's articles in *The Lethbridge Herald* included such topics as Waterton, local characters and Indian legends.

A cabin owner for a brief period, Middleton was also a three-time conqueror of Mount Cleveland and a friend to John George "Kootenai" Brown, Waterton's first official. Middleton's more than 50-year association with the park placed him squarely in the know and made him an influence with superintendents and others in the parks.

In 1932, he began 25 years of service with the Rotary Club of Cardston as its International Peace Park chairman. In 1948, he wrote a small book about the joining of the two parks that was sold for many years in the Great Northern hotel gift shops and was given away to visiting dignitaries.

After decades writing about others, the table was eventually turned. Clare Sheridan's *Redskin Interlude* describes some of his work with the Blackfeet, and *Chief Mountain, The Story of Canon Middleton* by Roberta J. Forsberg details his life and career. He is buried in the Waterton cemetery.

Hunter turned conservationist

Andy Russell, one of Alberta's best known authors and conservationists, was once a Waterton businessman whose job was to guide visitors over park trails. In the 1950s, as the park's saddle horse concessioner, Russell worked long and hard to spread the word about the wonders of Waterton.

Andy Russell

When he left the saddle horse business to others and set off on an illustrated lecture tour, he continued guiding people through the park—this time vicariously. The tours took him across the United States and Canada, capitalizing on his photography and experiences as a cowboy, trail guide and game hunter.

His first book, *Grizzly Country*, was published in 1967, followed by a dozen others on subjects such as water and wildlife conservation, the West and memoirs, all of which became bestsellers.

He later branched out into cinematography and broadcasting, becoming an eager advocate for Alberta's wild country. He has produced three feature-length films and written numerous articles for magazines and newspapers.

... and Brush

Bigger was best

John Fery (1859–1934) painted what he saw, transferring his impressions of Glacier mountain panoramas onto vast canvases.

From 1910 to 1913, Austrian-born Fery completed 347 oil paintings of Glacier, ranging in size from 40 inches (1 m) square to 40 by 192 inches (1 m by 4.8 m). Fery's work was for the Great Northern Railway, to be used in its "See America First" advertising campaign, and his paintings were displayed in its train stations across the United States.

One report indicates Fery's output was so prodigious that in 1913 the cost per painting to the railway was $31.70, based on his salary, supplies and accommodations.

Fery's work was not limited to Glacier. In the summer of 1926, he spent part of a week sketching in Waterton, also visiting Goat Haunt.

Courtesy, Karola Miener

Charlie Russell visits the Lewis (Glacier) Hotel in the 1920s.

The following summer, when the Prince of Wales Hotel opened in Waterton, scenes by Fery were prominently displayed all around the walls of the dining room.

During the 1950s and 1960s, many of the Fery paintings were removed from display when the Great Northern's hotels and train stations underwent major renovations.

Few people then thought of Fery as a major artist or even collectible, since his paintings were too big for an ordinary home. Browning, Montana, artist Bob Scriver had always admired them, though, and collected them for his museum, reportedly paying almost nothing. By the time Scriver died in 1999, he had collected some 35 Fery paintings.

Charlie's Glacier retreat

Western artist Charles M. Russell (1864–1926), first became acquainted with Lake McDonald even before Glacier became a national park.

In 1905, he and wife Nancy bought some land from Dimon Apgar and the next year they built what would become Bull Head Lodge.

This Russell summer home was visited by hundreds of friends, family and fellow artists, both well-known and obscure. It was agreeable company that Russell sought, not prestige. The couple also became regular visitors at the Glacier (Lewis) Hotel across the lake, where they would dine and dance, and Nancy would sell his art.

Russell's career is well documented at the C.M. Russell Museum in Great Falls, Montana, and in numerous books and publications about him, thanks in large part to Russell's outgoing personality, numerous handwritten and illustrated letters, his own poetry and books, and his large volume of works, including both paintings and sculptures. A statue of Russell resides in the U.S. Capitol rotunda, the only full-time artist so honored.

That Russell was a generous friend of many is legendary. One such example is the letterhead he created for W.N. Noffsinger's Park Saddle Horse Company showing a mountain trail ride. The letterhead was the only one Russell designed for a park concessioner and for a time included a short poem in appreciation of the horse.

Not only did Charlie Russell design this letterhead, he wrote a poem for it as well: "A MACHINE is made, A horse is born; No four-wheel brakes, No screaming horn ... But hoofs take trails, That wheels don't know, With saddle cinch, And latigo –X6"

Noffsinger (1861–1924) and Russell, both originally from Missouri, often spent time together at the company's Duck Lake Bar X6 Ranch, just a few miles east of Glacier.

Calendar man

German-born artist Winold Reiss (1886–1953) was fascinated with North American Indians, so much so that he emigrated to America and came to the West to study and paint them for the rest of his life.

Reiss' paintings of Blackfeet from a commission in 1927 so impressed Great Northern chairman Louis W. Hill and other railway officials that they decided to use the portraits for a company calendar the following year.

While the calendar also featured the work of other artists, such as Adolph Heinze (1887–1958), it would later be exclusively Reiss' Indian portraits featured on Great Northern calendars until they were discontinued by the railway in 1958.

199

The warm, sunset bronze of the flesh tones, the detail of the colorful costumes, and Reiss' Art Deco-stylized design motifs made the calendars instantly recognizable after only a few years, almost as much a signature of the Great Northern as its corporate goat logo.

The noteworthiness of Reiss' art, combined with his renown as an art instructor in New York, helped him attract enrolment in a summer art school at St. Mary Chalets in Glacier during the 1930s. The school specialized in painting and sculpture of Blackfeet, who modeled for the students and would pow-wow with them after classes.

Reiss' understanding and empathy for the Blackfeet, and personal relationships with many elders, earned him their lasting respect, and he was adopted into the tribe and given the name Beaver Child for his prolific output of portraits.

When he died, Reiss' ashes were scattered by his Indian friends on the Blackfeet reservation east of Glacier.

Sir Alexander Galt Museum and Archives

Donald Frache painted actor Paul Newman as Buffalo Bill in the 1970s. The paintings are said to now be in Newman's personal collection.

Working in Waterton

Donald Frache (1919–1994), whose ties to the park began when his father built a cabin in Waterton in 1928, became one of southern Alberta's most recognized artists. As it would happen, he would choose a Waterton topic to make a specialized debut in murals.

Frache studied at the Chouinard Art School in Los Angeles, California, and worked in New York City and Toronto before returning to his home town of Lethbridge, Alberta.

In 1954, in an effort to demonstrate his ability in large works, he completed a historical mural of the Upper Waterton Valley featuring John George "Kootenai" Brown and wife Olive, which was displayed briefly in the foyer of a Lethbridge movie theatre in connection with the showing of *River of No Return*.

Frache, who also painted many landscapes and illustrated book covers, went on to make a name in mural painting with works displayed at the Calgary International Airport, Aqua Court at Radium Hot Springs, British Columbia, and the Banff Springs Hotel in Banff National Park, among other venues.

His striking southern Alberta landscapes are still much sought after by private collectors, but he also painted many portraits, including one of actor Paul Newman as "Buffalo" Bill Cody in the Mayflower Film presentation *Buffalo Bill and the Indians.*

As for Frache's first mural, it was stored in his studio for 36 years after its theatre showing. In 1990, it was framed and put on permanent display at the Waterton Natural History Association's Heritage Centre.

Hans Reiss, left, taught sculpting at his brother's art school at St. Mary Chalets in the 1930s. His wood sculpture of a native, below, stood in front of Glacier Park Lodge.

Brother helping brother

During the 1930s, Winold Reiss ran a summer art school at the railway's underused St. Mary Chalets with the help of sculptor Carl Link (1887–1968) and Reiss' own brother, Hans Reiss (1885–1968). It was Hans, working as a climbing guide at Many Glacier Hotel, who suggested to Great Northern chairman Louis W. Hill that Winold would be a perfect artist for the railway's publicity needs, launching what would be nearly a 30-year collaboration.

Although overshadowed by his brother's efforts for the Great Northern, Hans Reiss was an artist of note in his own right and used the summer art school to create clay and wood sculptures of Blackfeet. Twelve of his clay models were eventually cast as bronzes and sold from his studio in Lake Tahoe, California, where he spent much of the rest of his life after leaving Glacier.

A legacy of Hans Reiss' work remains in the form of a stylized wooden sculpture of a Blackfeet Indian that was placed at the entrance to Glacier Park Lodge. Hans Reiss carved it at the St. Mary school and it was later moved to the hotel. The original has since been replaced by a copy, which stoically greets visitors to this day.

One of the Group of Seven

Alexander Young Jackson (1882–1974), best known as A.Y. Jackson, was a landscape impressionist who often traveled to Waterton from his home in eastern Canada to create new works.

Jackson was a member of Canada's Group of Seven, impression-ist artists whose ideals were to interpret the spirit of Canada and express it in paint. When the Group of Seven disbanded, Jackson came to Alberta to paint in 1937.

With a brother, Ernest, living in Lethbridge, A.Y. was motivated to linger in Alberta and explore artistic opportunities yet untouched. He was said to have considered the mountains as a background for an endless source of material for an artist. He quickly made friends and frequently stayed with those who had cabins in Waterton, including Mr. and Mrs. C. J. Bundy and Mr. and Mrs. Murton Harland.

Harland was reported as saying that Jackson often "moved his mountains. If Alex didn't like where they were, he's put them some-where else. It was the darnest thing."

Jackson produced many sketches of Waterton, finishing the works in oil when he returned home. He described the scenery as "most exciting."

Right subjects, wrong time

California artist Maynard Dixon (1875–1946) came to Glacier via New York. Following the San Francisco earthquake of 1906, which destroyed the artist's studio, Dixon moved to New York, where he met Montana's renowned artist Charles M. Russell in 1907. Russell, who was promoting his own work in the Big Apple, sparked Dixon's interest in the northern Rockies, and two summers later Dixon made his first trip to the region.

Dixon returned again after a 1912 meeting with Montana writer James Willard Schultz and at the encouragement of Russell, who said: "Now Dixon don't forget if you cut my range don't pass my camp."

Dixon would visit Russell and Glacier again in 1917, this time on a commission from Great Northern chairman Louis W. Hill to create illustrations that might be used in the railway's promotional efforts.

The result of the two-week tour of the park, and meetings with "the best Indians I have seen yet" (Curly Bear, Two Guns White Calf, Lazy Bear and Owen Heavy Breast), was 12 paintings that Dixon submitted to Hill for consideration. The scenes were of Glacier and

Blackfeet, but Hill didn't buy any—a matter of bad timing rather than Dixon's style.

U.S. railways had just been taken over by the government for the war effort and control of passenger traffic and advertising was in federal hands.

He made one big splash

If you have an opportunity to visit Montana's Capitol building in Helena, there's a four-foot by seven-foot (1.3 by 2.3 m) painting of Glacier, "Swift Current Lake," on the north wall of the old law library, now a legislative committee room. It is one of 10 Montana landscapes in the building done by Helena artist Ralph DeCamp (1858–1936).

DeCamp was initially commissioned in 1911 by the State of Montana to paint six scenic panels for the state law library (the other four panels were commissioned in the 1920s). Also creating scenes for the building were his friends Charlie Russell and Edgar Paxson (1852–1919). Russell, who had a summer home in Glacier, was to do images for the House of Representatives room, while Paxson's were for the lobby of the House of Representatives.

Russell was awed by DeCamp's mastery of landscapes, remarking: "That boy can sure paint the wettest water of anybody I know. You can hear his rivers ripple."

DeCamp worked full-time as a draftsman for the U.S. Surveyor General's Office in Helena, until retiring in 1924.

First art teacher

It was a small claim to fame for Waterton, but the results were widely admired when Edith Fanny Kirk (1856–1953) of Lethbridge, Alberta, immortalized park scenes beginning in July 1923.

For several consecutive summers, Kirk spent her vacation in Waterton taking advantage of the backcountry beauty spots to record them in oils, no mean feat for a woman in her sixties.

While in Waterton, Kirk favored the modestly priced Waterton Hotel and Chalets, where she spent several weeks at a time before returning to home where, as Lethbridge's first art teacher, she held classes in schools and taught privately.

Kirk's paintings were first displayed in the 1920s in the window of Lethbridge photographer A.E. Cross. She would later have many exhibitions in the city. While most of her works are now in private hands, in 1948 one of her paintings was presented to the City of Lethbridge by the Mathesis Club when a new city hall was opened.

Cutapuis

In the days when railroad was king, the first stop on any visit from the east to Glacier was usually Midvale (now called East Glacier Park). While Glacier Park Lodge dominated the view from the station and

Photos courtesy Joyce Clarke Turvey

Sculptor John L. Clarke may be best known by the name on his carvings, Catapuis, Blackfeet for Man-Who-Talks-Not. Scarlet fever left the artist, who had a studio in East Glacier Park, deaf and mute.

was the ultimate destination, a little shop on the main street of Midvale, on the other side of the tracks, was a must-see stop for tourists.

John L. Clarke (1881–1970), the son of Midvale founder Horace Clarke and his Blackfeet wife, Margaret First Kill, was a self-taught sculptor whose works, usually wood carvings or bronze sculptures of Glacier animals, were highly sought-after for their life-like qualities.

Clarke was profoundly deaf, the result of contracting scarlet fever when he was two years old, thus earning the Blackfeet name Cutapius, the Man-Who-Talks-Not. His wife Mamie was his interpreter, press secretary and business manager. They met when he was a packer and guide at his uncle Thomas Dawson's 4X Ranch while she was a cook at the rival Bar X6 Ranch.

Clarke's sculptures were exhibited in New York, London, Paris and at the World's Fair in Chicago in 1934, and ended up in the collections of such luminaries as President Warren G. Harding, John D. Rockefeller, Charlie Russell and Louis W. Hill.

Clarke's family claims that John's carvings of mountain goats were the inspiration for the Great Northern's corporate logo, also the unofficial symbol of Glacier.

Clarke's daughter, Joyce Turvey, opened an art gallery and museum in John's name in 1977 in East Glacier—a must-see stop for modern park visitors.

Prolific artist

Dudes who went on saddle horse trail rides in Glacier when Asa Lynn "Ace" Powell (1912–1978) was one of the guides often came home with more than just memories or photos.

Powell, a wrangler for six years in the 1930s for the Park Saddle Horse Company, usually took a pencil and roll of paper with him and he'd make sketches of people, and animals and scenes along the trip. At the end of the ride, Powell gave the sketches to dudes he'd gotten to know.

Asa "Ace" Powell worked as a "dude wrangler" in Glacier before turning to art.

Powell, who had grown up around Apgar and had known artist Charlie Russell, decided to devote himself full-time to art after the Second World War, first enroling at the University of Montana on the GI bill.

He wasn't satisfied with the courses and quit, taking the Famous Artists correspondence course instead.

He set up a studio and gallery in Hungry Horse, Montana, just west of Glacier, and during his lifetime would produce some 15,000 bronzes, wood carvings, oil, water color, pen and ink, and pencil sketches, making him possibly the most prolific artist associated with Glacier.

Powell's second and fourth wife, Nancy McLaughlin (1932–1985), was a successful artist in her own right.

One of their children, David Powell, has continued the family tradition and is also a successful artist with a studio in Simms, Montana.

This Powell pencil sketch was made in 1936 and given to Millie Perkins, who worked at Granite Park Chalets.

205

A woman of many talents

Annora Brown was a painter, writer, illustrator and naturalist of international fame who often hiked or rode the trails of Waterton seeking both information about flowers and inspiration for artworks.

Born and raised in Fort Macleod, Alberta, Brown had difficulty painting fast enough to keep up with the demand for her works, which ranged from landscapes to flowers to Indians in both oil and water colors.

One series of more than 200 paintings of Alberta wildflowers was commissioned by the prestigious Glenbow Foundation of Calgary, Alberta, but the pieces were privately purchased as fast as she could finish them. In the end, she had to paint a total of 500 works to keep up with requests and meet the quota of the commission.

In 1954, Brown's *Old Man's Garden*, a book she wrote and illustrated to tell some of the Indian lore and historic values of wild flowers in the early years of the country, became a first-of-its-kind reference. Brown's paintings and book were displayed and sold at Waterton's Kilmorey Lodge.

Brown's father was a member of the North West Mounted Police and was well acquainted with John George "Kootenai" Brown, forest ranger in charge of the park, but to whom he was not related.

Seen but not recognized

Ray Djuff collection

Joseph Scheuerle's painted portrait of Buffalo Body was used for a Great Northern Railway promotional stamp.

Joseph Scheuerle (1873–1948) might be considered Glacier's most noticed, yet unrecognized artist.

The Austrian-born artist/illustrator, who called Cincinnati home, was fascinated by Plains Indians and in 1907 started spending parts of his summers in Montana painting portraits of local natives.

In Glacier, Scheuerle met and befriended cowboy artist Charlie Russell, who spent his summers at a cabin by Lake McDonald.

The Indian portraits brought Scheuerle to the attention of Great Northern's Louis W. Hill, who purchased a few of the paintings of Blackfeet.

Some of Scheuerle's works were issued as "See America First" promotional stamps, and a portfolio of his native studies was printed for sale by the railway. But Scheuerle was, in the eyes of railway officials, superceded as a painter of the Blackfeet by the more stylish work of Winold Reiss of New York, and Scheuerle's material was no longer used after the mid-1920s.

Instead, Scheuerle found steady work producing illustrative sketches for railway brochures, humorous postcards about

This comical postcard of "camera hunting in Glacier" is the work of Joseph Scheuerle. The photographer looks remarkably like Tomer Hileman.

Glacier, and cartoon-style maps for Great Northern pamphlets. While some of his works were signed, many were simply initialed J.S.

From banking to backcountry

No single artist who created Waterton scenes ever knew as much about the backcountry as Bob Croskery. Tramping into the mountains was a labor of love for Croskery, who was always on the lookout for interesting views.

Croskery was introduced to Waterton by his wife Joan, whose family owned a cabin in the park for decades. A banker by profession, Croskery began painting in the late 1950s, using oils, studying art in both Canada and Europe, and later switching to watercolors, a medium he taught at Lethbridge Community College.

For many consecutive summers, he used Waterton as a summer art classroom, leading students on backcountry hikes to find inspiring locations to paint.

Croskery, who for several seasons sold his paintings in Waterton, continues to display his work at venues in southern Alberta.

The June 1964 flood was the worst of the 20th century in Waterton. Cabins were inundated, businesses disrupted and park facilities heavily damaged when the lake rose five feet (1.6 m) in one day and Cameron Creek overflowed its banks.

10 By the Numbers

Tall mountains, deep lakes, species of flora and fauna, events, natural and man-made features—you name it, the parks are filled with things that can be counted. Here is an assortment of items, arranged by subject, that have one thing in common: numbers.

But who's counting

4,000 Largest number of people ever served a meal (chili) at one time in Glacier, on July 15, 1933, for the opening and dedication ceremony at Logan Pass for Going-to-the-Sun Highway (as it was known then; it's now called Going-to-the-Sun Road). Chef Glen Montgomery created the chili from 500 pounds (226 kg) of beans, 125 pounds (56.7 kg) of hamburger, 100 pounds (45.4 kg) of onions, 36 gallons (136 litres) of tomatoes and 15 pounds (6.8 kg) of chili powder, not to mention salt and pepper. He needed an assistant to stir the nine washtubs that contained the meal and two more to stoke the wood stoves at a local Civilian Conservation Corps kitchen. Workers started hauling the chili to the pass 12 hours before the ceremony. Despite the preparations, there wasn't enough chili to go around. Fortunately, there were hot dogs and coffee to ensure everyone had something to eat and could enjoy a drink.

1,200 Probably the next largest group fed at a single time was on June 29, 1960, for a "chuck wagon barbecue" at Glacier Park Lodge for the 52nd annual Governors' Convention. The meal, consisting of beans, coleslaw, rolls, ice cream and cookies, was put on for the governors, their wives and state staff who attended the convention. Approximately 750 people were expected to attend the barbecue, but food was readied for hundreds of hangers-on and party crashers.

2,000 Number of people who camped in Waterton in the summer of 1910, some of whom stayed for two to three months.

11 Number of months it took the U.S. Congress and Canadian Parliament to pass individual pieces of legislation creating Waterton–Glacier International Peace Park. This world's first peace park was accomplished in large measure at the urging of the Rotary Clubs in Alberta and Montana.

2 Number of monuments in Waterton to honor forest ranger in charge John George "Kootenai" Brown (1839–1916). The first monument is Brown's tombstone, which marks his grave below the entrance road on the shore of Lower Waterton Lake.

Chris Morrison

John George "Kootenai" Brown's gravestone in Waterton. His two wives are buried on either side, but neither is named nor has a headstone.

Twenty years after his death, a group of Brown's friends, including Canon S.H. Middleton (1884–1964), Senator William A. Buchanan (1876–1954), Russell H. Bennett, Ernie Haug (1892–1952) and Arthur "Pop" Harwood (1876–1971), orchestrated the erection of a 10-foot (3 m) stone cairn with bronze plaque in the town. The monument was placed on a lot, set aside by the government, on the lakeshore side of Waterton Avenue, across from the RCMP barracks. The site and monument were dedicated as Kootenai Brown Memorial Park on July 5, 1936. Forty-nine years later, the 23-ton monument was moved to the Waterton marina to make way for a parking lot.

3 Number of swimming pools built in Waterton. The first, opened in 1924, was known as the Crystal Pool and was located immediately west of the Royal Canadian Mounted Police barrack on Cameron Falls Drive. The indoor pool, which was plagued with problems, operated intermittently until 1948.

The second pool was opened June 18, 1960, after years of lobbying by the town's business people. Built to Olympic standards, the new heated outdoor pool could accommodate 685 swimmers and included two diving boards, a children's wading pool, grassy areas for sunbathers, as well as locker and dressing rooms and caretaker's quarters. Built at a cost of more than $400,000, it was located on Cameron Falls Drive between Windflower and Clematis avenues. It was closed in 1993 because of continued financial losses. In 1997–98, the pool and its huge parking lot were re-leased and redeveloped into a new complex that includes the Waterton Lakes Lodge,

Alberta government photograph, Ray Djuff collection

More than 600 people could be accommodated at Waterton's swimming pool, which included a popular kiddies area as well an Olympic-sized main pool. The pool was replaced by a motel.

an international hostel and a health centre with a small indoor salt water pool. The pool is available to the public for a fee.

2 Number of hiking trails in Waterton or Glacier that cross the international boundary: Mother Duck Trail, from Cameron Lake via Boundary Creek to the lakeshore; and the Lakeshore Trail, from Waterton townsite to Goat Haunt and points south.

0 Number of times Charles Waterton (1782–1865) visited the park named for him.

0 Number of times anyone holding the title of Prince of Wales has visited the hotel in Waterton. The Prince of Wales in 1927 was Edward, son of King George V, and although Edward (1894–1972) owned the E.P. Ranch north of the park and

211

was in the area when the hotel opened, he declined to visit. Charles, eldest son of Queen Elizabeth and the present Prince of Wales, has visited Alberta on numerous occasions, but never Waterton.

2 Number of women to have worked as managers of the Prince of Wales Hotel: Lita Hamilton of Calgary, Alberta, during the summer of 1960, and Colleen Perrett of Mountain View, Alberta, who started in 2002 and continues in that position.

1 Number of mountains in Waterton named for a woman. The origin of the name Bertha Peak (8,005 ft, 2,440 m) is unconfirmed. One other mountain with a feminine name, Ruby Ridge (7,993 ft, 2,436 m), is named for its color. In Glacier, numerous natural features are named for women.

Land in reserve

203 Size in square miles (525.8 sq. km) encompassing Waterton Lakes National Park, the smallest national park in the Canadian Rockies.

9,353 Acres added to Glacier in 1953, bringing it to 1,013,594 acres (1,583 square miles or 4,100 sq. km). The enlargement of the park was the culmination of a land trade in which the State of Montana received 200,000 acres (80,935 hectares) of federal grazing land in exchange for the wooded lands lying along the west side of the park. Then Secretary of the Interior Douglas McKay dedicated the addition on July 18. Also participating in the ceremonies were the superintendents of Waterton and Glacier parks and state and provincial politicians.

21,986 Number of acres (8,897 hectares) of Glacier that were privately held in 1910, prior to the creation of the park. The Glacier Natural History Association was created in 1946, in part, to raise funds to assist in the acquisition of privately owned land in the park. Today, 382 acres (155 hectares) of Glacier remain in private hands.

0 Number of acres of Waterton privately held. Within the townsite, cottages owned by individuals are built on leased land which is owned by the government of Canada. All rights to the last privately owned land in the area known as Oil City, along the Akamina Parkway, were extinguished by purchase or expropriation by 1969.

$15   Amount charged by the government of Canada annually for leased waterfront lots in the Waterton townsite in 1911. Rear lots went for $10 a year. By 2000, the fees had increased more than 125 fold.

High and lows

3,150   feet: Lowest elevation (960 m) in Glacier, at the junction of the Middle and North forks of the Flathead River.

4,050   feet: Lowest elevation (1,234 m) in Waterton, on the Waterton River

9,547   feet: Highest spot in Waterton: Mount Blakiston (2,910 m)

10,466   feet: Highest spot in Glacier: Mount Cleveland (3,190 m). There are only six peaks in Glacier that exceed 10,000 feet: Cleveland, Mount Jackson (10,052 ft, 3,064 m), Kintla Peak (10,101 ft, 3,079 m), Mount Merritt (10,004 ft, 3,049 m), Mount Siyeh (10,014 ft, 3,052 m), and Mount Stimson (10,142 ft, 3,091 m).

94   feet: Height (28.6 m) of Lake Sherburne Dam, in the Swiftcurrent Valley near Many Glacier. It is a compacted earth fill structure, with a crest length of 1,086 feet (331 m). The total volume of material in the dam is 228,000 cubic yards (174,000 cu. m). The dam was built over four years, from 1914 to 1918, as part of the St. Mary River irrigation project.

Water, water everywhere

3   Number of lakes which lie in both Waterton and Glacier: Upper Waterton, Cameron and Crypt.

80   Number of lakes and ponds in Waterton. There are also more than 62 miles (100 km) of rivers and streams in the park.

234   Number of lakes in Glacier that are 2.5 acres (1 hectare) or more. Five of the lakes are greater than 1,000 acres (404 hectares). The largest is Lake McDonald, at 6,823 acres (2761 hectares)

487   Greatest depth, in feet (148.4 m), of Upper Waterton Lake, the deepest lake in the Canadian Rockies. This lake is 6.9 miles long (11.1 km), and half a mile (0.8 km) at its widest point.

Tomer Hileman postcard, Ray Djuff collection

Lake McDonald is the deepest and largest body of water in Glacier, which has 234 lakes that are 2.5 acres (1 hectare) or more. Bald eagles are regularly spotted patroling the lake's 10-miles (16 km) length in search of salmon and other fish.

437 Greatest depth in feet (133.1 m) of Lake McDonald, the deepest and largest lake in Glacier. Lake McDonald is 10 miles (16.1 km) long and over one mile (1.6 km) wide.

2 Number of watersheds in Waterton: the Belly and the Waterton. Both rivers are tributaries to the Saskatchewan River system, which empties into Hudson Bay.

2 Types of water habitats in Waterton and Glacier: lentic, or standing water, which includes ponds and lakes and marshes, and lotic, or running water, which is comprised of rivers and streams.

51 Number of people who have drowned in Glacier since 1913 when record keeping began. Five presumed drowned have never been found: Samantha Jones, 18, and Fred Huber Jr., 19, disappeared on Lake McDonald on July 1, 1923; James B. Pinney, 25, and John C. Provine, 33, on Kintla Lake on September 13, 1950; and James Krell, 42, disappeared on Lake McDonald on June 18, 1976. Kenneth W. Gelston, 22, fell from the top of St. Mary Falls into a crevasse on July 25, 1964, and was never seen again.

Roads for the masses

1 Number of roads which allow travelers to drive from the park gate to the Waterton townsite. Waterton is on a dead-end road, a fact that has kept visitation relatively low compared with Glacier, which sees three times as many tourists annually.

50 Minimum number of years an extension of the Akamina Parkway from Waterton to Glacier was discussed by various groups. It was first suggested in 1920 by Waterton superintendent G.A. Bevan, who envisioned a circular route over 250 to 300 miles (400 to 480 km) covering all of the most scenic areas of the two parks.

The route—with suggested variations over the years—never saw the light of day primarily because the British Columbia government refused to allow the road to cut into the southeastern portion of its province.

Had it been built, it would have been a monumentally expensive undertaking that would have irreparably changed a portion of the parks' backcountry.

4 Number of years it took to complete Chief Mountain International Highway. Opened on June 14, 1936, just three years after Going-to-the-Sun Road, the new highway was touted as the inter-park link, providing new vistas for motorists as well as a shorter, more direct route between Glacier and Waterton.

Clearing of the Canadian portion of the right-of- way began in 1932 as a winter project for unemployed men who lived in relief camps, Canada's answer to the Civilian Conservation Corps. Major work on the U.S. portion didn't begin until 1934. Hard surfacing was contracted in 1939. Over the years, this summer-only road has been widened and straightened in several places.

17 Number of years it took to complete Waterton's Akamina Parkway, from the townsite to Cameron Lake. The tough construction conditions, limited working season and lack of funds made progress slow.

Started in 1922, the road was passable in the summer of 1925, but many improvements, including both widening and ongoing repairs due to winter damage, were needed before it was considered a good road.

Progress was aided in 1931 with the arrival of 170 men hired as Depression relief laborers, and by 1939 the roadwork was largely completed.

Going-to-the-Sun Road

$1.5 million The original estimated cost to build the 52-mile (83.6 km) long Going-to-the-Sun Road. The final cost was $2.5 million.

$90 million The estimated cost to reconstruct and restore Going-to-the-Sun Road. While there has been intermittent work in the past decade to stabilize and patch parts of the road, a concerted reconstruction effort began in 2004 and is scheduled to take up to eight years.

$3 Base daily pay of workers who built Going-to-the-Sun Road. Room and board were provided to the workers on location.

3 Number of people killed during construction of Going-to-the-Sun Road. Charles Rudbergin was hanging by a rope on a cliff above the highway when he fell to the roadbed below in 1926. Carl Rosenquist was killed in 1931 by a falling rock. Gust Swanson was swept to his death in 1932 by a rock slide.

490,000 Pounds of explosives used in the construction of Going-to-the-Sun Road.

552,000 Number of cubic yards (422,000 cu. m) of rock removed to create the tunnels for Going-to-the-Sun Road.

The builders of Going-to-the-Sun Road were required to use numerous small blasts to shift rock rather than large ones that would have destroyed more of the landscape. The East Side tunnel was considered one of the most difficult tasks.

64 Inches workers could bore every 24 hours using the equipment available when working on tunnels for Going-to-the-Sun Road. The East Side Tunnel is 408 feet (124.3 m) long. The West Side Tunnel is 192 feet (58.5 m) long.

June 8 Average date on which Going-to-the-Sun Road is opened to traffic. The earliest date the road has been opened is May 23, in 1958 and 1992.

$1 million Revenue lost each day by the tourism industry in the Glacier Park area for each day the opening of Going-to-the-Sun Road is delayed beyond June 15. The latest recorded opening date was July 10, in 1943, due to reduced staffing during the Second World War. Since then, the latest date the road was opened was June 28, in 2002.

1 Number of days, on average, visitors spend in Glacier, usually driving Going-to-the-Sun Road and then departing, having "seen" the park.

Flora and fauna

24 Number of fish species in Waterton. Seventeen species are native and seven were introduced. Beginning in 1920, fish from Glacier's hatchery were brought to stock some of the lakes in the park. A hatchery was built in Waterton in 1928 to rear fish and to stock all of the park's lakes. In 1960, the hatchery was closed and stocking was discontinued.

22 Number of fish species in Glacier Park, including cutthroat trout, burbot (ling), northern pike, whitefish, kokanee salmon, brook trout, grayling, rainbow trout, lake trout (mackinaw), and bull trout (Dolly Varden).

52 Approximate weight in pounds (23.6 kg) of the largest lake trout ever caught in Waterton. Elenora Hunter caught the fish on July 8, 1920, using a bamboo pole near the Narrows. Mrs. Hunter and her husband Cal were longtime park residents and business operators.

18 million Number of fry released into the 500 lakes and streams of Glacier between 1912 and 1928. The greatest number of fish fry released in any one year during that period was 3.2 million in 1926. Officials claimed the park had the greatest density of fish of any similar-sized region in the world. The introduction of non-native species, such as lake trout, has meant the demise of the native bull trout, which is now listed as "threatened." It has also caused the inter-breeding of native west slope cutthroat with non-native Yellowstone cutthroat and rainbow trout.

Chris Morrison

Chris Morrison collection

Where fish live affects their size. Jeff Watson shows the size of a rainbow trout caught in high-altitude Twin Lakes. Dorothy Morrison caught her award-winning rainbow in 1941 in Upper Waterton Lake, where fish grow faster.

50,000 Number of cut throat trout shipped from the U.S. park service for planting in Cameron Lake in 1920. This first attempt was so feeble that the fish arrived in somewhat lifeless condition so they were deposited in Upper Waterton Lake rather than risk the arduous trip to Cameron. The next year, 20,000 fry were released in Crandell Lake because the road to Cameron was impassable and 10,000 were released in Cameron Creek. Another 60,000 young fish were slipped into the headwaters of Upper Waterton Lake and the program was deemed a success with only 25 per cent of the fish dying in transit.

61 Number of mammals species in Waterton. The largest, by weight, is the bison, which historically inhabited the eastern slopes of the mountains. The small demonstration herd is the only fenced wildlife in the park. Voles, mice-like animals, are among the lightest, weighing in at about 35 grams (one-and-a-half ounces).

57   Variety of mammals in Glacier. The park is home to a bio-
logically diverse collection of wildlife. Almost all of the larger
mammal species common to temperate North America, except
for the raccoon and opossum, can be found here. Raccoons
are found outside the park and haven't been noted with any
regularity in Glacier.

332   Estimated number of grizzly bears in Glacier, based on DNA
from hair samples gathered in the park. Due to statistical variation, however, the number of bears could range anywhere from
241 to 549. The previous estimate, conducted in the 1970s
and based only on sightings, placed Glacier's population of
grizzlies at 200. U.S. Geological Survey scientist Katherine
Kendall has been a leader in bear DNA studies and began a
new $2.1-million bear hair sampling program in 2004 across
eight million acres (3.2 million hectares) of Montana, including Glacier.

3   Number of cougars shot on February 10, 1994, after it was
discovered they'd taken up residence in a crawl space under a
vacant home in Glacier. The cats were a 135-pound (61.2 kg)
female and two 100-plus pound (45.4 kg) young. The den was
near two occupied houses and within 25 yards (22.8 m) of a
hill local children used for sledding, although local residents
said they never saw the cats until they had been shot.

20   Average number of years in the life span of a grizzly bear. At
age five or six, female grizzlies usually give birth for the first
time to two cubs and then again approximately every three
years. About 50 percent of the cubs will die a natural death
before they reach maturity.

16   Number of species of reptiles and amphibians in Glacier. They
include the Columbia spotted frog, long-toed salamander, western toad, tailed frog and pacific chorus frog. The stocking of fish
in previously fish-less lakes in the park has been blamed for the
loss and decline of several amphibians in parts of Glacier.

8   Number of reptiles and amphibians in Waterton: northwestern
toad, northern chorus frog, leopard frog, spotted frog, long-
toed salamander, tiger salamander, wandering garter snake and
prairie garter snake. There are no lizards, turtles or venomous
snakes in the park.

2   Number of times an amphibian migration has been recorded
in Glacier in the past decade: Once in the early 1990s in the

Nyack Flats area and again in 2002, when part of the Inside North Fork Road was closed to protect migrating toads.

241 Number of bird species found in Waterton.

272 Number of bird species found in Glacier.

0 Number of times wolves have been artificially relocated in Waterton. Wolves have, however, re-colonized on their own. In 1993, a pair of denning wolves near the Belly River raised seven pups. Prior to this, wolves had not been seen in the park since the 1950s.

639 The greatest number of eagles spotted in a single day in Glacier, recorded in November 5, 1981. Eagles are drawn to the park by kokanee salmon, which make their annual upstream journey on McDonald Creek to spawn and die. The kokanee run has since dwindled and only a few dozen eagles are seen annually.

6 Number of kokanee an eagle needs to eat each day just to maintain its weight, which averages about 10 pounds (4.5 kg).

54 Number of days of work lost on the rehabilitation project at Lake McDonald Lodge to minimize disruption to migrating bald eagles in the fall and early winter of 1988. During an additional 56 days, work was only allowed after dark on the advice of National Park Service naturalists.

24 Number of butterfly species observed in Glacier during a three-summer study, between 1987 and 1989. Types seen included *Colias nastes*, an arctic species, and *Euphydryas gilletti*, which thrives in wet meadows, where it deposits its eggs on a specific host plant, the *Lonicera involucrata* or twin-berry honeysuckle.

6 Number of weeks entomologists Helen and Edith Mauk of Lawrence, Massachusetts, spent in Glacier during the summer of 1924 chasing beetles. The pair said there were probably more than 18,000 known varieties of beetles in Glacier, more than in any other area of the world. Their collection was later to be exhibited at a national gathering of the American Entomological Society in Washington.

371 Number of species of spiders John Hancock, a researcher hired by Parks Canada, has identified in Waterton, as of August

2004. That number, compiled over a five-year period by Hancock, of Pincher Creek, Alberta, includes 52 species never previously noted in Alberta and two that are new to Canada.

1,200 Variety of plants in Glacier.

958 Number of plant species in Waterton, the most of any national park in the Canadian Rockies. Of 50 plant species considered rare in Canada, 30 are found in Waterton and they are found nowhere else in the country.

Beargrass is a variety of lily whose northern limit is Waterton.

500 Approximate age of the cedar-hemlock trees in the old-growth forest at Avalanche campground in Glacier. It's estimated the area last burned in 1516. By comparison, the cedars at the head of Lake McDonald date back to 1735, while those near Apgar and the park headquarters date from 1865.

Hiker's paradise

120 Approximate number of miles (192 km) of trails in Waterton.

1,070 Maximum number of miles (1,722 km) of trails in Glacier in 1940. This was comprised of 412 miles (663 km) of "tourist" trails and 658 miles of "fire" trails, many of the latter being paths cut by the Civilian Conservation Corps in the 1930s to every major area of the park to create access for firefighting purposes.

700 Approximate number of miles (1,125 km) of hiking trails in Glacier today. The 400 miles (644 km) of tourist trails remain. However, many fire trails created by the Civilian Conservation Corps have not been maintained. These paths can usually be found, but are sometimes overgrown.

30,000 Number of miles (48,279 km) DeWight Wanser rode over the trails of Glacier between 1924 and 1938. Employed by the Park Saddle Horse Company to establish and run tent camps on North Circle Tour, Wanser rode and led pack strings back and forth between his base camp at Cosley Lake (then known as Crossley Lake) and Many Glacier Hotel, where he picked up his supplies. Wanser's wife, Berith, ran the Crossley Lake camp, with its 18 tent houses that could accommodate up to 50 dudes.

Weather

20 Average wind speed in Waterton in miles per hour (32.2 km/h). One of the earliest recorded visits to Waterton was in 1858 by Lt. Thomas Blakiston (1832–1891), who noted Waterton's prevalent winds. He wrote: "This corner of the Mountains appeared to be a very windy spot, and when it was not blowing much on the plain, a strong breeze came from the south down the gorge which is the Upper Waterton Lake." Had Blakiston spent more time in the Waterton Valley, he would have discovered that a 20 mile per hour wind is a mere breeze.

Wind whips the water on Middle Waterton Lake, causing waves and spray that no sensible boater would attempt to navigate.

100 Highest wind speed in miles per hour (161 km/h) recorded in Waterton. A 90 mile per hour (145 km/h) wind nearly knocked down the Prince of Wales Hotel during its construction, in December 1926. "The east wing received the brunt of the strain, as the wind was slightly from the west and blew into the open end of this wing," Great Northern engineer Floyd

Parker wrote after the blizzard. "[I] figure the temporary six inch by six inch diagonal braces we places at the west end of the east wing was all that saved this wing."

60 Average inches (152.4 cm) of annual rainfall at Cameron Lake, the wettest place in the province of Alberta.

42 Average inches (106.7 cm) of annual rainfall in Waterton townsite.

29 Average inches (73.7 cm) of annual precipitation in West Glacier.

28 Average inches (71.1 cm) of annual precipitation in East Glacier Park.

225 Average number of inches (571 cm) of annual snowfall in Waterton townsite.

175 Average inches (444.5 cm) of annual snowfall in East Glacier Park.

136 Average inches (345.4 cm) of annual snowfall in West Glacier.

4 Number of feet (1.2 m) the level of Upper Waterton Lake rose in three hours on June 8, 1964, causing the worst flood in recorded memory in the park. The flooding was brought on by a deep snow pack in the mountains, melted by warm weather and accelerated by 10 inches (25.4 cm) of rain that fell in two days.

Waterton Avenue, the main street, was under a foot of water. All permanent residents and the operators of some businesses and staff members were moved to high ground at the Prince of Wales Hotel. Both water and sewer systems were badly damaged by the flood and temporary facilities were provided until June 16 when repairs were completed.

$4 million Cost to repair and restore buildings, utilities, roads, trails and 24 trail bridges in Glacier following the June 1964 flood.

3 Number of people trapped at Cameron Lake during the June 1964 flood. Seasonal warden Jim Van Tassell, his wife and year-old daughter were brought out of Cameron Lake station by horse and pack train. They had been cut off and without communication for six days when the road was washed out.

Fire ...

71,000   Number of acres (28,700 hectares) of forest the 2001 Moose Mountain fire burned in the North Fork River Valley. Of that, some 27,000 acres (10,9000 hectares) were inside Glacier.

0   Number of individual and commercial permits issued to morel mushroom pickers in Glacier. The practice is not allowed inside the park. Outside the park, however, in the spring of 2002, 1,290 commercial and 1,600 individual permits were issued by the Forest Service. Morel mushrooms, a highly desirable species which restaurants are willing to pay dearly for, have become a multi-million dollar industry. The fungus usually makes a prolific appearance in the spring and early summer the year after a forest fire.

145,000   Number of acres (58,700 hectares) of forest in Glacier destroyed in the summer of 2003 by a series of forest fires, making it the worst fire year in park history. The two main blazes, which started in July, were Wedge Canyon (53,315 acres, 21,575 hectares) and Robert (57,570 acres, 23,297 hectares). They persisted through the summer and were not extinguished or under control until September. The Robert fire forced several evacuations of Apgar and West Glacier, and its smoke forced repeated closures of Lake McDonald Lodge and Going-to-the-Sun Road. Fires are usually named after a nearby geographic location, but that wasn't the case for the Robert fire. The lookout on Huckleberry Mountain (6,593 ft, 2,010 m), who spotted the blaze on July 23, 2003, didn't know the protocol and when asked to christen the fire, he picked the name of his father, to whom he'd been writing a letter.

40,000   Number of acres (16,200 hectares) of forest destroyed in Glacier in the August 1929 Half Moon fire, which started about 10 miles (16 km) southwest of Glacier and blew toward Belton and Lake McDonald, just missing the park headquarters, then headed east toward Nyack. The lodgepole pines seen today on either side of the road between West Glacier and Apgar replaced the towering red cedar forest destroyed in the blaze.

7,640   Number of acres (3,092 hectares) of forest destroyed in August 1936 by Glacier's Heavens Peak fire, which swept over the Garden Wall and down the Swiftcurrent Valley, destroying a number of chalets, a tent museum and endangering Many Glacier Hotel. While not large compared to other fires, the

The Lethbridge Herald

Sofa Mountain Fire moved rapidly eastward from Waterton, forcing residents to be on high alert in case they were required to evacuate their homes. The fire took 16 days to bring under control.

damage was more noticeable because of the location and has left a greater legacy on living memory. Park staff and hotel workers feared a repeat of the Heavens Peak fire when a blaze in August 1967 swept along Going-to-the-Sun Road and up the west side of Mount Gould (9,553 ft, 2,912 m). It was contained before crossing the Continental Divide.

1 Number of fires which have been started in Glacier and spread to Waterton, forcing an evacuation order by the Royal Canadian Mounted Police. This 1935 fire, which was started by lightning near Boundary Creek and was fanned by a southerly wind, spread as far north as Bertha Creek before a change in the weather provided a north wind which saved the townsite of Waterton from certain destruction.

3,759   Number of acres (1,521 hectares) burned in Waterton's Sofa Mountain (8,251 ft, 2,515 m) forest fire of 1998. Driven by high winds, the fire burned for 16 days before being brought under control. At the fire's peak, 180 firefighters were employed using 13 bulldozers, seven water trucks and eight helicopters.

130   Number of years since the Sofa Mountain area had experienced a fire prior to the 1998 event.

$8 to $80   Cost per acre ($20 to $200 per hectare) to manage a prescribed burn in Waterton, depending on the size and nature of the burn. The park's first prescribed burn was done in the spring of 1989 and resulted in an increased quantity and quality of prairie habitat.

5,000   Number of acres (2,023 hectares) of burned forest cleared by the Civilian Conservation Corps between 1932 and 1939 in Glacier. Much of the cleared timber was cut at a CCC-built sawmill and sent to the Blackfeet reservation to be used as fence posts and telephone poles.

84,000   Number of man-days Civilian Conservation Corps members provided fighting fires in Glacier between 1932 and 1940. At its largest, the CCC force in Glacier numbered about 1,500. The men were paid $30 a month, of which $25 was sent to their families.

... and Ice

11,000   Approximate number of years ago that the last major ice sheet covering the Waterton–Glacier area melted to reveal the underlying rock, leaving as remnants the numerous small glaciers in Glacier. Scientists have estimated the ancient ice field that flowed out of the Two Medicine Valley was 48 miles (77 km) long and 30 miles (48 km) wide. In some places in the park, the ice fields were estimated to be 3,000 feet (914 m) deep.

0   Number of glaciers in Waterton.

150   Number of ice fields in Glacier in 1910, of which between 90 and 100 were considered glaciers.

50   Number of glaciers in Glacier today, 34 of which have names. Three other ice fields have names, but are smaller than th

U.S. Geological Survey's standard of 25 acres (10.1 hectares) to be called a glacier. There has been a 73 percent reduction in the area of the park covered by glaciers from 1850 to 1993. Only 6,672 acres (2,700 hectares) of glaciers remain of the 24,463 acres (9,900 hectares) which previously existed.

9   Number of glaciers within 100 miles (161 km) to the north, south or west of Glacier Park, making the grouping in Glacier remarkable for their number and isolation from similar features elsewhere in Canada or the United States. Glacier Park was named not for the ice fields in the park, but for the distinct ice-carved features of the area, such as the U-shaped valleys and cirques, or hanging valleys.

181   acres (73.2 hectares): Area of Grinnell Glacier in 2001, a reduction of 344 acres (139.2 hectares) since 1901. The loss of area in Grinnell Glacier in the previous 20 years is the equivalent of nine city blocks. Likewise the depth of the glacier has been reduced over time by roughly 90 per cent since 1901.

2030   Year by which a computer model has calculated the last glacier in Glacier Park will have melted based on present rates of increasing warming of the earth's atmosphere. Vice-President Al Gore, who hiked to Grinnell Glacier in 1997, made note of the glacier's shrinking size, using it as an example of global

Theories about the cause of global warming are hotly disputed, but evidence of it in Glacier is stark, especially the diminishing size of Grinnell Glacier. On the left, the glacier in the 1920s. On the right, a similar scene from the 1960s.

warming in his environmental platform during the 1998 presidential campaign. In a controversial outcome, Gore lost to Republican George W. Bush, who withdrew the United States from the Kyoto Protocol on Climate Change. The Kyoto Protocol would have limited carbon dioxide emissions in an attempt to slow or reverse global warming.

Geology

1.6 billion   Age of the Precambrian rock exposed at Waterton's Cameron Falls, making it the oldest exposed bedrock in the Canadian Rockies.

4   Number of principal formations of sedimentary rock that make up the bulk of the mountains in Glacier: Altyn (7,947 ft, 2,422 m), Appekunny (9,068 ft, 2,764 m), Grinnell (8,851 ft, 2,698 m) and Siyeh (10,014 ft, 3,052 m). The oldest is Altyn, a buff color, composed mainly of limestone and about 2,500 feet (762 m) thick. The Appekunny formation is about 3,000 feet (914 m) thick and composed of mostly green shales and argillites. The Grinnell formation averages 3,000 feet thick (914 m) and is mostly red. The Siyeh formation is up to 4,000 feet (1,219 m) thick and, as the youngest rock, is usually found at higher elevations.

95   Percentage of bedrock in Waterton that is sedimentary.

60   feet: The maximum thickness (18.3 m) of a fossilized reef of Protoerozoic algae found in the Siyeh rock formation. The algae lived in a sea that covered the area more than a billion years ago. The rock can be identified by concentric circles, or rosettes, each evidence of an algae colony of the genus *Collenia*.

Odds and Ends

60   Number of white Cadillacs provided by General Motors for the 52nd Annual Governors' Convention in 1960. GM also had on hand 140 Chevrolet cars for the wives of the governors and their staff. The National Governor's Association, which first met in 1908, continues to hold annual meetings.

13   Number of bullets held by the 9-mm Sigarms semi-automatic pistols carried by Glacier's rangers. The pistols replaced .357 Magnums that held six rounds. The rangers also have access to

Courtesy, Montana Highway Commission

General Motors supplied 60 white Cadillacs and 140 Chevrolet cars for the use of dignitaries at the 1960 Governors' Convention, held at Many Glacier Hotel.

40 mm and 45 mm sidearms, M-16 semiautomatic rifles, 12-gauge shotguns, pepper spray and collapsible batons. The last time rangers broke out their rifles was in October 1987, when they were searching for a sniper firing at cars on Going-to-the-Sun Road.

0 Number of sidearms carried by Waterton's wardens. Although issued rifles under special circumstances to tranquilize or, when necessary, destroy wildlife, wardens are forbidden by law from carrying pistols, although they also serve as authorized peace officers.

138 Number of peace parks that have been established worldwide since Waterton–Glacier became the first in 1932.

3 Number of major watersheds that originate in Glacier—Missouri, Columbia and Saskatchewan—making the park unique in North America and thus justifying the title "Crown of the Continent" given the park by George Bird Grinnell (1849–1938).

3 Number of borders joined in Waterton: Alberta, Montana and British Columbia just to the west of Cameron Lake.

277 Number of people who have died in Glacier as of June 2003. While the park was created in 1910, records on deaths have only been kept since 1913. After drowning, the second-leading cause of death is heart attacks, at 36.

10 Number of fatal bear attacks in Glacier's history. The first two were in August 1967 within hours of each other, in two separate locations in the park, and involving different bears on what became known as "the night of the grizzlies."

1 Number of fatal bear attacks in Waterton's history. It occurred on July 1, 1977. As a result, Parks Canada vastly improved the information on bears that it provided to visitors.

2,000 Number of people who visit Sperry Chalets each summer, both paying guests and hikers passing through.

$1 million Claimed cost of building a new, solar-powered, state-of-the-art, four-seater, composting outhouse at Sperry Chalets in 1998. What the claim ignores is that this figure included restoration work to Sperry Chalets. Nonetheless, it raised a stink with both Congress and the public as outrageous for such an out-of-the-way area visited by so few. Glacier's superintendent later said he wouldn't have spent the money at Sperry if the choice had been his, but vocal lobbyists and Congress forced his hand. The price was high because of the care taken

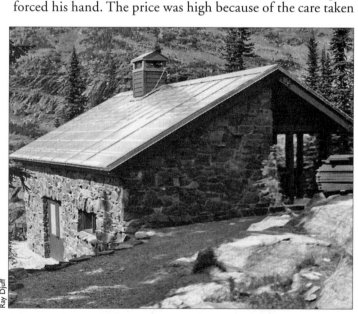

Reports of the so-called $1-million toilet at Sperry Chalets caused outrage in some quarters as a waste (no pun intended) of taxpayer dollars for the benefit of so few people, the hikers to this remote site.

with the environment, the difficulty of the work and the remoteness of the site, 6.5 miles (10.5 km) from the nearest road. About $300,000 of the $1 million was spent on 500 helicopter flights to haul in 1.5 million pounds (680,000 kg) of equipment, dirt, cement and other materials. What didn't need to be flown was packed in by mules. Prior to construction of the new outhouse, waste water had been collected in a holding tank and dumped over a cliff at the end of the season, polluting the environment.

Courtesy, Ford Motor Company

One of Glacier's red buses undergoes restoration at the Transportation Design and Manufacturing Company shop in Livonia, Michigan. Ford sponsored the estimated $6.5-million project.

34 Number of historic red buses in Glacier. There were originally 35 of the Model 706 buses bought from the White Motor Company of Cleveland between 1935 and 1939. One was wrecked in a crash. Ford Motor Company rebuilt 33 of the buses in 2000–2002. One, No. 78, was left in its original condition. While the "reds" are sometimes called "jammers" or "jammer buses," it is a misnomer. Jammers was the nickname for the drivers of the buses in the days when they had manual transmissions that required double-clutch shifting. Drivers who missed shifts were called "gear-jammers" or "jammers." The buses, which run between Lake McDonald and East Glacier Park, Many Glacier Hotel and Waterton, now have automatic transmissions.

Selected Bibliography

Buchholtz, C.W. *Man in Glacier*. 2nd Edition. West Glacier, Montana: Glacier Natural History Association, 1993.

Deittert, Gerald A. *Grinnell's Glacier: George Bird Grinnell and Glacier National Park*. Missoula, Montana: Mountain Press Publishing Company, 1992.

Dempsey, Hugh. *Indian Tribes of Alberta*. Calgary, Alberta: Glenbow Museum, 1979.

Edwards, J. Gordon. *A Climber's Guide to Glacier National Park*. Missoula, Montana: Mountain Press Publishing Co., 1984.

Fisher, Waneeta, *Waterton Resource Guide*. Waterton Lakes National Park: Parks Canada, 1997.

Getty, Ian. *The History of Human Settlement in Waterton Lakes National Park 1800-1937*. A research paper prepared for the Historic Parks Branch, Calgary Alberta: Parks Canada, 1971.

Great Northern Railway company records. Minnesota Historical Society, Saint Paul, Minnesota.

Hanna, Warren L. *Montana's Many Splendored Glacierland*. Seattle, Washington, Superior Publishing Company, 1976.

Hays, Howard, and H.A. Noble. *Drivers' Manual*. 8th edition. East Glacier Park, Montana: Glacier Park Transport Company, 1949.

Hill, Louis Warren. The business and personal papers of Louis W. Hill, James Jerome Hill Reference Library, St. Paul, Minnesota.

Lothian, W. F. *A Brief History of Canada's National Parks*. Ottawa: Supply and Services Canada, 1987.

National Archives of Canada: Files on Parks Canada and Waterton Lakes National Park. Ottawa.

Newspapers: *Calgary Herald, Daily Inter Lake, Great Falls Tribune, Hungry Horse News, The Lethbridge Herald, The Missoulian*.

Robinson, Donald. *Through the Years in Glacier National Park*. West Glacier, Montana: Glacier Natural History Association, Inc., 1960.

Rodney, William. *Kootenai Brown: His Life and Times*. Sidney, British Columbia: Gray's Publishing, 1969.

Ruhle, George C., *Guide to Glacier National Park*. Minneapolis, Minnesota: Campbell-Mithun, Inc., 1949.

INDEX

About the authors

Monika Djuff

A.E. Cross

Ray Djuff came to love Waterton and Glacier during a stint as an employee at the Prince of Wales Hotel in the 1970s. He's been back to the parks almost every year since, with family and friends in tow. When not researching and writing about the parks, he works as a journalist at the *Calgary Herald*. He is a graduate of the SAIT and the University of Calgary.

Chris Morrison has been writing in Alberta for the last 35 years, specializing in Waterton and Glacier for more than half that. She's been on the trail, in the lakes and on top of the mountains and still can't get enough of the place. She is a graduate of the University of Oregon, School of Journalism.